HE SAID, THEY SAID...

- Caroline Scott Keener -

HE SAID, THEY SAID...

The Wisdom of the Wise,
The Experience of the Ages

atmosphere press

Published by Atmosphere Press

Cover design by Ronaldo Alves

atmospherepress.com

To Him
who is able to keep you from falling,
and to present you faultless
before the presence of his glory
with exceeding joy.
To the only wise God our Savior,
be glory and majesty, dominion and power,
both now and ever.
Amen.

Jude 24-25

For Mother,
Jean Bradsher Scott,
whose legacy is her loyalty,
her integrity,
and her devoted love.

July 18, 1925 – February 14, 2022

Yet not to thine eternal resting-place
Shalt thou retire alone, nor couldst thou wish
Couch more magnificent. Thou shalt lie down
With patriarchs of the infant world — with kings,
The power of the earth — the wise, the good
Fair forms, and hoary seers of ages past,
All in one mighty sepulchre.

So live, that when thy summons comes to join
The innumerable caravan, which moves
To that mysterious realm, where each shall take
His chamber in the silent halls of death,
Thou go not, like the quarry-slave at night,
Scourged to his dungeon, but, sustained and soothed
By an unfaltering trust, approach thy grave,
Like one who wraps the drapery of his couch
About him, and lies down to pleasant dreams.

"Thanatopsis"
William Cullen Bryant

TABLE OF CONTENTS

God...

A SPECIAL NOTE OF THANKS

There is one to whom I owe a particular debt of gratitude which I can never repay.

After several years of work on this book, I was finally ready to share it. But first, I wanted someone to read the "finished" product and give me feedback. I knew exactly whom to ask: Sherrill Dalton Grant—"Muffin" to all who know her best and love her most.

She is a dear friend of more than 25 years. An avid reader, Muffin is meticulous, disciplined, and devout.

When I asked her if she would read my book, she immediately said that she would be delighted. I thanked her profusely, and as I handed over the three-inch-thick, five-pound notebook, I said, "If you see any errors, please mark them and I'll make the corrections."

Soon she told me that she was enjoying the book. As the months passed, she sent positive updates: "I'm at 'L' now and I'm really loving this book!" "I'm at 'T' and have a list of people I want to give a copy to." "I'm very close to the end, and you really do need to get this published."

While I appreciated her comments, I was beginning to think that this was taking more time than I had expected. Maybe this book was too long. Or too boring. Or something.

That "something" was the hundreds—or thousands—of mistakes Muffin was finding and correcting!

Muffin turns out to be more than a wonderful friend. She is an eagle-eyed grammarian and, well, a saint.

She saw every error of omission and commission: every misspelled word and grammatical slip, every faulty comma, period, semicolon, ellipse, quotation mark, parentheses, or extra space.

Had I realized the enormity of the task, I would never have asked Muffin for this "favor." Once I understood the scope of what she had done, I apologized. "No," Muffin said. "I have loved this! I do not have one creative bone in my body, but I am able to see these kinds of things. And, the timing of this project is perfect."

While tirelessly editing this book, Muffin valiantly fought battles of her own with courage and faith. Every day that I have known her, Muffin has modeled a godly life. She has done so with joy—even in the midst of sorrow.

Muffin, although I can never adequately express my gratitude for the gifts of your friendship and your precious time, I will offer these words of the 19th-century Frenchman, Jean Massieu:

"Gratitude is the memory of the heart."

You are in my heart. **– Carolee**

From the rising of the sun,
to the place where it sets,
the name of the Lord be praised.

Psalm 113:3

PREFACE

"Thank God I have the seeing eye, that is to say, as I lie in bed I can walk step by step on the fells and rough land seeing every stone and flower and patch of bog and cotton pass where my old legs will never take me again."

Beatrix Potter, 1866 – 1943

For more than thirty years, daily walks have been a defining part of my life, and those who know me best know that about me. Even people I do not know well sometimes comment, "I saw you walking yesterday" or "We haven't actually met, but I often see you walking." Sometimes, people express concern by saying, "I haven't seen you out walking lately."

Each comment reminds me of someone who was a fixture in my universe many years ago. I only knew her as the very elderly lady who seemed to walk for hours each day. It was impossible to go anywhere in our town without seeing her on the sidewalks. Her familiar posture and determined gait were easily recognizable even from a distance. I can remember thinking in those naïve days, "There must be something wrong with her. Who would spend so many hours like that?" Now, it has occurred to me: I have become that woman!

And what a blessing!

We lovers of daily walks are in good company. From ancient times many have touted the pleasure and benefits of a daily walk.

"We ought to take outdoor walks, to refresh and raise our spirits by deep breathing in the open air."

Seneca, 4BC – 65AD

"If the body be feeble, the mind will not be strong. The sovereign invigorator of the body is exercise, and of all the exercises walking is best. Walking is the best possible exercise. Habituate yourself to walk very far."

Thomas Jefferson, 1743 – 1826
Letter to Martha Jefferson, August 27, 1786

"Give me odorous at sunrise a garden of beautiful flowers where I can walk undisturbed."

Walt Whitman, 1819 – 1892
Poem, "Give Me the Splendid Silent Sun" (1865)

John Muir, the famed naturalist, prolific writer, and perhaps the greatest walker of all time, traveled vast expanses of this world on foot. In his writings he expressed his sense of intimacy with God through the majesty of His Creation. As a child from a devout Scottish home, he was required to read the Bible everyday, eventually memorizing most of the Old Testament and all of the New. A lover of Scripture, the explorer of nature wrote that he also came to see another "primary source for understanding God: The Book of Nature." According to his biographer, Denis C. Williams, Muir saw nature as a great teacher, "revealing the mind of God," and this belief became the central theme of his later journeys and the subtext of his nature writing.

"Oh, these vast, calm, measureless mountain days in whose light everything seems equally divine, opening a thousand windows to show us God."

John Muir, 1838 – 1914
My First Summer in the Sierra (1911)
*(Williams, Denis C (2002). *God's Wilds: John Muir's Vision of Nature*. College Station: Texas A&M University Press. ISBN 1585441430.)

The earth's beauty does indeed inspire and lead me from thoughts of gratitude to prayers of thanks and praise to Him, the Creator, who gave me life, sustains my life, and is the very source of all that is good, perfect, and beautiful. Far more ably than I, others have expressed their own experience of the power of the majesty of the Creation to move us beyond ourselves to an awareness of the very presence of the Creator.

"The best remedy for those who are afraid, lonely or unhappy is to go outside, somewhere they can be quiet, alone with the heavens, nature and God. Because only then does one feel that all is as it should be."

Anne Frank, 1929 – 1945
Diary Entry Wednesday, February 23, 1942
The Diary of a Young Girl, June 14, 1942 – August 1, 1944 (1947)

"We say, then, to anyone who is under trial, give Him time to steep the soul in His eternal truth. Go into the open air, look up into the depths of the sky, or out upon the wideness of the sea, or on the strength of the hills that is His also; or, if bound in the body, go forth in the spirit; spirit is not bound. Give Him time and, as surely as dawn follows night, there will break upon the heart a sense of certainty that cannot be shaken."

Amy Carmichael, 1867 – 1951
Elisabeth Elliot, *A Chance to Die: The Life and Legacy of Amy Carmichael* (1987)

"Why must people kneel down to pray? If I really wanted to pray I'll tell you what I'd do. I'd go out into a great big field all alone or in the deep, deep woods and I'd look up into the sky—up—up—up—into that lovely blue sky that looks as if there was no end to

its blueness. And then I'd just feel a prayer."

Lucy Maud Montgomery, 1874 – 1942
Anne of Green Gables (1908)

Years ago a respected and beloved teacher, Patty Crossley, encouraged me to approach God in prayer, beginning with adoration and thanksgiving, thus focusing on Him, His power, goodness, and love rather than on myself, my needs, my concerns.

"Each time, before you intercede, be quiet first, and worship God in His glory. Think of what He can do, and how He delights to hear the prayers of His redeemed people. Think of your place and privilege in Christ, and expect great things!"

Andrew Murray, 1828 – 1917

"By turning your eyes on God in meditation, your whole soul will be filled with God. Begin all your prayers in the presence of God."

Saint Francis de Sales, 1567 – 1622

Accepting the wisdom of the "praise first" pattern of prayer, I made it my habit to begin my daily walks and prayers by focusing my thoughts on the innumerable attributes of God, naming one for each letter of the alphabet, A-Z, and giving Him thanks for each.

Over time, I realized that certain particular truths about Him continued to be most meaningful to me as I practiced this pattern, and now I have begun my prayers for almost 30 years by speaking these words to God daily, virtually unchanged. These A-Z thoughts, words, and prayers are now fixed, not only in my mind but in my heart, and continue to give me encouragement, strength, and solace no matter the circumstances of a given day. I have learned that spending the first few minutes of prayer in praise and thanksgiving—shifting my focus from me/my/I to Him—is transformative, changing my perspective and changing me.

This pattern of first offering adoration and thanksgiving reminds me that in my prayers and in all things, no matter the circumstances of the moment, I must learn to think first and always of God, to be mindful of His continuous presence, power, and love. To recall His promises, to remember His mercies, and to come to Him in faith, learning anew each day to trust Him, and to know that as He has been, He will always be, my ample portion, in this life and in the life to come. The quotations collected here remind me to recall His faithfulness in the past, anticipate His sufficiency in all things, and to never fall victim to "spiritual amnesia."

May these words strengthen and encourage you on the paths of your own life, and may you experience the blessing described by the psalmist:

"He has laid my boundaries in pleasant places."

Psalm 16:61

My paternal great-grandfather, John Thomas Lea, wrote in our family Bible on December 29, 1912 the following words of encouragement, hope, and love for those dearest to him. I offer to you, my beloved family, my faithful friends, and all who may read these pages, his words which express my heart's desire as well:

"One more request is to each of my children, strive to meet me in heaven, and also to all my relations and friends, my prayer is that we meet again where we will never say good-bye".

CSK
May 5, 2021

A NOTE TO THOSE WITH WHOM I HAVE SHARED THE PATH

Though most of my "walking life" has been spent on the familiar sidewalks of our Greensboro and Charlotte neighborhoods and at our beloved Grandfather Mountain, I have had wonderful opportunities to take my walks in other beautiful, but faraway places. It is pure pleasure to recall those paths of beauty and the joy of having shared many of them with others who are so dear to me.

It's a long way from
the well-worn path to the little waterfall on the farm in Milton,
the home of my childhood (and my heart's home),
to the high walkway of the Sydney Harbor Bridge.

From the lake trail at Jasper Lodge
to the banks of the Nile and the endless sands surrounding the pyramids.

From the sidewalks of Manhattan and the shoreline of Larchmont
to the Great Wall of China.

From the vast Cairngorms and the windswept Orkneys
to Buenos Aires and Mendoza.

From the frigid base of Aconcagua
to the soft white sand of Nevis.

From the Teton Valley at Driggs
to the dunes of Dubai.

From the shores of the Gulf of Oman
to the sacred cemetery on the cliffs of Normandy.

From the turquoise beauty of Kailua beach
to the foothills of the Rockies at Calgary.

From the sidewalks of London and Paris and Rome,
and the steep steps of Tuscan hill towns,
to the walkways of the Pacific coast's

Golden Gate, Lions Gate, and Deception Pass bridges.

From the sandy white beaches of Contadora
to the Outback and Ayers Rock.

From the peak of Cook's Look
to the massive high crater of Haleakala.

From St. Petersburg and Moscow
to Milford Sound.

From Lakeville to Luxor to Lake Louise.

Over all these years, in all these places and others near and far, in times of joy and sorrow, I have spent untold hours walking this earth, reveling in the beauty of Creation, awed by the sure sense of God's presence and power and majesty.

God has indeed "laid my boundaries in pleasant places."

"The wisdom of the wise, and the experience of the ages,
may be preserved by quotation."

Isaac Disraeli, 1766 – 1848

Almighty God, for you all things are possible; nothing is too hard for you.

Ah, Sovereign Lord, you have made the heavens and the earth by your great power and your outstretched arm. Nothing is too hard for you.

Jeremiah 32:17

JOB 42:2
I know that you can do all things; no purpose of yours will be thwarted.

PSALM 71:18
Even when I am old and gray, do not forsake me, O God, until I declare your power to the next generation, your might to all who are to come.

PSALM 89:8
O Lord God Almighty, who is like you? You are mighty, O Lord, and your faithfulness surrounds you.

PSALM 91:1, 2
He who dwells in the shelter of the Most High will rest in the shadow of the Almighty.

PSALM 93:4
Mightier than the thunder of the great waters, mightier than the breakers of the sea – the Lord on high is mighty.

PSALM 105:4
Look to the Lord and seek his strength; seek his face always.

PSALM 145:3
Great is the Lord and most worthy of praise; his greatness no one can fathom. One generation shall praise your works to another, and shall declare your mighty acts. On the glorious splendor of your majesty and on your wonderful works, I will meditate. Men shall speak of the power of your awesome acts, and I will tell of your greatness.

ISAIAH 6:3
Holy, holy, holy is the Lord Almighty, the whole earth is full of his glory.

ISAIAH 9:6
For unto us a child is born, unto us a son is given, and the government will be upon his shoulders. And he will be called Wonderful Counselor, Mighty God, Everlasting Father, Prince of Peace.

ISAIAH 40:26
Lift up your eyes on high and see who has created these stars, the One who leads forth their host by number, He calls them all by name; because of the greatness of His might and the strength of His power, not one of them is missing.

ISAIAH 46:9 – 10
"Remember the former things, those of long ago; I am God, and there is no other; I am God, and there is none like me. I make known the end from the beginning, from ancient times,

what is still to come. I say, 'My purpose will stand and I will do as I please.'"

ISAIAH 47:4
Our Redeemer—the Lord Almighty is his name—is the Holy One of Israel.

JEREMIAH 32:18, 19
O great and powerful God, whose name is the Lord Almighty, great are your purposes and mighty are your deeds.

JEREMIAH 32:27
"I am the Lord, the God of all flesh. Is anything too hard for me?"

AMOS 4:13
He who forms the mountains, creates the wind, and reveals his thoughts to man, he who turns dawn to darkness and treads the high places of the earth—the Lord Almighty is his name.

MATTHEW 19:26
Jesus looked at them and said, "With God all things are possible."

LUKE 1:37
The angel said to Mary, "Nothing is impossible with God."

LUKE 18:27
Jesus replied, "What is impossible with men is possible with God."

JOHN 16:33
"I have said these things to you, that in me you may have peace. In the world you will have tribulation. But take heart; I have overcome the world."

1 CORINTHIANS 2:5
That your faith should not stand in the wisdom of men, but in the power of God.

2 CORINTHIANS 1:20
For no matter how many promises God has made, they are "Yes" in Christ. And so through him, the "Amen" is spoken by us to the glory of God.

2 CORINTHIANS 12:9
But he said to me, "My grace is sufficient for you, for my power is made perfect in weakness." Therefore, I will boast all the more gladly about my weaknesses, so that Christ's power may rest on me.

EPHESIANS 3:20
Now to him who is able to do exceedingly abundantly above all that we ask or think, according to the power that works within us....

EPHESIANS 6:10
Finally, be strong in the Lord and in his mighty power.

PHILIPPIANS 4:13
I can do all things through him who strengthens me.

PHILIPPIANS 4:19
And my God will meet all your needs according to the riches of his glory in Christ Jesus.

REVELATION 1:8
"I am the Alpha and the Omega," says the Lord God, "who is, and was, and is to come, the Almighty."

REVELATION 4:8
Holy, holy, holy is the Lord God Almighty, who was, and is, and is to come.

REVELATION 19:6
Our Lord God Almighty reigns.

"Possible things are easy to believe. The Glorious Impossibles are what bring joy to our hearts, hope to our lives, and songs to our lips."

Madeleine L'Engle, 1918 – 2007
The Glorious Impossible (1990)

"Almighty and eternal Lord God, the great Creator of heaven and earth, and the God and Father of our Lord Jesus Christ; look down from heaven in pity and compassion upon me thy servant, who humbly prostrate myself before thee."

George Washington, 1732 – 1799
Editor, W. Herbert Burk; *Washington's Prayers* (1907)

"It is impossible for one to despair who remembers that his helper is omnipotent."

Jeremy Taylor, 1613 – 1667
Josiah Hotchkiss Gilbert; *Dictionary of Burning Words of Brilliant Writers* (1895)

"God works powerfully, but for the most part gently and gradually."

John Newton, 1725 – 1807
Ed., Harold J. Chadwick; *The Amazing Works of John Newton* (2009)

"It is the duty of all nations to acknowledge the Providence of Almighty God, to obey his will, to be grateful for his benefits and

humbly implore his protection and favor. I am sure there never was a people who had more reason to acknowledge a divine interposition in their affairs, than those of the United States; and I should be pained to believe that they have forgotten that agency which was so often manifested during the revolution; or that they failed to consider the omnipotence of Him, who is alone able to protect them. He must be worse than an infidel that lacks faith, and more than wicked, that has not gratitude enough to acknowledge his obligations."

George Washington 1732 – 1799
Letter to Brigadier-General Nelson, August 20,1778,
Ford's Writings of George Washington, Vol. VII (1890)

"Only he shakes the heavens and from its treasures takes out the winds. He joins the waters and the clouds and produces the rain. He does all those things. Only he realizes miracles permanently."

Michael Servetus, 1511 – 1553

"There is a signature of wisdom and power impressed on the works of God, which evidently distinguishes them from the feeble limitations of men—not only the splendor of the sun, but the glimmering light of the glowworm."

John Newton, 1725 – 1807
Newton's "Messiah Sermon Series,"
Sermon No. 5 (circa 1785 – 1786)

"I have found that there are three stages in every great work of God: first, it is impossible, then it is difficult, then it is done."

James Hudson Taylor, 1832 – 1905
Leslie T. Lyall; *A Passion for the Impossible: The Continuing Story of the Mission Hudson Taylor Began* (1965)

"Beware in your prayers, above everything else, of limiting God, not only by unbelief, but by fancying that you know what He can do. Expect unexpected things "above all that we ask or think."

Andrew Murray, 1828 – 1917 Yes, indicates copy
The Ministry of Intercession: A Plea for More Prayer (1898)

"I plainly told them, 'Be ye sincerely converted, and with your whole heart, to the Lord our God, for nothing is impossible to Him, that he may today send food on your road, even until you are satisfied, because He has everywhere abundance.' And, with God's help, it was so done: Behold! A herd of swine appeared in the road before our eyes."

Saint Patrick, 385 – 431

"Faith sees the invisible, believes the unbelievable, and receives the impossible."

Corrie ten Boom, 1892 – 1983
Jesus is Victor (1985)

"Here lies the tremendous mystery— that God should be all-powerful, yet refuse to coerce. He summons us to cooperation. We are honored in being given the opportunity to participate in his good deeds. Remember how he asked for help in performing his miracles: Fill the water pots, stretch out your hand, distribute the loaves."

Elisabeth Elliot, 1926 – 2015
Gateway to Joy (1998)

"All nature is full of God. He is enthroned in Light: he creates darkness: he hath his way in the whirlwind, fendeth abroad his lightnings, giveth snow like wool, scattereth the hoar-frost like ashes,

and casteth forth his ice like morsels! Who can stand before his cold? Who can thunder with a voice like God? It is He who distils the rain from his bottles, who opens the bubbling fountains, who covers the fields with grass, and the hills with flocks, who spins out the fleecy air, and spreads forth the liquid plains, who refreshes us with his wings, lights us with the sun, and entertains us with his table, richly furnish'd with all the dainty of heaven."

Wellins Calcott, 1726 – 1779
Thoughts Moral and Divine Upon Various Subjects (1766)

"To know the mighty works of God, to comprehend His wisdom and majesty and power; to appreciate, in degree, the wonderful workings of His laws, surely all this must be a pleasing and acceptable mode of worship to the Most High, to whom ignorance cannot be more grateful than knowledge."

Nicolaus Copernicus, 1473 – 1543
Louis E. Van Norman, *Poland: The Knight Among Nations* (1908)

"Faith is a grasping of Almighty power;
The hand of man laid on the arm of God;
The grand and blessed hour in which the things impossible to me
Become the possible, O Lord, through Thee."

Anna Elizabeth Hamilton, 1843 – 1875
J.H. Gilbert; *Dictionary of Burning Words of Brilliant Writers* (1895)

B

You, O Lord, are my breath and bread of life, the giver and sustainer of my life. All the days ordained for me were written in your book before even one came to be.

The Lord God formed the man from the dust of the earth and breathed into his nostrils the breath of life, and the man became a living being.

Genesis 2:7

Jesus said to them, "I am the bread of life."

John 6:35

For you created my inmost being, you knit me together in my mother's womb. All the days ordained for me were written in your book before one of them came to be.

Psalm 139:6, 16

EXODUS 16:4 - 7
Behold, I am about to rain bread from heaven - a day's portion - and in the morning you shall see the glory of the Lord.

DEUTERONOMY 30:20
"Love the Lord your God, that you may obey his voice, and that you may cling to him, for he is your life and the length of your days."

NEHEMIAH 9:6
You give life to everything and the multitudes of heaven worship you.

JOB 10:12
You have granted me life and steadfast love, and your care has preserved my spirit.

JOB 12:10
In his hand is the life of every creature and the breath of all mankind.

JOB 33:4
The Spirit of God has made me; the breath of the Almighty gives me life.

PSALM 3:5
I lie down and sleep; I wake again because the Lord sustains me.

PSALM 16:11
You make known to me the path of life; in your presence there is fullness of joy; at your right hand are pleasures forevermore.

PSALM 51:10 – 12
Create in me a pure heart, O God, and renew a steadfast spirit within me. Do not cast me from your presence or take your Holy Spirit from me. Restore to me the joy of your salvation and grant me a willing spirit to sustain me.

PSALM 54:4
Surely God is my help; the Lord is the one who sustains me.

PSALM 55:22
Cast your cares and burdens on the Lord and he will sustain you; he will never let the righteous to be moved.

PSALM 91:14 - 16
"Because he loves me," says the Lord, "I will rescue him; I will protect him, for he acknowledges my name. He will call on me, and I will answer him; I will be with him in trouble, I will deliver him and honor him. With long life I will satisfy him and show him my salvation."

PSALM 103:1 - 5
Bless the Lord, O my soul, all that is within me, bless his holy name! Bless the Lord, O my soul, and forget not all his benefits: who forgives all your sins, who heals all your diseases, who redeems your life from the pit and crowns you with loving-kindness and tender mercies, who satisfies your mouth with good things, so that your youth is renewed like the eagle's.

PSALM 104:13 - 15
From your lofty abode you water the mountains; the earth is satisfied with the fruit of your work. You cause the grass to grow for the livestock and plants for man to cultivate, that he may bring forth food from the earth and wine to gladden the heart of man, oil to make his face shine and bread to strengthen man's heart.

PSALM 104:24, 27
How many are your works, O Lord! In wisdom you made them all; the earth is full of your creatures. These all look to you to give them their food at the proper time.

PSALM 107:9
Let them give thanks to the Lord for his unfailing love and his wonderful deeds for mankind, for he satisfies the thirsty and fills the hungry with good things.

PSALM 145:15 – 16
The eyes of all look to you, and you give them their food at the proper time. You open your hand and satisfy the desires of every living thing.

PSALM 147:7
He upholds the cause of the oppressed and gives food to the hungry.

PSALM 150:6
Let everything that has breath praise the Lord.

PROVERBS 30:7 – 9
Two things I ask of you, O Lord; do not refuse me before I die: Keep falsehood and lies far from me; give me neither poverty nor riches, but give me only my daily bread. Otherwise, I may have too much and disown you and say, “Who is the Lord?” Or I may become poor and steal and dishonor the name of my God.

ECCLESIASTES 9:7
Go, eat your food with gladness, and drink your wine with a joyful heart, for God has already approved what you do.

ISAIAH 42:5
This is what God the Lord says—he who created the heavens and stretched them out, who spread out the earth and all that comes out of it, who gives breath to its people, and life to those who walk on it: “I, the Lord, have called you in righteousness; I will take hold of your hand.”

ISAIAH 46:3 - 4
Listen to me, you whom I have upheld since you were conceived, and have carried since your birth. Even to your old age and gray hairs I am he, I am he who will sustain you. I have made you and I will carry you; I will sustain you and I will rescue you.

ISAIAH 55:10 - 11
As the rain and the snow come down from heaven, and do not return to it without watering the earth and making it bud and flourish, so that it yields seed for the sower and bread for the eater, so is my word that goes out from my mouth: it will not return to me empty, but will accomplish what I desire and achieve the purpose for which I sent it.

JEREMIAH 1:5
"Before I formed you in the womb I knew you, before you were born, I set you apart; I appointed you as a prophet to the nations."

MATTHEW 4:4
Jesus answered, "Man does not live on bread alone, but on every word that comes from the mouth of God."

MATTHEW 6:11
Jesus taught them to pray, saying, "Give us this day our daily bread."

MATTHEW 6:25 - 26
Jesus said, "Therefore I tell you, do not be anxious about your life, or what you will eat or drink; or about your body, what you will wear.... Look at the birds of the air; they do not sow or reap or store away in barns, and yet your heavenly Father feeds them. Are you not much more valuable than they?"

JOHN 6:27, 32 - 33, 35

Jesus answered, "Do not labor for food that perishes, but for food that endures to eternal life which the Son of Man will give you .... it is my Father who gives you the true bread from heaven. For the bread of God is he who comes down from heaven and gives life to the world .... I am the bread of life. He who comes to me will never be hungry, and he who comes to me will never be thirsty."

JOHN 6:47 - 51

Jesus said, "Very truly I tell you, the one who believes has eternal life. I am the bread of life. Your forefathers ate the manna in the desert, yet they died. But here is the bread that comes down from heaven, which a man may eat and not die. I am the living bread that came down from heaven. If anyone eats of this bread, he will live forever. This bread is my flesh, which I will give for the life of the world."

ACTS 17:24 - 25

The God who made the earth and everything in it is the Lord of heaven and earth and does not live in temples made by hands. And, he is not served by human hands, as if he needed anything, because he himself gives all men life and breath and everything else.

ACTS 17:27 - 28

... [H]e is not far from any one of us: For in him we live and move and have our being.

PHILIPPIANS 4:19

And my God will meet all your needs according to the riches of his glory in Christ Jesus.

"Blessed art Thou,
O God of the universe,
who bringeth forth bread from the earth."

A Traditional Hebrew Blessing

"God is great.
God is good.
Let us thank Him for our food.
By His hand we all are fed.
Give us Lord our daily bread.
Amen."

A Child's Blessing
Traditional

"We are all mere beggars showing other beggars where to find bread."

Martin Luther, 1483 – 1546

"There are people in the world so hungry, that God cannot appear to them except in the form of bread."

Mahatma Gandhi, 1869 – 1948
The Spirituality of Bread (2007)

"The sky is the daily bread of the eyes."

Ralph Waldo Emerson, 1803 – 1882
Journal entry, May 25, 1943

"Let there be work, bread, water, and salt for all."

Nelson Mandela, 1918 – 2015
Inaugural Address, May 10, 1994

"In the Lord's Prayer, the first petition is for daily bread. No one can worship God or love his neighbor on an empty stomach."

Woodrow Wilson 1856 – 1924
Speech at Economic Club Dinner, New York, May 23, 1912

"We who lived in concentration camps can remember the men who walked through the huts comforting others, giving away their last piece of bread."

Viktor E. Frankl, 1905 – 1997
Man's Search for Meaning (1946)

"Here is bread, which strengthens man's heart,
and therefore is called the staff of Life."

Matthew Henry, 1662 – 1714
"Psalm 104," *Matthew Henry's Commentary on the Whole Bible* (1710)

"The hunger for love is much more difficult to remove than the hunger for bread."

Mother Teresa, 1910 – 1997
Interview, "TIME Magazine" (December 4, 1989)

"Man lives by affirmation even more than he does by bread."

Victor Hugo, 1802 – 1885
Les Misérables (1862)

"To eat bread without hope is still slowly to starve to death."

Pearl S. Buck, 1892 – 1973
To my daughters, with love (1967)

"I have no taste for corruptible food, nor for the pleasures of this life. I desire the Bread of God, which is the Flesh of Jesus Christ, who was of the seed of David, and for drink I desire His Blood, which is love incorruptible."

Ignatius of Antioch, 50 – 108
"Epistle to the Romans" (circa 105)

"Spiritual power is hidden power, locked in the silence of the soul. We cannot force it to come at command of will. But when in extremity our strength is as water, our will as the sighing of the wind, when we yield all physical being and lean hard on the spiritual strength within us, the soul's strength rises to assure us as the sun rises over the rim of night. This spiritual strength is man's inheritance, the eternal power granted him at Creation. It is God's breath within him. On that strength we can go forward; we can take whatever comes and know that it is well with us always."

Angelo Patri, 1876 – 1965
Article, "Magic", *Redbook Magazine* (July 1938)

"Everyone needs beauty as well as bread, places to play and pray, where nature heals and gives strength to body and soul alike."

John Muir, 1838 – 1914
The Yosemite (1912)

"When you arise in the morning, think of what a precious privilege it is to be alive—to breathe, to think, to enjoy, to love."

Marcus Aurelius, 121 – 180
Personal Writings, *Meditations*, 161 – 180
Translated from the Greek, by R. Graves (1811)

Breathe on Me, Breath of God

Breath on me, breath of God
Fill me with life anew,
That I may love what Thou dost love,
And do what Thou wouldst do.

Breathe on me, Breath of God,
Until my heart is pure,
Until with Thee I will one will,
To do and to endure.

Breathe on me, Breath of God,
Till I am wholly Thine,
Until this earthly part of me
Glows with Thy fire divine.

Breathe on me, Breath of God,
So shall I never die,
But live with Thee the perfect life
Of Thine eternity.

Edwin Hatch, 1835 – 1899
Hymn (1878)

Break Thou the Bread of Life

Break Thou the bread of life, dear Lord, to me,
As Thou didst break the loaves beside the sea;
Beyond the sacred page I seek Thee, Lord;
My spirit pants for Thee, O living Word!

Bless Thou the truth, dear Lord, to me, to me,
As Thou didst bless the bread by Galilee;
Then shall all bondage cease, all fetters fall;
And I shall find my peace, my all in all.

Thou art the bread of life, O Lord, to me,
Thy holy Word the truth that saveth me;
Give me to eat and live with Thee above;
Teach me to love Thy truth, for Thou art love.

Oh, send Thy Spirit, Lord, now unto me,
That He may touch my eyes, and make me see:
Show me the truth concealed within Thy Word,
And in Thy Book revealed I see the Lord.

Mary Lathbury, 1841 – 1913
Verses 3–4, Alexander Groves 1842 – 1909
Hymn (1877)

C

In the beginning, O God, you created the heavens and the earth. By your word all things were made. The heavens, the earth, and all therein belong to you.

In the beginning, God created the heavens and the earth.

Genesis 1:1

The earth is the Lord's and everything therein, the world and all who live in it; for he founded it upon the seas and established it upon the waters.

Psalm 24:1

In the beginning, you laid the foundation of the earth and the heavens are the works of your hands.

Psalm 105:25

Through him all things were made;
without him nothing was made that has been made.

John 1:3

GENESIS 1:16
God made two great lights—the greater light to govern the day and the lesser light to govern the night. He also made the stars.

GENESIS 1:27
So God created mankind in his own image, in the image of God he created them; male and female he created them.

NEHEMIAH 9:6
You alone are the Lord. You have made the heavens, even the highest heavens, with all their starry host, the earth and all that is on it, the seas and all that is in them. You give life to all of them; and the heavenly host bows down before you.

PSALM 19:1 - 4
The heavens declare the glory of God; the skies proclaim the work of his hands. Day after day they pour forth speech; night after night they display knowledge. There is no speech or language where their voice is not heard. Their voice goes out into all the earth, their words to the end of the world.

PSALM 33:6, 9
By the word of the Lord were the heavens made, the starry hosts by the breath of his mouth.... For he spoke and it came to be; he commanded and it stood firm.

PSALM 89:11
The heavens are yours, and yours also the earth; you founded the world and all that is in it.

PSALM 90:2
Before the mountains were brought forth, or ever you had formed the earth and the world, from everlasting to everlasting you are God.

PSALM 104:24 - 25
O Lord, how manifold are your works! In wisdom you have made them all; the earth is full of your creatures. Here is the sea, great and wide, which teems with creatures innumerable, living things both great and small.

PSALM 139:13 - 14
For you created my inmost being; you knit me together in my mother's womb. I praise you for I am fearfully and wonderfully made; your works are wonderful, I know that full well.

PSALM 146:5 - 6
Blessed is he whose help is the God of Jacob, whose hope is in the Lord his God, the Maker of heaven and earth, the sea, and everything in them—the Lord who remains faithful forever.

PROVERBS 3:19 - 20
By wisdom the Lord laid the earth's foundations, by understanding he set the heavens in place; by his knowledge the deeps were divided, and the clouds let drop their dew.

ECCLESIASTES 11:5
As you do not know the path of the wind, or how a body is formed in a mother's womb, so you cannot understand the work of God, the Maker of all things.

ISAIAH 40:25 - 26, 28
"To whom will you compare me? Or who is my equal," says the Holy One. "Lift your eyes and look to the heavens: Who

created all these? He who brings out the starry host one by one, and calls them each by name. Because of his great power and mighty strength, not one of them is missing.... Do you not know? Have you not heard? The Lord is the everlasting God, the Creator of the ends of the earth."

ISAIAH 44:24
This is what the Lord says—your Redeemer, who formed you in the womb: "I am the Lord who has made all things, who alone stretched out the heavens, who spread out the earth by myself."

ISAIAH 45:12
"It is I who made the earth and created mankind upon it. My own hands stretched out the heavens; I marshaled their starry hosts."

ISAIAH 48:12 - 13
"I am he; I am the first and the last. My own hands laid the foundations of the earth, and my right hand spread out the heavens; when I summon them, they all stand up together."

ISAIAH 64:8
Yet, O Lord, you are our Father. We are the clay, you are the potter; we are all the work of your hand.

JEREMIAH 10:12
God made the earth by his power; he founded the world by his wisdom and stretched out the heavens by his understanding.

JEREMIAH 32:17
Ah, Sovereign Lord, you have made the heavens by your great power and outstretched arm. Nothing is too hard for you.

JEREMIAH 33:2 - 3
This is what the Lord says, He who made the earth, the Lord who formed it and established it - the Lord is his name: "Call to me and I will answer you and tell you great and unsearchable things you do not know."

JEREMIAH 51:15
He made the earth by his power; he founded the world by his wisdom and stretched out the heavens by his understanding.

ACTS 17:24 - 25
The God who made the earth and everything in it is the Lord of heaven and earth and does not live in temples made by hands. And he is not served by human hands, as if he needed anything, because he himself gives all men life and breath and everything else.

ROMANS 1:20
For since the creation of the world God's invisible qualities - his eternal power and divine nature - have been clearly seen, being understood from what has been made, so that men are without excuse.

1 CORINTHIANS 11:12
For as woman came from man, so also is man born of woman. But everything comes from God.

COLOSSIANS 1:15 - 17
The Son is the image of the invisible God, the firstborn over all creation. For by him all things were created: things in heaven and on earth, visible and invisible, whether thrones or powers or rulers or authorities; all things were created by him and for him. He is before all things and in him all things hold together.

HEBREWS 1:10
And, You, Lord, laid the foundation of the earth in the beginning, and the heavens are the work of your hands.

HEBREWS 11:3
By faith we understand that the universe was created at God's command, so that what is seen was not made out of what was visible.

REVELATION 4:11
You are worthy, our Lord and God, to receive glory and honor and power, for you created all things and by your will they were created and have their being.

"Thank you for the world so sweet;
Thank you for the food we eat,
Thank you for the birds that sing;
Thank you, God, for everything.
Amen."

Miss Edith Rutter-Leatham, Victorian Poet
A Child's Grace

"World, do you know your Creator?
Seek Him in the heavens.
Above the stars He must dwell."

Ludwig von Beethoven, 1770 – 1827
Symphony No.9, Opus 125 (1824)

"God creates out of nothing. Wonderful you say. Yes, to be sure, but He does what is still more wonderful: He makes saints out of sinners."

Søren Kierkegaard, 1813 – 1855
Journals (July 7,1838)

"Tread softly! All the earth is holy ground."

Christina Rossetti, 1830 – 1894
"Later Life: A Double Sonnet of Sonnets" (1881)

"Earth's crammed with heaven,
And every common bush afire with God;
But only he who sees, takes off his shoes,
The rest sit round it and pluck blackberries,
And daub their natural faces unaware."

Elizabeth Barrett Browning, 1806 – 1861
"Aurora Leigh" (1856)

"Praised be You, my Lord, through Sister Moon and the stars;
in the heavens, you have made them bright, precious and fair."

Saint Francis of Assisi, died 1226

"There is a God-shaped vacuum in the heart of every man which cannot be filled by any created thing, but only by God, the Creator, made known through Jesus."

Blaise Pascal, 1623 – 1662
Pensées (1670)

"If we discover a desire within us that nothing in this world can satisfy, we should begin to wonder if perhaps we were created for another world.

C. S. Lewis, 1898 – 1963
Mere Christianity (1952)

"Man was created to praise, reverence, and serve God our Lord and in this way to save his soul. The other things on Earth were created for man's use, to help him reach the end for which he was created."

Saint Ignatius of Loyola, 50 – 108
The Spiritual Exercises of Ignatius of Loyola (1548)

"God dwells in his creation, and is everywhere indivisibly present in all his works. He is transcendent above all his works even while he is immanent within them."

A.W. Tozer, 1897 – 1963
The Pursuit of God (1948)

"There is a signature of wisdom and power impressed on the works of God, which evidently distinguishes them from the feeble imitations of men. Not only the splendor of the sun, but the glimmering light of the glowworm, proclaims his glory."

John Newton, 1725 – 1807
Newton's "Messiah Sermon Series,"
Sermon No. 5 (circa 1785–1786)

"Almighty and eternal Lord God, the great Creator of heaven and earth, and the God and Father of our Lord Jesus Christ; look down from heaven in pity and compassion upon me thy servant, who humbly prostrate myself before thee."

George Washington, 1732 – 1799
W. Herbert Burk; *Washington's Prayers* (1907)

"God writes the Gospel not in the Bible alone, but also in trees, and in the flowers and clouds and stars."

Martin Luther, 1483 – 1546
Attributed

"Some people, in order to discover God, read books. But there is a very great book: the appearance of created things. Look above you! Look below you! Note it. Read it. God whom you want to discover never wrote that book with ink. Instead, he set before you the things he had made. Can you ask for a louder voice than that?"

Saint Augustine, 354 – 430
Ed., G. Moran; "Sermon 126," *Miscellanea Augustiniana* (Rome 1930)

"All creation is a symphony of praise to God."

Sainte Hildegard of Bingen, 1098 – 1179
Scivias (1141 – 1151)

"I can see how a man might look down upon the earth and be an atheist, but I cannot conceive how a man could look up into the heavens and say there is no God."

Abraham Lincoln, 1809 – 1865
Magazine Article, "The New Education,"
Vol. XVI, No.1 (January 1903)

"The laws of nature are but the mathematical thoughts of God."

Euclid, circa 365 – 300 BC

"The world will never starve for want of wonders."

Gilbert Keith Chesterton, 1874 – 1936
Tremendous Trifles (1909)

"The universe is neither centered on the earth nor the sun. It is centered on God."

Alfred Noyes, 1880 – 1958
Attributed

"God knows the deepest places of our being, it is He who has shaped it with his very hands."

Saint Augustine, 354 – 430
Confessions (397 – 400)

"Heaven wheels above you, displaying to you her eternal glories, and still your eyes are on the ground."

Dante Alighieri, 1265 – 1321

"Behold the beauty of the day. The shout of color to glad color, rocks and trees, and sun and seas, and wind and sky: All these are God's expression, art work of His hand, which men must love ere they can understand."

Richard Hovey, 1864 – 1900
Richard Hovey and Bliss Carman; "The Gift of Art,"
Last Songs of Vagabondia (1900)

"In the beginning God created the heaven and the earth... The extraordinary, the marvelous thing about Genesis is not how unscientific it is, but how amazingly accurate it is. How could the ancient Israelites have known the exact order of an evolution that wasn't to be formulated for thousands of years? Here is a truth that cuts across barriers of time and space."

Madeleine L'Engle, 1918 – 2007
"The Expanding Universe." Newberry Award
Acceptance Speech, 1963
Award for her book, *A Wrinkle in Time* (1962)

"Heaven is under our feet as well as over our heads."

Henry David Thoreau, 1837 – 1861
Journals (1884)

"For me, the idea of a creation is not conceivable without invoking the necessity of design. One cannot be exposed to the law and order of the universe without concluding that there must be design and purpose behind it all....My experiences with science led me to God. They challenge science to prove the existence of God. But must we really light a candle to see the sun?"

Wehrner von Braun, 1912 – 1977
"Letter to the California State Board of Education,"
September 14, 1972

"Were it not for God, we would be in this glorious world with grateful hearts and no one to thank."

Christina Rossetti, 1830 – 1894
Attributed

"The God who created, names, and numbers the stars in the heavens also numbers the hairs of my head. He pays attention to very big things and to very small ones. What matters to me matters to Him, and that changes my life."

Elisabeth Elliot, 1926 – 2015
Passion and Purity (1984)

"This most beautiful system of the sun, planets, and comets, could only proceed from the counsel and dominion of an intelligent and powerful Being. A Heavenly Master governs all the world as Sovereign of the universe. We are astonished at Him by reason of His perfection; we honor Him and fall down before Him because of His unlimited power. From blind physical necessity which is always and everywhere the same, no variety adhering to time and place could evolve, and all variety of created objects which represent order and life in the universe could happen only by the willful reasoning of its original Creator, Whom I call the Lord God."

Isaac Newton, 1643 – 1727
The Principia: Mathematical Principles of Natural Philosophy (1687)

"True prayer is neither a mere mental exercise nor a vocal performance. It is far deeper than that—it is a spiritual transaction with the Creator of Heaven and Earth. Prayer is not a hard requirement—it is the natural duty of a creature to its creator, the simplest homage that human need can pay to divine liberality."

Charles Spurgeon, 1834 – 1892
Sermon, "The Throne of Grace," Metropolitan Tabernacle, Newington, November 19, 1871

"The fullness of joy is to behold God in everything."

Julian of Norwich, born 1342

"It is remarkable how few people seem to derive any pleasure from the beauty of the sky."

John Lubbock, 1834 – 1913
The Pleasures of Life (1890)

"If our Creator has so bountifully provided for our existence here, which is but momentary, and for our temporal wants, which will soon be forgotten, how much more must He have done for our enjoyment in the everlasting world?"

Hosea Ballou, 1771 – 1852
Maturin M. Ballou, *Biography of Rev. Hosea Ballou* (1854)

"Never lose an opportunity of seeing anything beautiful. Beauty is God's hand-writing—a way-side sacrament; welcome it in every fair face, every fair sky, every fair flower, and thank Him for it, the fountain of all loveliness, and drink it in, simply and earnestly, with all your eyes; it is a charmed draught, a cup of blessing."

Charles Kingsley, 1819 – 1875
From the Journal, *Politics for the People* (1848)

"I cannot look around me without being struck with the analogy observable in the works of God. I find the Bible written in the style of His other books of Creation and Providence. The pen seems in the same hand. I see it, indeed, write at times mysteriously in each of these books; thus, I know that mystery in the works of God is only another name for my ignorance. The moment, therefore, that I become humble, all becomes right."

Richard Cecil, 1495 – 1553
J.H. Gilbert; *Dictionary of Burning Words and Brilliant Writers* (1895)

This is My Father's World

This is my Father's world, And to my list'ning ears,
All nature sings, and round me rings, The music of the spheres.
This is my Father's world: I rest me in the thought
Of rocks and trees, of skies and seas— His hand the wonders wrought.

This is my Father's world: The birds their carols raise,
The morning light, the lily white, Declare their Maker's praise.
This is my Father's world: He shines in all that's fair;
In the rustling grass I hear Him pass, He speaks to me everywhere.

This is my Father's world: Oh, let me ne'er forget
That though the wrong seems oft so strong, God is the ruler yet.

Maltbie Babcock, 1858 – 1901
Hymn (1901)

How Great Thou Art

O Lord my God, when I in awesome wonder
Consider all the works Thy hand hath made,
I see the stars, I hear the mighty thunder,
Thy pow'r throughout the universe displayed,

Chorus:

Then sings my soul, My Savior God, to Thee,
How great Thou art! How great Thou art!
Then sings my soul, My Savior God, to Thee,
How great Thou art! How great Thou art!

When through the woods and forest glades I wander
And hear the birds sing sweetly in the trees,
When I look down from lofty mountain grandeur
And hear the brook and feel the gentle breeze,

And when I think, that God, His Son not sparing;
Sent Him to die, I scarce can take it in,
That on a Cross, my burdens gladly bearing,
He bled and died to take away my sin.

When Christ shall come, with shouts of acclamation,
And take me home, what joy shall fill my heart!
Then I shall bow in humble adoration
And there proclaim, "My God, how great Thou art!"

Carl Gustaf Boberg, 1859 – 1940
From his poem, "O Great God" (1891)
Translated by Stuart K. Hine (1949)

All Things Bright and Beautiful

All things bright and beautiful,
All creatures great and small,
All things wise and wonderful:
The Lord God made them all.

Each little flow'r that opens,
Each little bird that sings,
He made their glowing colors,
He made their tiny wings.

The purple-headed mountains,
The river running by,
The sunset and the morning
That brightens up the sky.

The cold wind in the winter,
The pleasant summer sun,
The ripe fruits in the garden,
He made them every one.

The tall trees in the greenwood,
The meadows where we play,
The rushes by the water,
To gather every day.

He gave us eyes to see them,
And lips that we might tell
How great is God Almighty,
Who has made all things well.

Cecil Frances Alexander, 1819 – 1895
Hymn (1848)

You, Lord, are my deliverer from darkness and death to light and eternal life.

For you have delivered me from death and my feet from stumbling, that I may walk before God in the light of life.

Psalm 56:13

"I am the light of the world. Whoever follows me will never walk in darkness, but will have the light of life."

John 8:12

Declare the praises, proclaim the excellencies of him who called you out of darkness into his marvelous light.

1 Peter 2:9

2 SAMUEL 22:2, 29
The Lord is my rock, my fortress and my deliverer.... You, Lord, are my lamp; the Lord turns my darkness into light.

JOB 12:22
He reveals the deep things of darkness and brings utter darkness into the light.

JOB 33:28
He redeemed my soul from going down to the pit, and I will live to enjoy the light.

PSALM 3:8
From the Lord comes deliverance. May your blessing be on your people.

PSALM 16:11
You have made known to me the path of life; you will fill me with joy in your presence, with eternal pleasures at your right hand.

PSALM 18:2
The Lord is my rock, my fortress and my deliverer; my God is my rock, in whom I take refuge. He is my shield and the horn of my salvation, my stronghold.

PSALM 18:28
You, O Lord, keep my lamp burning; my God turns my darkness into light.

PSALM 27:1
The Lord is my light and my salvation; whom shall I fear? The Lord is the stronghold of my life; of whom shall I be afraid?

PSALM 34:7
The angel of the Lord encamps around those who fear him, and he delivers him.

PSALM 36:9
For with you is the fountain of life; in your light we see light.

PSALM 40:17
Lord, you are my help and my deliverer.

PSALM 80:19
Restore us, Lord God Almighty; make your face shine on us, that we may be saved.

PSALM 86:13
For great is your love toward me; you have delivered me from the depths of the grave.

PSALM 91:14 - 16
Because he loves me, I will deliver him; because he knows my name, I will protect him. When he calls out to me, I will answer him; I will be with him in trouble. I will deliver him and honor him. With long life I will satisfy him and show him my salvation.

PSALM 103:1 - 5
Bless the Lord, O my soul, and all that is within me, bless his holy name. Bless the Lord, O my soul and forget not all his benefits—who forgives all your sins and heals all your diseases, who redeems your life from the pit, and crowns you with love and compassion, who satisfies your desires with good things so that your youth is renewed like the eagle's.

PSALM 116:8
For you, O Lord, have delivered my soul from death, my eyes from tears, my feet from stumbling.

PSALM 139:12
Even the darkness will not be dark to you; the night will shine like the day, for darkness is as light to you.

ISAIAH 9:2
The people walking in darkness have seen a great light; on those living in the land of the shadow of death, a light has dawned.

ISAIAH 5:20
Woe unto them that call evil good, and good evil; that put darkness for light, and light for darkness; that put bitter for sweet, and sweet for bitter.

ISAIAH 60:19
No longer will you need the sun to shine by day, nor the moon to give its light by night, for the Lord your God will be your everlasting light, and your God will be your glory.

MICAH 7:8
Though I have fallen, I will rise. Though I sit in darkness, the Lord will be my light.

MATTHEW 6:13
Jesus taught them, saying, "Lead us not into temptation but deliver us from evil."

MATTHEW 7:13 – 14
Jesus said to them, "Enter by the narrow gate; for wide is the gate and broad is the way that leads to destruction, and there are many who go in by it. But small is the gate and narrow the road that leads to life, and only a few find it."

JOHN 1:4 – 5
In him was life, and that life was the light of men. The light shines in the darkness, but the darkness has not understood it.

JOHN 3:16
Jesus said, "For God so loved the world that he gave his only begotten Son, that whosoever believes in him shall not perish but have eternal life."

JOHN 5:24
Jesus said to them, "Verily I say to you, he who hears my voice and believes in him who has sent me has everlasting life, and shall not come to judgment, but has passed from death into life."

JOHN 6:47
Jesus said, "He who believes has everlasting life."

JOHN 6:63
Jesus said to them, "It is the Spirit who gives life; the flesh profits nothing. The words that I speak to you are spirit, and they are life."

JOHN 6:68 – 69
Simon Peter answered him, "Lord, to whom shall we go? You have the words of eternal life. We believe and know that you are the Holy One of God."

JOHN 8:12
Jesus said, "I am the light of the world. Whoever follows me will never walk in darkness, but will have the light of life."

JOHN 10:10
Jesus said to them, "I am come that you may have life and have it more abundantly."

JOHN 10:27 – 28
Jesus told them, "My sheep listen to my voice; I know them and they follow me. I give them eternal life, and they will never perish, and no one will snatch them out of my hand."

JOHN 12:46
Jesus spoke to them, saying, "I have come into the world as a light, so that no one who believes in me should stay in darkness."

JOHN 14:6
Jesus said to them, "I am the way, the truth, and the life. No one comes to the Father except through me."

JOHN 17:3
Jesus prayed, "Now this is eternal life: that they may know you, the only true God and Jesus Christ whom you have sent."

ROMANS 6:23
The gift of God is eternal life in Christ Jesus our Lord.

1 CORINTHIANS 15:55
Where, O death, is your victory? Where, O death, is your sting?

2 CORINTHIANS 4:6
For God, who said, "Let light shine out of the darkness," made his light shine in our hearts to give us the light of the knowledge of the glory of God in the face of Christ.

2 CORINTHIANS 4:16 - 18
Therefore, we do not lose heart. Though outwardly we are wasting away, yet inwardly we are being renewed day by day. For our light and momentary troubles are achieving for us an eternal glory that far outweighs them all. So we fix our eyes not on what is seen but on what is unseen. For what is seen is temporary, but what is unseen is eternal.

EPHESIANS 5:8 - 9
For you were once darkness, but now you are light in the Lord. Live as children of light.

COLOSSIANS 1:13 - 14
For he has delivered us from the power of darkness and brought us into the kingdom of the Son he loves, in whom we have redemption, the forgiveness of sins.

2 TIMOTHY 1:9 - 10
He has saved us and called us to a holy life—not because of anything we have done but because of his own purposes and grace. This grace was given us in Christ Jesus before the beginning of time, but it has now been revealed through the appearing of our Savior, Christ Jesus, who has destroyed death and brought life and immortality to light through the gospel.

1 JOHN 1:2, 5
The life appeared; we have seen it and testify to it, and we proclaim to you the eternal life, which was with the Father and has appeared to us.... This is the message we have heard from him and declare to you: God is light and in him there is no darkness at all.

1 JOHN 2:25
And this is the promise that He has promised us: eternal life.

1 JOHN 5:11
And this is the testimony: God has given us eternal life, and this life is in his Son.

1 JOHN 5:20
And we know that the Son of God has come and has given us an understanding, that we may know Him who is true; and we are in Him who is true, in His Son Jesus Christ. This is the true God and eternal life.

JUDE 21
Keep yourselves in God's love as you wait for the mercy of our Lord Jesus Christ to bring you to eternal life.

REVELATION 21:4
He will wipe away every tear from their eyes, and death shall be no more, neither shall there be mourning, nor crying, nor pain anymore, for the former things have passed away.

REVELATION 21:6
Then He said to me, "It is done. I am the Alpha and the Omega, the beginning and the end I will give to the one who thirsts from the spring of the water of life without cost."

"O Holy Spirit, descend plentifully into my heart.
Enlighten the dark corners of this neglected dwelling and scatter thy cheerful beams."

Saint Augustine, 354 – 430
"Prayer to the Holy Spirit"

"Let your door stand open to receive Him, unlock your soul to Him, offer Him a welcome in your mind, and then you will see the riches of

simplicity, the treasures of peace, the joy of grace. Throw wide the gates of your heart, stand before the sun of the everlasting light. . . .”

Saint Ambrose, died 397
“Exposition of Psalm 118” (circa 386 – 390)

“The guilty one is not he who commits the sin, but he who causes the darkness.”

Victor Hugo, 1802 – 1885
Les Misérables (1862)

“Great and glorious God, and Thou Lord Jesus, I pray you shed abroad your light in the darkness of my mind. Be found of me, Lord, so that in all things I may act only in accordance with Thy holy will.”

Saint Francis of Assisi, died 1226

“Look at how a single candle can both defy and define the darkness.”

Anne Frank, 1929 – 1945
The Diary of a Young Girl (1947)

“All the darkness in the world cannot extinguish the light of a single candle.”

Saint Francis of Assisi, died 1226

“For death is no more than a turning of us over from time to eternity.”

William Penn, 1644 – 1718
More Fruits of Solitude: Being the Second Part of Reflections and Maxims Relating to the Conduct of Human Life (circa 1692)

"Once a man is united with God, how could he not live forever?"

C. S. Lewis, 1898 – 1963
Mere Christianity (1952)

"How sweet is rest after fatigue! How sweet will heaven be when our journey is ended."

George Whitefield, 1714 – 1770
Letters of George Whitefield, for the Period 1734–1742 (1771)

"For a small reward, a man will hurry away on a long journey; while for eternal life, many will hardly take a single step."

Thomas à Kempis, 1380 – 1471
Imitation of Christ (1418 – 1427)

"Give light, and the darkness will disappear of itself."

Desiderius Erasmus, 1466 – 1536
Attributed

"It is not death that we should fear, but we should fear never beginning to live."

Marcus Aurelius, 121 – 180
Meditations (161 – 180)

"In order for the light to shine so brightly, the darkness must be present."

Francis Bacon, 1561 – 1626
Attributed

"Truly, it is in darkness that one finds the light, so when we are in sorrow, then this light is nearest of all to us."

Meister Eckhart, 1260 – 1328
Attributed

"Darkness cannot drive out darkness; only light can do that.
Hate cannot drive out hate; only love can do that."

Martin Luther King, Jr., 1929 – 1968
"Loving Your Enemies," Dexter Avenue Baptist Church,
Montgomery, Alabama Nov.17, 1957

"For it is in giving that we receive,
it is in pardoning that we are pardoned,
and it is in dying that we are born to eternal life."

Saint Francis of Assisi, died 1226

"Hope is being able to see that there is light despite all of the darkness."

Desmond Tutu, 1931 – 2021
"The Priest," *NY Times Magazine* (March 7, 2010)

"I will love the light for it shows me the way, yet I will endure the darkness because it shows me the stars."

Og Mandino, 1923 – 1996
The Greatest Salesman in the World (1968)

"The trouble is, people do not know that Christ is a Deliverer. They forget that the Son of God came to keep them from sin as well as to forgive it."

Dwight L. Moody, 1837 – 1899
Anecdotes and Illustrations (1876)

"And Faith, not knowledge, builds for every man,
In his own consciousness,
The ultimate, bright Heaven of his hope,
The realm of joy, the goal of his desire.

No weaker hand can lead the errant soul
From Doubt's dark labyrinth into the light,
And up the starry heights whereon is God."

Andrew Downing, 1815 – 1852
"The Sphinx," *The Trumpeter and Other Poems* (1897)

"There are two ways of spreading light:
to be the candle or the mirror that reflects it."

Edith Wharton, 1862 – 1937
"Veaslius in Zante," *Artemis to Actaeon: And Other Verses* (1909)

"Even the darkest night will end and the sun will rise"

Victor Hugo, 1802 – 1885
Les Misérables (1862)

I can see that in the midst of death, life persists. In the midst of untruth, truth persists. In the midst of darkness, light persists. Hence, I gather that God is life, truth, light. He is love. He is the supreme good.

Mahatma Gandhi, 1869 – 1948
"On God," Kingsley Hall, London, October 20, 1931

"The darkness around us might somehow light up if we would first practice using the light we have in the place we are."

Henry Haskins, 1875 – 1957
Meditations in Wall Street (1940)

"Maybe you have to know the darkness before you can appreciate the light."

Madeleine L'Engle, 1918 – 2007
A Ring of Endless Light (1980)

"To love beauty is to see light."

Victor Hugo, 1802 – 1885
Les Misérables (1862)

"What causes night in our souls may leave stars."

Victor Hugo, 1802 – 1885
Ninety-Three (1874)

"We can easily forgive a child who is afraid of the dark;
the real tragedy of life is when men are afraid of the light."

Plato, circa 448 – 348 BC

"Though my soul may set in darkness, it will rise in perfect light;
I have loved the stars too fondly to be fearful of the night."

Sarah Williams, 1814 – 1868
"The Old Astronomer," *Twilight Hours: A Legacy of Verse* (1868)

"Our Christian wisdom is to name the darkness as darkness, and the Light as light, and to learn how to live and work in the Light so that 'the darkness does not overcome it.'" (John 1:5)

Richard Rohr, born 1943
Meditation 8, *Preparing for Christmas with Richard Rohr* (1988)

My True Father,
I set my hopes upon You alone,
And I only ask You, God,
For my Soul salvation.
Let Your Holy Will
Be my strengthening on this way,
For my life without You is a mere empty moment,

And only serving You leads to Eternal life.
Amen!

Saint Agapit of Pechersk, 11th Century
"Prayer for the Soul"

"Christianity asserts that every individual human being is going to live forever and this must be either true or false. Now there are a good many things which would not be worth bothering about if I were going to live only seventy years, but which I had better bother about very seriously if I am going to live forever."

C. S. Lewis 1898 – 1963
Mere Christianity (1952)

"It's best to be with those in time that we hope to be with in eternity."

Thomas Fuller, 1608 – 1661

"May Christ bring us all together to everlasting life."

Saint Benedict, 480 – 550
Rule of Benedict (515)

"I believe the promises of God enough to venture an eternity on them."

Isaac Watts, 1674 – 1748
"Cheering Thoughts for the Sick and Weary,"
General Baptist Magazine, No.1, 1876

"We know but little now about the conditions of the life that is to come. But what is certain is that love must last. God, the Eternal God, is love. Covet therefore that everlasting gift, that one thing which it is certain is going to stand, that one coinage which will be current in the universe when all other coinages of all of the nations shall be useless and unhonored."

Henry Drummond, 1851 – 1897
The Greatest Thing in the World (1870)

"Divine Wisdom, intending to detain us some time on earth, has done well to cover with a veil the prospect of the life to come; for if our sight could clearly distinguish the opposite bank, who would remain on this tempestuous coast of time?"

Madame de Stael, 1766 – 1817
Ed., Tryon Edwards; *A Dictionary of Thoughts: A Cyclopedia of Laconic Quotations* (1891)

"No one is as capable of gratitude as one who has emerged from the kingdom of darkness."

Elie Wiesel, 1928 – 2016
Nobel Peace Prize Acceptance Speech, Oslo, Norway, December 10, 1986

Lead, Kindly Light

Lead, kindly Light
amid the encircling gloom,
Lead Thou me on!
The night is dark, and I am far from home –
Lead Thou me on!
Keep Thou my feet;
I do not ask to see
The distant scene, one step enough for me.
So, lead me onward, Lord, and hear my plea.

John Henry Newman, 1801 – 1890
From the Hymn (1833)

"Lord, make me an instrument of thy peace.
Where there is hatred, let me sow love,
Where there is injury, pardon;
Where there is doubt, faith;
Where there is despair, hope;

Where there is darkness, light;
Where there is sadness, joy.
O Divine Master, grant that I may not so much seek
to be consoled as to console,
to be understood as to understand,
to be loved, as to love.
For it is in giving that we receive,
It is in pardoning that we are pardoned,
and it is in dying that we are born to eternal life.
Amen,"

Saint Francis of Assisi, died 1226
"The Peace Prayer of Saint Francis"

From everlasting to everlasting thou art God.

Lord, you have been our dwelling place throughout all generations. Before the mountains were born or you brought forth the earth and the world, from everlasting to everlasting you are God.

Psalm 90:1 – 2

GENESIS 21:33
Abraham planted a tamarisk tree in Beersheba, and there he called upon the name of the Lord, the Eternal God.

DEUTERONOMY 33:27
The eternal God is your refuge, and underneath are the everlasting arms.

1 CHRONICLES 29:10
Praise be to you, O Lord, God of our father Israel, from everlasting to everlasting.

NEHEMIAH 9:5
Stand up and praise the Lord your God who is from everlasting to everlasting.

JOB 37:26
Behold, God is great, and we know him not; the number of his years is unsearchable.

PSALM 33:11
But the plans of the Lord stand firm forever, the purposes of his heart through all generations.

PSALM 41:13
Blessed be to the Lord, the God of Israel, from everlasting to everlasting. Amen and Amen.

PSALM 48:14
For this God is our God forever and ever; He will be our guide even to the end.

PSALM 90:2, 4
Before the mountains were brought forth or ever you had formed the earth and the world, from everlasting to everlasting you are God. For a thousand years in your sight are but as yesterday when it is past, or as a watch in the night.

PSALM 102:24, 27
Your years go on through all generations. But you remain the same, and your years will not come to an end.

PSALM 145:13
Your kingdom is an everlasting kingdom and your dominion endures through all generations.

ISAIAH 26:4
Trust in the Lord forever, for the Lord is the Rock eternal.

ISAIAH 40:28
Do you not know? Have you not heard? The Lord is the everlasting God, the Creator of the ends of the earth. He will not grow weary and his understanding no one can fathom.

ISAIAH 48:12
Listen to Me, O Jacob, even Israel whom I called; I am He, I am the first, I am also the last.

ISAIAH 57:15
For thus says the high and exalted One who lives forever, whose name is Holy, "I dwell on a high and holy place, and also with the contrite and lowly of spirit in order to revive the spirit of the lowly and to revive the heart of the contrite."

DANIEL 6:26
The God of Daniel is the living God and he endures forever; his kingdom will not be destroyed, his dominion will never end.

MATTHEW 24:35
Jesus said to his disciples, "Heaven and earth will pass away, but my words will never pass away."

JOHN 8:58
"I tell you the truth," Jesus answered, "before Abraham was born, I am!"

ROMANS 8:38 – 39
For I am sure that neither death nor life, nor angels nor rulers, nor things present nor things to come, nor powers, nor height nor depth, nor anything else in all creation, will be able to separate us from the love of God in Christ Jesus our Lord.

2 CORINTHIANS 4:18
So, we fix our eyes not on what is seen but on what is unseen. For what is seen is temporary, but what is unseen is eternal.

1 TIMOTHY 1:17
Now to the King eternal, immortal, and invisible, the only God, be honor and glory forever and ever. Amen.

HEBREWS 1:10 – 12
In the beginning, O Lord, you laid the foundations of the earth, and the heavens are the work of your hands. They will perish, but you remain; they will all wear out like a garment. You will roll them up like a robe; like a garment they will be changed. But you remain the same, and your years will never end.

HEBREWS 13:8
Jesus Christ is the same yesterday, today, and forever.

2 PETER 3:8
But do not forget this one thing, dear friends: With the Lord a day is like a thousand years and a thousand years are like a day.

REVELATION 1:8
"I am the Alpha and the Omega," says the Lord God, "who is, and who was, and who is to come, the Almighty."

"It is not in time that precede all times, O Lord. You precede all past times in the sublimity of an ever-present reality. You have made all times and are before all times."

Augustine, 354 – 430

"God and all attributes of God are eternal."

Baruch Spinoza, 1632 – 1677
Ethics (1677)

"God is Alpha and Omega in the great world, let us endeavor to make him so in the little world; let us practice to make him our last thought at night when we sleep; and our first in the morning when we awake; so shall our fancy be sanctified in the night, and our understanding rectified in the day; so shall our rest be peaceful, and our labors prosperous; our life pious, and our death glorious."

Wellins Calcott, 1726 – 1779
Thoughts Moral and Divine (1761)

"Almighty and eternal Lord God, the great Creator of heaven and earth, and the God and Father of our Lord Jesus Christ, look down from heaven in pity and compassion upon me thy servant, who humbly prostrate myself before thee."

George Washington, 1732 – 1799
W. Herbert Burk; "Wednesday Morning Prayer,"
Washington's Prayers (1907)

"Oh, eternal and everlasting God, direct my thoughts, words, and work. Wash away my sins in the immaculate blood of the Lamb and purge my heart by Thy Holy Spirit. Daily, frame me more and more in the likeness of Thy son, Jesus Christ, that living in Thy fear, and dying in Thy favor, I may in Thy appointed time obtain the resurrection of the justified unto eternal life. Bless, O Lord, the whole race of mankind and let the world be filled with the knowledge of Thee and Thy son, Jesus Christ."

George Washington, 1732 – 1799
W. Herbert Burk; "Monday Morning Prayer,"
Washington's Prayers (1907)

"None can comprehend eternity but the eternal God. Eternity is an ocean, whereof we shall never see the shore; it is a deep, where we can find no bottom; a labyrinth from whence we cannot extricate ourselves and where we shall never lose the door."

Thomas Boston, 1676 – 1732
Human Nature in Its Fourfold State (1720)

"The everlasting God has become our Father, and the moment we realize that, it transforms everything".

Martyn Lloyd-Jones, 1899 – 1981
Spiritual Depression–Its Causes and Cures (1965)

"Now may the God and Father of our Lord Jesus Christ, and the eternal high priest himself, the Son of God, Jesus Christ, build you up in faith and truth and in all gentleness and in all freedom from anger and forbearance and steadfastness and patient endurance and purity."

Polycarp, 65 – 155

"For if there's no everlasting God, there's no such thing as virtue, and there's no need of it."

Fyodor Dostoevsky, 1821 – 1881
The Brothers Karamazov (1880)

"I believe the promises of God enough to venture an eternity on them."

Isaac Watts, 1674 – 1748
J.H. Gilbert; *Dictionary of Burning Words and Brilliant Writers* (1895)

"I believe in the immortality of the soul because I have within me eternal longings."

Helen Keller, 1880 – 1968
Midstream: My Later Life (1929)

"In Him alone lie our security, our confidence, our trust. A spirit of restlessness and resistance can never wait, but one who believes he is loved with an everlasting love, and knows that underneath are the everlasting arms, will find strength and peace."

Elisabeth Elliot, 1926 – 2015
Quest for Love: True Stories of Passion and Purity (1996)

"The difference God's timelessness makes is that this now (which slips away from you even as you say the word now) is for Him infinite."

C. S. Lewis, 1898 – 1963
"To Miss Breckenridge: from Magdalen College," August 1, 1949
The Letters of C. S. Lewis (1966)

"My God, I am yours for time and eternity. Teach me to cast myself entirely into the arms of your loving Providence with a lively, unlimited confidence in your compassionate, tender pity. Grant, O most merciful Redeemer, that whatever you ordain or permit may be acceptable to me. Take from my heart all painful anxiety; let nothing sadden me but sin, nothing delight me but the hope of coming to the possession of You, my God and my all, in your everlasting kingdom. Amen."

Suscipe of Catherine McAuley, 1778 – 1841
Also known as the "Act of Resignation"

O God, Our Help in Ages Past

O God, our help in ages past,
Our hope for years to come,
Our shelter from the stormy blast,
And our eternal home!

Beneath the shadow of Thy throne
Still may we dwell secure;
Sufficient is Thine arm alone,
And our defense is sure.

Before the hills in order stood,
Or earth received her frame,
From everlasting Thou art God,
To endless years the same.

A thousand ages in Thy sight
Are like an evening gone;
Short as the watch that ends the night
Before the rising sun.

The busy tribes of flesh and blood,
With all their cares and fears,
Are carried downward by the flood,
And lost in following years.

Thy Word commands our flesh to dust:
"Return, ye sons of men!"
All nations rose from earth at first
And turn to earth again.

Time, like an ever-rolling stream,
Bears all its sons away;
They fly forgotten as a dream
Dies at the opening day.

Our God our help in ages past,
Our hope for years to come,
Be Thou our guard while life shall last,
And our eternal home.

Isaac Watts, 1674 – 1748
Hymn (1708)

You are faithful, O Lord, to a thousand generations of those who love you and are called by your name.

Know therefore that the Lord your God is God, the faithful God who keeps covenant and steadfast love with those who love him and keep his commandments, to a thousand generations.

Deuteronomy 7:9

He remembers his covenant forever, the word he commanded for a thousand generations.

1 Chronicles 16:15

GENESIS 28:15
I am with you and will watch over you wherever you go; I will not leave you until I have done what I have promised you.

EXODUS 34:6
And he passed in front of Moses, proclaiming, "The Lord, the Lord, the compassionate and gracious God, slow to anger, abounding in love and faithfulness."

DEUTERONOMY 31:6
Be strong and courageous, do not be afraid or tremble at them, for the Lord your God is the one who goes with you; he will never leave you or forsake you.

DEUTERONOMY 32:4
He is the Rock, his works are perfect, and all his ways are just. A faithful God who does no wrong, upright and just is he.

PSALM 25:10
All the ways of the Lord are loving and faithful for those who keep the demands of his covenant.

PSALM 33:4
For the word of the Lord is right and true; he is faithful in all he does.

PSALM 33:11
The counsel of the Lord stands forever, the purposes of his heart through all generations.

PSALM 36:5
Your love, Lord, reaches to the heavens, your faithfulness to the skies.

PSALM 57:2 - 3
I cry out to God Most High, to God who fulfills his purpose for me. He sends from heaven and saves me... God sends his steadfast love and his faithfulness!

PSALM 57:10
For great is your love, reaching to the heavens; your faithfulness reaches to the skies.

PSALM 68:19
Praise be to the Lord, to God our Savior, who daily bears our burdens.

PSALM 86:15
But you, O Lord, are a compassionate and gracious God, slow to anger, abounding in love and faithfulness.

PSALM 89:1 - 2
I will sing of the Lord's great love forever; with my mouth I will make your faithfulness known through all generations. I will declare that your love stands firm forever, that you have established your faithfulness in heaven itself.

PSALM 89:5
And the heavens will praise thy wonders, O Lord: Thy faithfulness also in the assembly of the holy ones.

PSALM 89:8
You are mighty, O Lord, and your faithfulness surrounds you.

PSALM 89:14
Righteousness and justice are the foundations of your throne; love and faithfulness go before you.

PSALM 89:33 - 35
I will not take my love from him, nor will I ever betray my faithfulness. I will not violate my covenant nor alter what my lips have uttered. Once for all I have sworn by my holiness.

PSALM 90:1
Lord, you have been our dwelling place throughout all generations.

PSALM 91:4
He will cover you with his feathers, and under his wings you will find refuge; his faithfulness will be your shield and your rampart.

PSALM 100:4 - 5
Enter into his gates with thanksgiving, and into his courts with praise: be thankful unto him, and bless his name. For the Lord is good; his love endures forever and his faithfulness continues through all generations.

PSALM 115:1
Not to us, O Lord, not to us but to your name be the glory, because of your love and faithfulness.

PSALM 117:1 - 2
Praise the Lord, all you nations; extol him all you peoples. For great is his love toward us, and the faithfulness of the Lord endures forever.

PSALM 119:90
Your faithfulness endures through all generations; you established the earth and it endures.

PSALM 121:3
He will not allow your foot to slip; he who keeps you will not slumber.

PSALM 138:8
The Lord will perfect that which concerns me; Thy lovingkindness, O Lord, is everlasting. Do not forsake the works of thy hands.

PSALM 145:13 – 14
Your kingdom is an everlasting kingdom, and your dominion endures through all generations. The Lord is faithful to all his promises and loving toward all he has made. The Lord upholds all those who fall and lifts up all who are bowed down.

PSALM 146:5 – 6
Blessed is he whose help is the God of Jacob, whose hope is in the Lord his God, the Maker of heaven and earth, the sea, and everything in them—the Lord who remains faithful forever.

ISAIAH 41:10
"Do not fear for I am with you; do not look anxiously about you, for I am your God. I will strengthen you, surely I will help you, surely I will uphold you with my righteous right hand."

ISAIAH 43:1 – 3
But now, this is what the Lord says, he who created you, he who formed you: "Do not fear, for I have redeemed you; I have summoned you by name; you are mine. When you pass through the waters, I will be with you; and when you pass through the rivers, they will not sweep over you. When you walk through the fire, you will not be burned; the flames will not set you ablaze. For I am the Lord your God, the Holy One of Israel, your Savior."

LAMENTATIONS 3:22 – 23
Because of the Lord's great love we are not consumed, for his compassions never fail. They are new every morning; great is your faithfulness. The steadfast love of the Lord never ceases; his mercies never come to an end; they are new every morning; great is your faithfulness.

MATTHEW 28:20
Jesus said to them, "And surely I am with you always, even to the end of the age."

LUKE 1:45
Blessed is she who has believed that what the Lord has said to her will be accomplished.

1 CORINTHIANS 1:9
God, who has called you into fellowship with his Son, Jesus Christ our Lord, is faithful.

1 CORINTHIANS 10:13
No temptation has overtaken you that is not common to mankind. God is faithful, and he will not let you be tempted beyond what you can bear, but with the temptation he will also provide the way of escape, that you may be able to endure it.

2 CORINTHIANS 1:20
For no matter how many promises God has made, they are "Yes" in Christ.

PHILIPPIANS 1:6
Be confident of this, that he who began a good work in you will carry it on to completion.

PHILIPPIANS 4:19
But my God shall supply all your needs according to his riches in glory by Christ Jesus.

1 THESSALONIANS 5:23 - 24
May God himself, the God of peace, sanctify you through and through. May your whole spirit, soul, and body be kept blame-

less at the coming of the Lord Jesus Christ. The one who calls you is faithful, and he will do it.

2 THESSALONIANS 3:3
But the Lord is faithful, and he will strengthen you and protect you from the evil one.

2 TIMOTHY 2:13
If we are faithless, he will remain faithful, for he cannot deny himself.

2 TIMOTHY 4:17
But the Lord stood with me and gave me strength.

HEBREWS 10:23
Let us hold resolutely to the hope we confess, for He who promised is faithful.

HEBREWS 13:5
Keep your life free from love of money, and be content with what you have, for he has said, "I will never leave you nor forsake you."

1 JOHN 1:9
If we confess our sins, he is faithful and just and will forgive our sins and purify us from all
unrighteousness.

"The glory of God's faithfulness is that no sin of ours has ever made Him unfaithful."

Charles Spurgeon, 1834 – 1892
"The Novelties of Divine Mercy," Sermon No. 3170 (November 11, 1909)

"He who sends the storm steers the vessel."

Thomas Adams, Puritan, 1583 – 1652

"In God's faithfulness lies eternal security."

Corrie ten Boom, 1892 – 1983
This Day is the Lord's (1980)

"God's strength behind you, His concern for you, His love within you, and His arms beneath you are more than sufficient for the job ahead of you."

William Arthur Ward, 1921 – 1994
Attributed

"The whole of the past is embraced by the word 'forgiveness'; the whole of the future is preserved in the faithfulness of God."

Dietrich Bonhoeffer, 1906 – 1945
Ethics (1949)

"...when we have been brought very low and helped, sorely wounded and healed, cast down and raised again, have given up all hope, and been suddenly snatched from danger, and placed in safety, and when these things have been repeated to us and in us a thousand times over, we begin to learn to trust simply to the word and power of God, beyond and against appearances...."

John Newton, 1725 – 1807
"Letter #II to Mrs. _____," September, 1764
John Newton and Richard Cecil, *The Works of Reverend John Newton Vol. I* (1847)

"The thoughtful believer recalls God's faithfulness in the past when confronted by any new threat. Part of spiritual maturity is strong sense of one's own history."

Max Anders, born 1947
"Deuteronomy," *Holman Old Testament Commentary, #3* (2002)

"O Lord, thou knowest how busy I am this day.
If I forget thee, do not thou forget me."

1st Baron Jacob Astley of Redding, 1579 – 1652
"Battle Prayer at the Battle of Edgehill," Sunday, October 23, 1642

"He hath never failed thee yet.
Never will his love forget.
O fret not thyself nor let
Thy heart be troubled,
Neither let it be afraid."

Amy Carmichael, 1867 – 1951
Elisabeth Elliot, *Shadow of the Almighty: The Life and Testament of Jim Elliot* (1958)

"In the same way the sun never grows weary of shining, nor a stream of flowing, it is God's nature to keep his promises. Therefore, go immediately to His throne and say, 'Do as you promised.'"

Charles H. Spurgeon, 1834 – 1899
January 15th Devotion, *Morning by Morning* (1891)

"He will keep His word—the gracious One, full of grace and truth— no doubt of it. He said, "Him that cometh unto me, I will in nowise cast out," and "Whatsoever ye shall ask in my name I will give it." He WILL keep His word: then I can come and humbly present my petition, and it will be all right. Doubt is here inadmissible, surely." –D.L.

David Livingstone, 1813 – 1873
Journal entry May 13, 1872
The Last Journals of David Livingstone, Central Africa, 1865 – 1873 (1874)

"Believers are inclined to attribute their successes to their godliness when it would be more accurate to connect them to God's faithfulness."

Max Anders, born 1947
Deuteronomy, Holman Old Testament Commentary, Vol. 3 (2002)

"God's faithfulness is stronger than our unfaithfulness and our infidelities."

Pope Francis, born 1936
Twitter

"God is not a deceiver that He should offer to support us, and then, when we lean upon Him, should slip away from us."

Augustine, 354 – 430

"Faith is the virtue by which, clinging to the faithfulness of God, we lean upon him, so that we may obtain what he gives to us."

William Ames, 1576 – 1633

"The same everlasting Father who cares for you today will care for you tomorrow and every day. Either he will shield you from suffering or give you unfailing strength to bear it. Be at peace then and put aside all anxious thoughts and imaginings."

Francis de Sales, 1567 – 1662

"To be assured of our salvation is no arrogant stoutness. It is faith. It is devotion. It is not presumption. It is God's promise."

Augustine, 354 – 430

"God is not proud. He stoops to conquer, He will have us even though we have shown that we prefer everything else to Him."

C. S. Lewis, 1898 – 1963
The Problem of Pain (1940)

"All God's giants have been weak men and women who have gotten hold of God's faithfulness."

Hudson Taylor, 1832 – 1905

"God does not give us everything we want, but He does fulfill His promises, leading us along the best and straightest paths to Himself."

Dietrich Bonhoeffer, 1906 – 1945
Ed., Eberhard Bethge: Letter, August 14, 1944, *Letters and Papers From Prison* (1970)

"He who has led, will lead
All through the wilderness;
He who hath fed will feed…
He who hath heard thy cry
Will never close His ear;
He who hath marked thy faintest sigh
Will not forget thy tear.
He loveth always, faileth never,
So rest on Him today."

Amy Carmichael, 1867 – 1951
Elisabeth Elliot, *A Chance to Die: The Life and Legacy of Amy Carmichael* (1987)

Great is Thy Faithfulness

Great is Thy faithfulness, O God my Father,
There is no shadow of turning with Thee;
Thou changest not, Thy compassions, they fail not
As Thou hast been, Thou forever wilt be.

Refrain:
Great is Thy faithfulness!
Great is Thy faithfulness!
Morning by morning new mercies I see;
All I have needed Thy hand hath provided.
Great is Thy faithfulness, Lord, unto me!

Summer and winter, and springtime and harvest,
Sun, moon and stars in their courses above,
Join with all nature in manifold witness
To Thy great faithfulness, mercy and love.

Pardon for sin and a peace that endureth,
Thine own dear presence to cheer and to guide;
Strength for today and bright hope for tomorrow,
Blessings all mine, with ten thousand beside!

Thomas O. Chisholm, 1866 – 1960
Hymn (1923)

Lord, you are gracious and compassionate. You bind the wounds of the brokenhearted; you stoop to lift us up.

But you are a forgiving God, gracious and compassionate,
slow to anger and abounding in love.

Nehemiah 9:17

The Lord is close to the brokenhearted and saves those
who are crushed in spirit.

Psalm 34:18

Your right hand sustains me; you stoop down to make me great.

Psalm 18:35

EXODUS 34:6
And he passed in front of Moses, proclaiming, "The Lord, the Lord, the compassionate and gracious God, slow to anger, abounding in love and faithfulness"....

2 SAMUEL 22:36
You give me your shield of victory; you stoop down to make me great.

PSALM 30:5
For his anger is but for a moment, and his favor is for a lifetime. Weeping may tarry for the night, but joy comes with the morning.

PSALM 68:19
Praise be to the Lord, to God our Savior, who daily bears our burdens.

PSALM 86:15
But you, O Lord, are a compassionate and gracious God, slow to anger, abounding in love and faithfulness.

PSALM 103:1 - 5
Praise the Lord, O my soul; all my inmost being, praise his holy name. Praise the Lord, O my soul, and forget not all his benefits—who forgives all your sins and heals all your diseases, who redeems your life from the pit and crowns you with love and compassion, who satisfies your desires with good things so that your youth is renewed like the eagle's.

PSALM 103:8 - 14
The Lord is compassionate and gracious, slow to anger, abounding in love. He will not always accuse, nor will he harbor his anger forever; he does not treat us as our sins deserve or repay us according to our iniquities. For as high as the heavens are above the earth, so great is his love for those who fear him; as far as the east is from the west, so far he has removed our transgressions from us. As a father has compassion on his children, so the Lord has compassion on those who

fear him; for he knows how we are formed, he remembers that we are dust.

PSALM 116:2
Because he bends down to listen, I will pray as long as I have breath.

PSALM 116:5
The Lord is gracious and righteous; our God is full of compassion.

PSALM 145:8 - 9
The Lord is gracious and compassionate, slow to anger and rich in love. The Lord is good to all; he has compassion on all he has made.

PSALM 145:14
The Lord upholds all who fall and lifts up all who are bowed down.

PSALM 147:3
The Lord heals the brokenhearted and binds up their wounds.

ISAIAH 30:18 - 19
Yet the Lord longs to be gracious to you; he rises to show you compassion. For the Lord is a God of justice. Blessed are all who wait for him!... How gracious he will be when you cry for help! As soon as he hears he will answer you.

ISAIAH 40:11
He tends his flock like a shepherd: He gathers the lambs in his arms and carries them close to his heart; he gently leads those who have young.

ISAIAH 40:29
He gives strength to the weary and increases the power of the weak.

ISAIAH 54:8
"But with everlasting kindness I will have compassion on you," says the Lord your Redeemer.

ISAIAH 55:7
Let the wicked forsake his way and the unrighteous man his thoughts; and let him return to the Lord, and He will have compassion on him, and to our God, for He will abundantly pardon.

ISAIAH 57:15
For this is what the high and lofty One says—he who lives forever, whose name is holy: "I live in a high and holy place, but also with him who is contrite and lowly in spirit, to revive the spirit of the lowly and to revive the heart of the contrite."

ISAIAH 145:8
The Lord is gracious and compassionate, slow to anger and rich in love.

LAMENTATIONS 3:22 - 23
Because of the Lord's great love we are not consumed, for his compassions never fail. They are new every morning; great is your faithfulness.

JOHN 1:14, 16 - 17
And the Word became flesh and dwelt among us. We have seen his glory, the glory of the one and only Son, who came down from the Father, full of grace and truth.... For from his

fullness we have all received grace upon grace. For the law was given through Moses; grace and truth came through Jesus Christ.

ROMANS 5:1 – 2
Therefore, since we have been justified through faith, we have peace with God through our Lord Jesus Christ, through whom we have gained access by faith into this grace in which we now stand.

ROMANS 5:21
So just as sin ruled over all people and brought them to death, now God's wonderful grace rules instead, giving us right standing with God and resulting in eternal life through Jesus Christ our Lord.

ROMANS 11:36
For from Him and through Him and for Him are all things. To Him be the glory forever! Amen.

2 CORINTHIANS 1:3 – 4
Praise be the God and Father of our Lord Jesus Christ, the Father of compassion and the God of all comfort, who comforts us in all our troubles, so that we can comfort those in any trouble with the comfort we ourselves have received from God.

2 CORINTHIANS 12:9 – 10
But he said to me, "My grace is sufficient for you, for my power is made perfect in weakness." Therefore, I will boast all the more gladly about my weaknesses, so that Christ's power may rest on me. That is why, for Christ's sake, I delight in weaknesses, in insults, in hardships, in persecutions, in difficulties. For when I am weak, then I am strong.

EPHESIANS 2:4 - 5
But because of his great love for us, God who is rich in mercy, made us alive in Christ even when we were dead in our transgressions—it is by grace you have been saved.

EPHESIANS 2:7 - 10
...[T]he incomparable riches of God's grace [are] expressed in his kindness to us in Christ Jesus, for it is by grace that you have been saved, through faith—and this not from yourselves, it is the gift of God—not by works so that no one can boast. For we are God's workmanship, created in Christ Jesus to do good works, which God prepared in advance for us to do.

EPHESIANS 4:32
Be kind and compassionate to one another, forgiving each other, just as in Christ God forgave you.

COLOSSIANS 3:12 - 14
Holy and dearly loved children, clothe yourselves with compassion, kindness, humility, gentleness and patience. Bear with each other and forgive whatever grievances you may have against one another. Forgive as the Lord forgave you. And over all these virtues put on love, which binds them all together in perfect unity.

TITUS 2:11
For the grace of God has appeared, bringing salvation to all people.

HEBREWS 4:16
Let us approach the throne of grace with confidence, so that we may receive mercy, and receive grace in our time of need.

1 PETER 5:7
Cast all your cares and anxieties on him because he cares for you.

1 PETER 5:10 - 11
And the God of all grace who called you to eternal glory in Christ—to him be the power forever and ever. Amen.

2 PETER 3:18
Grow in the grace and knowledge of our Lord and Savior Jesus Christ. To him be the glory both now and forever. Amen.

"Grace is the free, undeserved goodness and favor of God to mankind."

Matthew Henry, 1662 – 1714
Commentary of the Whole Bible (1706)

"God tempers the wind to the shorn lamb."

Laurence Sterne, 1713 – 1768
A Sentimental Journey Through France and Italy (1768)

"May the perfect grace and eternal love of Christ our Lord be our never-failing protection and help."

Saint Ignatius of Loyola, 1491 – 1556
"Letter of Perfection" (1547)

"Almighty and eternal Lord God, the great Creator of heaven and earth, and the God and Father of our Lord Jesus Christ; look down from heaven in pity and compassion upon me thy servant, who humbly prostrate myself before thee."

George Washington, 1732 – 1799
W. Herbert Burk; *Washington's Prayers* (1907)

"Intoxicated with unbroken success, we have become too self-sufficient to feel the need of redeeming and preserving grace, too proud to pray to the God who made us."

Abraham Lincoln, 1809 – 1865
Proclamation Appointing a National Fast Day
Washington, D.C., March 30, 1863

"I would rather make mistakes in kindness and compassion than work miracles in unkindness and hardness."

Mother Teresa, 1910 – 1997
A Gift for God: Prayers and Meditations (1975)

"Spirit of God, descend upon my heart
wean it from earth; through all its pulses move;
stoop to my weakness, mighty as thou art,
and make me love thee as I ought to love."

George Croly, 1780 – 1860
From the Hymn, "Spirit of God, Descend Upon My Heart" (1854)

"Grace, then, is grace—that is to say, it is sovereign, it is free, it is sure, it is unconditional, it is everlasting."

Alexander Whyte, 1836 – 1921
Commentary on the Shorter Catechism (1883)

"And what is grace? Grace is the free favor of God, the undeserved bounty of the ever-gracious Creator against whom we have offended, the generous pardon, the infinite, spontaneous loving-kindness of the God who has been provoked and angered by our sin, but who, delighting in mercy, and grieving to smite on the creatures whom he has made, is ever ready to pass by transgression, iniquity, and sin, and to save his people from all the evil consequences of their guilt."

Charles Haddon Spurgeon, 1834 – 1892
Sermon No. 3115, Delivered on the Lord's Day Evening,
November 1, 1874
Metropolitan Tabernacle, Newington

"Forgive, forget. Bear with the faults of others as you would have them bear with yours. Be patient and understanding. Life is too short to be vengeful or malicious."

Phillips Brooks, 1835 – 1893
A.V.G. Allen, *Memories of His Life with Extracts from His Letters and Notebooks* (1907)

"God is not proud. He stoops to conquer. He will have us even though we have shown that we prefer everything else to Him."

C. S. Lewis, 1898 – 1963
The Problem of Pain (1940)

"I have had prayers answered—most strangely so sometimes—but I think our Heavenly Father's loving-kindness has been even more evident in what He has refused me."

Lewis Carroll, 1832 – 1898
"Letter: To an invalid, Christ Church," Oxford, November 1885
Lewis Carroll and Lancelyn Green,
The Selected Letters of Lewis Carroll (1982)

"Man is born broken. He lives by mending. The grace of God is glue."

Eugene O'Neill, 1888 – 1953
Play, "The Great God Brown," First performed 1926

"How far you go in life depends on your being tender with the young, compassionate with the aged, sympathetic with the striving, and tolerant of the weak and strong. Because, someday in your life you will have been all of these."

George Washington Carver, born circa 1864 – 1943
Attributed

"Grace can pardon our ungodliness and justify us with Christ's righteousness; it can put the Spirit of Jesus Christ within us; it can help us when we are down; it can heal us when we are wounded; it can multiply pardons, as we through frailty multiply transgressions."

John Bunyan, 1628 – 1688
Ed., Jeremiah Chaplin; *The Riches of Bunyan*, (1850)

"By God's grace, I am what I am."

Saint Benedict, died 547
Rule of Benedict (516)

"If the Lord be with us, we have no cause of fear. His eye is upon us, His arm over us, His ear open to our prayer –His grace sufficient, His promise unchangeable."

John Newton, 1725 – 1807
Letters to the Rev. Mr. R_____, Letter 1, April 15, 1776
Cardiphonia, Or, The Utterance of the Heart: In the Course of a Real Correspondence (1780)

"I believe that the root of almost every schism and heresy from which the Christian church has ever suffered, has been the effort of men to earn, rather than to receive, their salvation."

John Ruskin, 1819 – 1900
J.H. Gilbert, *Dictionary of Burning Word and Brilliant Writers* (1895)

"Laughter is the closest thing to the grace of God."

Karl Barth, 1886 – 1968
Ed., Robert I. Fitzhenry; *The Harper Book of Quotations* (1993)

"A sensible friend who will unsparingly criticize you from week to week will be a far greater blessing to you than a thousand

undiscriminating admirers if you have sense enough to bear his treatment, and grace enough to be thankful for it."

Charles Haddon Spurgeon, 1834 – 1892
"The Blind Eye and the Deaf Ear," *Lectures to My Students* (1869)

"The repeated promises in the Qur'an of the forgiveness of a compassionate and merciful Allah are all made to the meritorious, whose merits have been weighed in Allah's scales, whereas the gospel is good news of mercy to the undeserving. The symbol of the religion of Jesus is the cross, not the scales."

John Stott, 1921 – 2011
Authentic Christianity (1995)

"Cheap grace is the preaching of forgiveness without requiring repentance, baptism without church discipline, communion without confession, absolution without personal confession.
Cheap grace is grace without discipleship, grace without the cross, grace without Jesus Christ."

Dietrich Bonhoeffer, 1906 – 1945
The Cost of Discipleship (1937)

"For grace is given not because we have done good works, but in order that we may be able to do them."

Saint Augustine, 354 – 430

"Grace puts its hand on the boasting mouth, and shuts it once and for all."

Charles H. Spurgeon, 1834 – 1892
Sermon No. 318, "High Doctrine," June 3, 1860

"Grace and sin are quarrelsome neighbors."

Charles H. Spurgeon, 1834 – 1892
Treasury of David (1869)

"Compassion asks us to go where it hurts, to enter into the places of pain, to share in brokenness, fear, confusion, and anguish. Compassion challenges us to cry out with those in misery, to mourn with those who are lonely, to weep with those in tears. Compassion requires us to be weak with the weak, vulnerable with the vulnerable, and powerless with the powerless. Compassion means full immersion in the condition of being human."

Henri J. M. Nouwen, 1932 – 1996
Words of Hope and Healing (2005)

"True goodness is not merely impulsive, but rational and considerate—It will therefore pause, and be at some trouble to inquire what service, and how best may it be rendered.... Goodness should be willing to give time, and thought, and patience, and even labor, not mere money and kind words and compassionate looks."

George Washington Bethune, 1805 – 1862
The Fruit of the Spirit (1839)

"Search Scripture through, and you must, if you read it with a candid mind, be persuaded that the doctrine of salvation by grace alone is the great doctrine of the word of God."

Charles H. Spurgeon, 1834 – 1892
The Treasury of David: An Original Exposition of the Book of Psalms, Vol. I (1869)
Exposition of Psalm 3:8

I am not what I ought to be—ah, how imperfect and deficient! I am not what I wish to be—I abhor what is evil, and I would cleave to what is good! I am not what I hope to be—soon, soon shall I put off mortality, and with mortality all sin and imperfection. Yet, though I am not what I ought to be, nor what I wish to be, nor what I hope to be, I can truly say, I am not what I once was; a slave to sin and Satan; and I can heartily join with the apostle, and acknowledge, "By the grace of God I am what I am."

John Newton, 1725 – 1807
"The Christian Spectator," Vol. 3 (1821)

"Until he extends the circle of his compassion to all living things, man will not himself find peace."

Albert Schweitzer, 1875 – 1965
Kulturphilosophie (1923)

"Compassion is the basis of morality."

Arthur Schopenhauer, 1788 – 1860
On the Basis of Morality (1840)

"Compassion is the chief law of human existence."

Fyodor Dostoevsky, 1821 – 1996
The Idiot (1869)

"The word comfort is from two Latin words meaning "with" and "strong"—He is with us to make us strong. Comfort is not soft, weakening commiseration; it is true, strengthening love."

Amy Carmichael, 1867 – 1951
Kohila: the shaping of an Indian nurse (1939)

"Jesus, thou art all compassion,
pure, unbounded love thou art;
visit us with thy salvation;
enter every trembling heart."

Charles Wesley, 1707 – 1788
From the Hymn, "Love Divine, All Loves Excelling" (1747)

"No act of kindness, no matter how small, is ever wasted."

Aesop, died 564 BC
"The Lion and the Mouse"

"What wisdom can you find that is greater than kindness?"

Jean-Jacques Rousseau, 1712 – 1798
Confessions (1782)

"You cannot do a kindness too soon,
for you never know how soon it will be too late."

Ralph Waldo Emerson, 1803 – 1882
The Conduct of Life (1860)

"Be kind, for everyone you meet is fighting a harder battle."

Plato, circa 428 – 348 BC

"Moved by grace, we turn toward God."

Catechism of the Catholic Church

"You may call God love, you may call God goodness.
But the best name for God is compassion."

Meister Eckhart, 1260 – 1328
Attributed

"If there is any kindness I can show, or any good thing I can do to any fellow being, let me do it now, and not deter or neglect it, as I shall not pass this way again."

Anonymous Proverb,
"Household Words: A Weekly Journal", 1859
(English magazine edited by Charles Dickens)
Circulated as Quaker saying at least since 1869

"The man who labors to please his neighbor for his good to edification has the mind that was in Christ. It is a sinner trying to help a sinner."

Richard Cecil, 1748 – 1810
J.H. Gilbert; *Dictionary of Burning Words of Brilliant Writers* (1895)

"Even a feeble, but kind and tender man, will effect more than a genius, who is rough and artificial."

Richard Cecil, 1748 – 1810
J.H. Gilbert; *Dictionary of Burning Words of Brilliant Writers* (1895)

"The grandest operations, both in nature and in grace, are the most silent and imperceptible."

Richard Cecil, 1748 – 1810
J.H. Gilbert; *Dictionary of Burning Words of Brilliant Writers* (1895)

"Knowledge is folly unless grace guide it."

George Herbert, 1593 – 1633
J.H. Gilbert; *Dictionary of Burning Words of Brilliant Writers* (1895)

"In the New Testament grace means God's love in action towards men who merited the opposite of love. Grace means God moving heaven and earth to save sinners who could not lift a finger to save themselves."

J. I. Packer, 1926 – 2020
Knowing God (1973)

"Consider how much you owe to his forgiving grace, that after ten thousand affronts he loves you as infinitely as ever."

Charles H. Spurgeon, 1834 – 1892
February 3rd Morning Devotion, *Morning and Evening* (1865)

"Grace comes into the soul as the morning sun into the world; first a dawning, then a light, and at last the sun in its full and excellent brightness."

Thomas Adams, 1583 – 1652
Ed., John Brown; *Sermons of Thomas Adams: The Shakespeare of Puritan Theologians* (1909)

"And that is the wonder of all wonders, that God loves the lowly.... God is not ashamed of the lowliness of human beings. God marches right in. He chooses people as his instruments and performs his wonders where one would least expect them. God is near to lowliness; he loves the lost, the neglected, the unseemly, the excluded, the weak and broken."

Dietrich Bonhoeffer, 1906 – 1945
Ed., Jana Riess; *God is in the Manger: Reflections on Advent and Christmas* (2010)

"With His healing hand on a broken heart,
And the other on a star,
Our wonderful God views the miles apart,
And they seem not very far.
There is hope and help for our sighs and tears,
For the wound that stings and smarts;
Our God is at home with the rolling spheres,
And at home with broken hearts."

Manie Payne Ferguson, 1850 – 1932
Mrs. Charles E. Cowman, February 19th Devotion, *Springs in the Valley*, (1939)

Amazing Grace

Amazing grace! (how sweet the sound)
That saved a wretch like me!
I once was lost, but now am found,
Was blind, but now I see.

'Twas grace that taught my heart to fear,
And grace my fears reliev'd;
How precious did that grace appear
The hour I first believ'd!

Thro' many dangers, toils, and snares,
I have already come;
'Tis grace hath brought me safe thus far,
And grace will lead me home.

The Lord has promis'd good to me,
His word my hope secures;
He will my shield and portion be
As long as life endures.

Yes, when this flesh and heart shall fail
And mortal life shall cease;
I shall possess, within the veil,
A life of joy and peace.

The earth shall soon dissolve like snow,
The sun forbear to shine;
But God, who call'd me here below,
Will be forever mine.

– (The lines below are said by some to be misattributed,
not written by Newton.) –

When we've been there ten thousand years,
Bright shining as the sun,
We've no less days to sing God's praise,
Than when we first begun.

John Newton, 1725 – 1807
Olney Hymns, 1779

Holy, holy, holy art thou, O Lord our God. Only thou art holy.

Holy, holy, holy is the Lord God Almighty; the whole earth is full of his glory.

Isaiah 6:3

EXODUS 3:5 – 6
"Do not come any closer," God said. "Take off your shoes, for the place where you are standing is holy ground." Then he said, "I am the God of your father, the God of Abraham, the God of Isaac and the God of Jacob." At this, Moses hid his face, because he was afraid to look at God.

EXODUS 15:11
Who is like you, O Lord, among the gods? Who is like you, majestic in holiness, awesome in glorious deeds, doing wonders?

LEVITICUS 19:2
"Be holy because I, the Lord, your God, am holy."

1 SAMUEL 2:2
There is no one holy like the Lord, there is no one besides you; there is no one like our God.

1 CHRONICLES 16:10 – 11
Glory in his holy name; let the hearts of those who seek the Lord rejoice. Look to the Lord and his strength; seek his face always.

PSALM 29:2
Ascribe to the Lord the glory due his name; worship the Lord in the splendor of his holiness.

PSALM 77:13
Your way, O God, is holy. What god is great like our God?

PSALM 89:33 – 35
"I will not take my love from him, nor will I ever betray my faithfulness. I will not violate my covenant nor alter what my lips have uttered. Once for all I have sworn by my holiness."

PSALM 99:2 – 3
The Lord is great in Zion; he is exalted over all the peoples. Let them praise your great and awesome name! Holy is he!

PSALM 99:5
Exalt the Lord our God and worship at his footstool; holy is he.

PSALM 105:3 – 4
Glory in his holy name; let the hearts of those who seek the Lord rejoice. Look to the Lord and his strength; seek his face always.

ISAIAH 40:25 – 26
"To whom will you compare me? Or who is my equal?" says the Holy One.

ISAIAH 43:1 - 3
But now, this is what the Lord says—he who created you, he who formed you: "Do not fear, for I have redeemed you; I have summoned you by name; you are mine. When you pass through the waters, I will be with you; and when you pass through the rivers, they will not sweep over you. When you walk through the fire, you will not be burned; the flames will not set you ablaze. For I am the Lord your God, the Holy One of Israel, your Savior."

ISAIAH 57:15
For this is what the high and lofty One says—he who lives forever, whose name is holy: I live in a high and holy place, but also with him who is contrite and lowly in spirit, to revive the spirit of the lowly and to revive the heart of the contrite.

JOHN 6:68 - 69
Simon Peter answered him, "Lord, to whom shall we go? You have the words of eternal life. We believe and know that you are the Holy One of God."

JOHN 17:11
Jesus prayed, "I will remain in the world no longer, but they are still in the world, and I am coming to you. Holy Father, protect them by the power of your name, the name you gave me, so that they may be one as we are one."

REVELATION 4:8
Holy, Holy, Holy is the Lord God Almighty, who was, and is, and is to come.

REVELATION 15:3 - 4
Great and marvelous are your deeds, Lord God Almighty. Just and true are your ways, King of the ages. Who will not fear

you, O Lord, and bring glory to your name? For you alone are holy.

"Holiness: the 'mysterium tremendum': or 'awe inspiring mystery.'"

Otto Rudolph, 1869 – 1937
The Idea of the Holy (1917]

"Holiness consisteth not in a cowl or in a garment of gray. When God purifies the heart by faith, the market is sacred as well as the sanctuary; neither remaineth there any work or place which is profane."

Martin Luther, 1483 – 1546
Edward P. Day; *Day's Collacon: An Encyclopaedia of Prose Quotations* (1884)

"Nothing whatever pertaining to godliness and real holiness can be accomplished without grace."

Saint Augustine, 354 – 430

"Tread softly! All the earth is holy ground."

Christina Rossetti, 1830 – 1894
"Later Life: A Double Sonnet of Sonnets" (1881)

"The essence of true holiness consists in conformity to the nature and will of God."

Samuel Lucas, 1805 – 1870
Ed., Tryon Edwards; *A Dictionary of Thought* (1908)

"On a handful of occasions the Bible repeats something to the third degree. To mention something three times in succession is to elevate it

to the superlative degree. Only one attribute of God is elevated to the third degree. The Bible says that God is holy, holy, holy. Not that He is merely holy, or even holy, holy. He is holy, holy, holy."

R.C. Sproul, 1939 – 2017
The Holiness of God (2000)

"Holiness is not some lofty experience, unattainable except to those who can leap the stars, but it is rather a lowly experience, which lowly people in the lowly walks of life, can share with Jesus by letting his mind be in them."

Samuel Logan Brengle, 1860 – 1936
Hindrance to Holiness (1897)

"Breathe in me, O Holy Spirit, that my thoughts may all be holy.
Act in me, O Holy Spirit, that my work, too, may be holy.
Draw my heart, O Holy Spirit, that I love but what is holy.
Strengthen me, O Holy Spirit, to defend all that is holy.
Guard me, then, O Holy Spirit, that I always may be holy."

Saint Augustine, 354 – 430
Augustine's "Prayer to the Holy Spirit"

"For You are holy, our God, and to You we give glory, to the Father and the Son and the Holy Spirit, now and forever."

John Chrysostom, died 407
The Divine Liturgy of St John Chrysostom

Holy, Holy, Holy

Holy, holy, holy! Lord God Almighty!
Early in the morning our song shall rise to Thee;
holy, holy, holy, merciful and mighty!
God in three Persons, blessed Trinity!

Holy, holy, holy! All the saints adore Thee,
Casting down their golden crowns around the glassy sea;
Cherubim and seraphim falling down before Thee,
Who was, and is, and evermore shall be.

Holy, holy, holy! Though the darkness hide Thee,
Though the eye of sinful man Thy glory may not see;
Only Thou art holy; there is none beside Thee,
Perfect in pow'r, in love, and purity.

Holy, holy, holy! Lord God Almighty!
All Thy works shall praise Thy Name, in earth, and sky, and sea;
Holy, holy, holy; merciful and mighty!
God in three Persons, blessed Trinity!

Reginald Heber, 1783 – 1826
Hymn (1826)

I

You, O Lord, are infinite in every aspect of your being, transcending all that we can imagine or comprehend. You dwell in inapproachable light.

He determines the number of the stars and calls them each by name. Great is the Lord and mighty in power; his understanding is infinite.

Psalm 147:4–5

Ah, Sovereign Lord, you have made the heavens and the earth by your outstretched arm. Nothing is too hard for you.

Jeremiah 32:17

Oh, the depth of the riches of the wisdom and the knowledge of God! How unsearchable his judgments and his paths beyond tracing out! Who has known the mind of the Lord? Or who has been his counselor? Who has ever given to God that God should repay him? For from him and through him and for him are all things. To him be glory forever! Amen.

Romans 11:33–36

DEUTERONOMY 29:29
The secret things belong to the Lord our God, but the things revealed belong to us and our children forever.

1 KINGS 8:27 (SOLOMON'S PRAYER)
But will God indeed dwell on earth? Behold, heaven, the highest heaven cannot contain you.

JOB 5:9
He performs wonders that cannot be fathomed, miracles that cannot be counted.

JOB 11:7 - 9
Can you fathom the mysteries of God? Can you probe the limits of the Almighty? They are higher than the heavens above—what can you do? They are deeper than the depths of the grave—what can you know? Their measure is longer than the earth and wider than the sea.

JOB 11:17
Can you find out the deep things of God? Can you find out the limit of the Almighty?

JOB 15:8
Do you limit wisdom to yourself?

JOB 36:22
God is exalted in his power. Who is a teacher like him?

JOB 37:23
The Almighty is beyond our reach and exalted in power, the number of his years is unsearchable.

JOB 42:1 – 3
Then Job replied to the Lord: "I know that you can do all things; no purpose of yours can be thwarted. You asked, 'Who is this that obscures my plans without knowledge?' Surely I spoke of things I did not understand, things too wonderful for me to know."

PSALM 44:21
...he knows the secrets of the heart.

PSALM 92:5
How great are your works, O Lord, how profound your thoughts!

PSALM 104:2
The Lord wraps himself in light as with a garment; he stretches out the heavens like a tent.

PSALM 115:3
But our God is in the heavens; He does whatever He pleases.

PSALM 139:1 – 4, 6
O Lord, you have searched me and you know me. You know when I sit and when I rise; you perceive my thoughts from afar. You discern my going out and my lying down; you are familiar with all my ways. Before a word is on my tongue you know it completely.... Such knowledge is too wonderful for me, too lofty for me to attain.

PSALM 145:3
Great is the Lord and most worthy of praise; his greatness no one can fathom.

ECCLESIASTES 3:11
He has made everything beautiful in its time. He also has set eternity in the hearts of men: yet they cannot fathom what God has done from beginning to end.

ECCLESIASTES 8:17
Then I saw all that God has done. No one can comprehend what goes on under the sun. Despite all his efforts to search it out, man cannot discover its meaning. Even if a wise man claims to know, he cannot really comprehend it.

ECCLESIASTES 11:5
As you do not know the path of the wind, or how the body is formed in the womb, so you cannot understand the work of God, the Maker of all things.

ISAIAH 40:12 - 14
Who has measured the waters in the hollow of his hand, or with the breadth of his hand marked off the heavens? Who has held the dust of the earth in a basket, or weighed the mountains on the scales and the hills in a balance? Who has understood the mind of the Lord, or instructed him as counselor? Whom did the Lord consult to enlighten him, and who taught him the right way? Who was it that taught him knowledge or showed him the path of understanding?

ISAIAH 40:28 - 29, 31
Do you not know? Have you not heard? The Lord is the everlasting God, the Creator of the ends of the earth. He will not grow tired or weary, and his understanding no one can fathom. He gives strength to the weary and increases the power of the weak.... Those who hope in the Lord will renew their strength. They will soar on wings like eagles; they will run and not grow weary, they will walk and not be faint.

ISAIAH 55:8 - 9

"For my thoughts are not your thoughts, neither are my ways your ways," declares the Lord. "As the heavens are higher than the earth, so are my ways higher than your ways and my thoughts than your thoughts."

DANIEL 2:20 - 22

Praise be to the name of God for ever and ever; he changes times and seasons; he sets up kings and deposes them. He gives wisdom to the wise and knowledge to the discerning. He reveals deep and hidden things; he knows what lies in darkness, and light dwells with him.

MICAH 4:12

The nations do not know the thoughts of the Lord: they do not understand his plan.

1 CORINTHIANS 2:9 - 10

No eye has seen, no ear has heard, no mind has conceived what God has prepared for those who love him, but God has revealed it to us by his Spirit. The Spirit searches all things, even the deep things of God.

1 CORINTHIANS 2:16

For who has known the mind of the Lord that he may instruct him?

EPHESIANS 3:20 - 21

Now to Him who is able to do exceedingly abundantly above all that we ask or think, according to the power that works in us, to Him be glory in the church by Christ Jesus to all generations, forever and ever. Amen.

PHILIPPIANS 2:5
Your attitude should be that of Christ Jesus, who being in very nature God, did not consider equality with God something to be grasped.

1 TIMOTHY 6:16
The King of kings and Lord of lords, who alone is immortal and lives in unapproachable light, whom no one has seen or can see. To him be honor and might forever. Amen.

HEBREWS 4:13
Nothing in all creation is hidden from God's sight.

1 JOHN 3:20
If our hearts condemn us, God is greater than our hearts, and he knows everything.

REVELATION 1:8
"I am the Alpha and the Omega," says the Lord God, "who is and was is to come, the Almighty."

"'Finitum non capax infiniti' = 'The finite cannot contain the infinite.'"

A Philosophical Axiom of the Reformation, 1517 – 1648

"By God, I mean a being absolutely infinite—that is, a substance consisting in infinite attributes, of which each expresses eternal and infinite essentiality."

Baruch Spinoza, 1632 – 1677
Ethics (1677)

"We know that God is everywhere; but certainly we feel His presence most when His works are on the grandest scale spread before us;

and it is in the unclouded night-sky, where His worlds wheel their silent course, that we read clearest His infinitude, His omnipotence, His omnipresence."

Charlotte Brontë, 1816 – 1855
Jane Eyre (1847)

"In Christ was united the human and the divine. His mission was to reconcile God to man, and man to God; to unite the finite with the infinite."

Ellen G. White, 1827 – 1915
"The Sufferings of Christ", Pamphlet No. 169 (1882)

"The angels are lost in perpetual contemplation of an infinite glory."

Viktor Frankl, 1905 – 1997
Man's Search for Meaning (1946)

"God is that infinite All of which man knows himself to be a finite part."

Leo Tolstoy, 1828 – 1910
Diary Entry, November 1, 1910

"None can comprehend eternity but the eternal God."

Thomas Boston, 1676 – 1732
Sermon, "The Doctrine of Hell," "Part IV – The Eternity of the Whole"
Human Nature in Its Fourfold State (1730)

"The infinity of God is not mysterious, it is only unfathomable; not concealed, but incomprehensible; it is a clear infinity, the darkness of the pure unsearchable sea."

John Ruskin, 1819 – 1900
Modern Painters, Vol. II (1846)

"Anyone who does not believe in miracles is not a realist."

David Ben-Gurion, 1886 – 1973
A variant from Ben-Gurion's Interview on CBS, October 5, 1956

"Faith is an act of a finite being who is grasped by, and turned to, the infinite."

Paul Tillich, 1886 – 1965
Dynamics of Faith (1957)

"The riddles of God are more satisfying than the solutions of man."

G.K Chesterton, 1874 – 1936
Introduction to the Book of Job (1907)

"If you have understood, then what you have understood is not God."

Saint Augustine, 354 – 430
"Sermons on the New Testament," Sermon No. 67, 412

"The laws of nature are but the mathematical thoughts of God."

Euclid, born mid-fourth century

"There is a signature of wisdom and power impressed on the works of God, which evidently distinguishes them from the feeble limitations of men – not only the splendor of the sun, but the glimmering light of the glowworm."

John Newton, 1725 – 1807
Newton's "Messiah Sermon Series,"
Sermon No. 5 (circa 1785 – 1786)

"Surely God would not have created such a being as man with an ability to grasp the infinite, to exist only for a day! No, no, man was made for immortality."

Abraham Lincoln, 1809 – 1865
Lincoln's words to friends, 1856
Quoted by Isaac Newton Arnold, "The Layman's Faith,"
Paper read before the Philosophical Society of Chicago, Saturday, December 16, 1882

"Beauty itself is but the sensible image of the infinite; that all creation is a manifestation of the Almighty; not the result of caprice, but the glorious display of his perfection."

George Bancroft, 1800 – 1891
"The Necessity, the Reality, and the Promise of the Progress of the Human Race"
Address to the New York Historical Society, November 20, 1854

"The important thing is not to stop questioning. Curiosity has its own reason for existence. One cannot help but be in awe when he contemplates the mysteries of eternity, of life, of the marvelous structure of reality. It is enough if one tries merely to comprehend a little of this mystery each day."

Albert Einstein, 1879 – 1955
From Ed. William Miller's memoir on the life of Einstein
"Life Magazine," May 2, 1955

"An infinite God can give all of himself to each of his children. He does not distribute himself that each may have a part, but to each one he gives all of himself as fully as if there were no others."

A.W. Tozer, 1897 – 1963
February 26th Devotion, *Mornings with Tozer* (2008)

"Christianity, if false, is of no importance, and if true, of infinite importance. The only thing it cannot be is moderately important."

C. S. Lewis, 1898 – 1963
Mere Christianity (1952)

"God's gifts put man's best dreams to shame."

Elizabeth Barrett Browning, 1806 – 1861
"Sonnet 26," *Sonnets from the Portuguese* (1850)

"Don't use words too big for the subject. Don't say 'infinitely' when you mean 'very'; otherwise, you'll have no word left when you want to talk about something really infinite."

C. S. Lewis, 1898 – 1963
Eds., Mead and Dorsett; "Letter to Joan," June 26, 1956,
Letters to Children (1985)

"As well might a gnat seek to drink in the ocean, as a finite creature to comprehend the Eternal God. A God whom we could understand would be no God. If we could grasp Him, He could not be infinite. If we could understand Him, He could not be divine."

Charles H. Spurgeon, 1834 – 1892
Sermon No. 291, December 25, 1859

"In God you come up against something which is in every respect immeasurably superior to yourself. Unless you know God as that—and, therefore, know yourself as nothing in comparison—you do not know God at all."

C. S. Lewis, 1898 – 1963
Mere Christianity (1952)

"To Catholic, Orthodox, and some Protestant Christians, communion involves partaking of the physical real presence of God in the bread and wine of the Eucharist. By contrast, the Torah draws the Jew into engagement with God's infinite mind. Torah learning is the definitive Jewish mode of communion with God."

Rabbi Meir Soloveichik, 1971
Article, "Torah and Incarnation," *First Things*, October, 2010

"Infinite wisdom planned that redemption should be by the cross. Infinite wisdom brought Jesus to the cross in due time. He was crucified by the determinate counsel and foreknowledge of God."

J.C. Ryle, 1816 – 1900
Old Paths (1877)

"I know that mystery in the works of God is only another name for my ignorance. The moment that I become humble, all becomes right."

Richard Cecil, 1748 – 1810
The Miscellanies of Richard Cecil, Vol II (1847)

"There are only two ways to live your life. One is as though nothing is a miracle. The other is as if everything is."

Albert Einstein, 1879 – 1955
Robert E. Hinshaw, *Living with Nature's Extremes: The Life of Gilbert Fowler White* (2006)

"I would rather live in a world where my life is surrounded by mystery than live in a world so small that my mind could comprehend it."

Harry Emerson Fosdick, 1878 – 1969
Riverside Sermons (1958)

"Whatever may be the mysteries of life and death, there is one mystery which the cross of Christ reveals to us, and that is the infinite and absolute goodness of God. Let all the rest remain a mystery so long as the mystery of the cross of Christ gives us faith for all the rest."

Charles Kingsley, 1819 – 1875
J.H. Gilbert, *Dictionary of Burning Words of Brilliant Writers* (1895)

"Beware of doubt—faith is the subtle chain that binds us to the Infinite."

Elizabeth Oakes Smith, 1806 – 1893
The Poetical Writings of Elizabeth Oakes Smith (1846)

"I believe not only in 'special providences,' but in the whole universe as one infinite complexity of 'special providences.'"

Charles Kingsley, 1819 – 1875
J.H. Gilbert; *Dictionary of Burning Words of Brilliant Writers* (1895)

"God moves in a mysterious way, His wonders to perform.
He plants His footsteps in the sea and rides upon the storm."

William Cowper, 1731 – 1800
Hymn, "God Moves in a Mysterious Way," 1773
John Newton, *Twenty-six Letters on Religious Subjects; to which are added Hymns* (1774)

"It is impossible for a man to despair who remembers that his Helper is omnipotent."

Jeremy Taylor, 1613 – 1667

"God is a Spirit, in and of himself infinite in being, glory, blessedness, and perfection; all-sufficient, eternal, unchangeable, incomprehensible, everywhere present, almighty, knowing all things,

most wise, most holy, most just, most merciful and gracious, longsuffering, and abundant in goodness and truth."

Westminster Larger Catechism. 1647
In answer to Question 7, "What is God?

Immortal, Invisible, God only Wise

Immortal, invisible, God only wise,
in light inaccessible hid from our eyes,
most blessed, most glorious, the Ancient of Days,
almighty, victorious, thy great name we praise.

Unresting, unhasting, and silent as light,
nor wanting, nor wasting, thou rulest in might;
thy justice like mountains high soaring above
thy clouds which are fountains of goodness and love.

To all life Thou givest, to both great and small;
In all life Thou livest, the true life of all;
We blossom and flourish as leaves on the tree,
And wither and perish, but nought changeth Thee.

Great Father of glory, pure Father of light,
thine angels adore thee, all veiling their sight;
all praise we would render; O help us to see
'tis only the splendor of light hideth thee!

Walter C Smith, 1824 – 1908
Hymn (186)

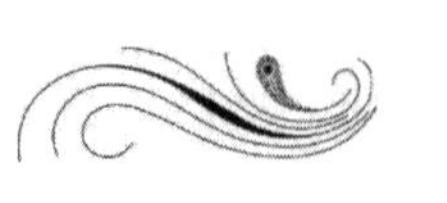

J

Lord Jesus, thou art the Christ, the Son of the living God.

Isaiah's Prophecy

The people walking in darkness have seen a great light;

on those living in the land of the shadow of death, a light has dawned.

For unto us a child is born, to us a son is given, and the government will be upon his shoulders. And he will be called Wonderful Counselor, Mighty God, Everlasting Father, Prince of Peace.

Of the increase of his government there shall be no end.

He will reign on David's throne and over his kingdom, establishing and upholding it with justice and righteousness from that time on and forever.

The zeal of the Lord will accomplish this.

Isaiah 9:2, 6 – 7

The Annunciation

In the sixth month, God sent the angel Gabriel to Nazareth, a town in Galilee, to a virgin pledged to be married to a man named Joseph, a descendant of David.

The virgin's name was Mary. The angel went to her and said,
"Greetings, you who are highly favored! The Lord is with you."
Mary was greatly troubled at his words and wondered what kind
of greeting this might be.

But the angel said to her, "Do not be afraid, Mary, you have found
favor with God. You will be with child and give birth to a son,
and you will give him the name Jesus.

He will be great and will be called the Son of the Most High.

The Lord God will give him the throne of his father, David,
and he will reign over the house of Jacob forever;
his kingdom will never end."

"How will this be," Mary asked the angel, "since I am a virgin?"
The angel answered, "The Holy Spirit will come upon you,
and the power of the Most High will overshadow you.
So the Holy One to be born will be called the Son of God.

Even Elizabeth your relative is going to have a child in her old age,
and she who was said to be barren is in her sixth month.
For nothing is impossible with God."

"I am the Lord's servant," Mary answered.

"May it be to me as you have said." Then the angel left her.

Luke 1:26 – 38

For God so loved the world that he gave His only begotten Son
that whosoever believeth in Him should not perish,
but have everlasting life.

John 3:16

MATTHEW 1:16
Jacob was the father of Joseph, the husband of Mary, by whom Jesus was born, who is called the Messiah.

MATTHEW 3:16 - 17
As soon as Jesus was baptized, he went up out of the water. Suddenly the heavens were opened, and he saw the Spirit of God descending like a dove and resting on him. And a voice from heaven said, "This is My beloved Son, in whom I am well pleased!"

MATTHEW 14:32 - 33
And when they got into the boat, the wind ceased. Then those who were in the boat worshiped him saying, "Truly you are the Son of God."

MATTHEW 16:15 - 17
"But what about you?" Jesus asked. "Who do you say I am?" Simon Peter answered, "You are the Christ, the Son of the living God." Jesus replied, "Blessed are you, Simon son of Jonah! For this was not revealed to you by flesh and blood, but by my Father in heaven."

MATTHEW 17:4 - 6 **The Transfiguration**
Peter said to Jesus, "Lord, it is good that we are here. If you wish, I will put up three shelters—one for you, one for Moses, and one for Elijah." While he was still speaking, a bright cloud enveloped them, and a voice from the cloud said, "This is my beloved Son, with whom I am well pleased; listen to him." When the disciples heard this, they fell facedown, terrified.

MATTHEW 26:63 - 64
But Jesus remained silent. And the high priest said to him, "I adjure you by the living God, tell us if you are the Christ, the Son of God." "I am He," replied Jesus.

JOHN 1:1 - 4
In the beginning was the Word, and the Word was with God, and the Word was God. He was with God in the beginning.

Through him all things were made; without him nothing was made that has been made. In him was life, and that life was the light of all mankind. The light shines in the darkness, and the darkness has not overcome it.

JOHN 1:14
And the Word became flesh and dwelt among us. We have seen his glory, the glory of the One and Only, who came from the Father, full of grace and truth.

JOHN 1:17
For the law was given through Moses; grace and truth came through Jesus Christ.

JOHN 6:68 - 69
Simon Peter replied, "Lord, to whom would we go? You have the words of eternal life. We believe and know that you are the Holy One of God."

JOHN 10:30
Jesus said, "I and the Father are one."

JOHN 11:25 - 27
Jesus said to Martha, "I am the resurrection and the life. Whoever believes in me, though he dies, yet shall he live, and everyone who lives and believes in me shall never die. Do you believe this?" "Yes, Lord," she answered. "I believe that you are the Christ, the Son of God, who was to come into the world."

JOHN 14:6
Jesus answered, "I am the way and the truth and the life. No one comes to the Father except through me."

JOHN 14:15
Jesus said to them, "If you love me, keep my commandments."

JOHN 17:3
"Now this is eternal life: that they may know you, the only true God and Jesus Christ whom you have sent."

JOHN 20:26 - 29
Though the doors were locked, Jesus came and stood among them and said, "Peace be with you." Then he said to Thomas, "Put your finger here; see my hands. Reach out your hand and put it into my side. Stop doubting and believe." Thomas said to him, "My Lord and my God!" Then Jesus told him, "Because you have seen me, you have believed; blessed are those who have not seen and yet have believed."

JOHN 20:30 - 31
Jesus did many other miraculous signs in the presence of his disciples which are not recorded in this book. But these are written that you may believe that Jesus is the Christ, the Son of God, and that by believing you may have life in his name.

ROMANS 1:1 - 4
Paul, a servant of Christ Jesus, called to be an apostle, set apart for the gospel of God, which he promised beforehand through his prophets in the holy Scriptures, concerning his Son, who was descended from David, according to the flesh and was declared to be the Son of God in power according to the Spirit of holiness by his resurrection from the dead, Jesus Christ our Lord.

ROMANS 6:23
For the wages of sin is death, but the gift of God is eternal life through Christ Jesus our Lord.

1 CORINTHIANS 1:26 - 31

Brothers and sisters, think of what you were when you were called. Not many of you were wise by human standards; not many were influential; not many were of noble birth. But God chose the foolish things of the world to shame the wise; God chose the weak things of the world to shame the strong. God chose the lowly things of this world and the despised things—and the things that are not—to nullify the things that are, so that no one may boast before him. It is because of him that you are in Christ Jesus, who has become for us wisdom from God—that is, our righteousness, holiness and redemption. Therefore, as it is written: "Let the one who boasts boast in the Lord."

1 CORINTHIANS 8:6

For us there is but one God, the Father from whom all things came and for whom we live; and there is but one Lord, Jesus Christ, through whom all things came and through whom we live.

PHILIPPIANS 2:9 - 11

Therefore, God exalted him to the highest place and gave him the name that is above every name, that at the name of Jesus every knee should bow, in heaven and on earth and under the earth, and every tongue acknowledge that Jesus Christ is Lord, to the glory of God the Father.

COLOSSIANS 1:15 - 20

The Son is the image of the invisible God, the firstborn over all creation. For in him all things were created: things in heaven and on earth, visible and invisible, whether thrones or powers or rulers or authorities; all things have been created through him and for him. He is before all things, and in him all things hold together. And he is the head of the body, the church; he is the beginning and the firstborn from among the dead, so that in everything he might have the supremacy. For God was pleased to have all his fullness dwell in him, and through him to reconcile to himself all things, whether things on earth or things in heaven, by making peace through his blood shed on the cross.

COLOSSIANS 2:9
For in Christ all the fullness of the Deity lives in bodily form.

1 TIMOTHY 2:5
God our Savior wants all to be saved and to come to a knowledge of the truth. For there is one God and one mediator between God and men, the man Jesus Christ, who gave himself as a ransom for all.

1 PETER 1:3
Blessed be the God and Father of our Lord Jesus Christ! By his great mercy he gave us new birth into a living hope through the resurrection of Jesus Christ from the dead, that is, into an inheritance imperishable, undefiled, and unfading. It is reserved in heaven for you....

1 JOHN 4:10
In this is love, not that we loved God, but that He loved us and sent His Son to be the propitiation for our sins.

1 JOHN 4:14
We have seen and testify that the Father has sent the Son to be the Savior of the world.

1 JOHN 5:5
Who is it that overcomes the world? Only he who believes that Jesus is the Son of God.

1 JOHN 5:20
We know also that the Son of God has come and has given us understanding, so that we may know him who is true. And we are in him who is true by being in his Son Jesus Christ. He is the true God and eternal life.

JUDE 24 - 25
To Him who is able to keep you from falling, and to present you faultless before the presence of his glory with exceeding joy. To the only wise God our Savior, be glory and majesty, dominion and power, both now and ever. Amen.

"Hail the heaven-born Prince of Peace!
Hail the Sun of Righteousness!
Light and life to all He brings,
Risen with healing in his wings
Mild He lays His glory by
Born that man no more may die
Born to raise the sons of earth
Born to give them second birth."

Charles Wesley, 1707 – 1778
Hymn, Stanza 3, "Hark! The Herald Angels Sing" (1739)

"Look for Christ and you will find Him, and with Him everything else."

C. S. Lewis, 1898 – 1963
Mere Christianity (1952)

"Although my memory is fading, I remember two things very clearly: I am a great sinner and Christ is a great Savior."

John Newton, 1725 – 1807
Out of the Depths: The Autobiography of John Newton,
Revised by Dennis R. Hillman (2003)

"The Son of God became a man to enable men to become sons of God."

C. S. Lewis, 1898 – 1963
Mere Christianity (1952)

*"Take from the Bible the Godship of Christ,
and it would be but a heap of dust."*

Henry Ward Beecher, 1813 – 1887
Ed., Edna Dean Proctor; *Life Thoughts* (1858)

"Jesus, Son of the Eternal God, have mercy on me."

Michael Servetus, died 1553
(Last words before being burned alive for "heresy"
upon a pyre of his own books.)

"There is not a square inch in the whole domain of our human existence over which Christ, who is Sovereign over all, does not cry: 'Mine!'"

Abraham Kuyper, 1837 – 1920
Inaugural Address, Opening of the Free University of Amsterdam, October 20, 1880

"A Christian has no need of any law in order to be saved, since through faith we are free from every law. Thus, all the acts of a Christian are done spontaneously, out of a sense of pure liberty."

Martin Luther, 1483 – 1546
"A Treatise of Christian Liberty" (1520)

"If Jesus is not God, then there is no Christianity, and we who worship Him are no more than idolaters. Conversely, if He is God, those who say He was merely a good man, or even the best of men,

are blasphemers. More serious still, if He is not God, then He is a blasphemer in the fullest sense of the word. If he is not God, He is not even good."

J. Oswald Sanders, 1902 – 1992
Christ Incomparable (1952)

"I want to take the word Christianity back to Christ himself, back to that mighty heart whose pulse seems to throb through the world today, that endless fountain of charity out of which I believe has come all true progress and all civilization that deserves the name. I go back to that great Spirit which contemplated a sacrifice for the whole of humanity. That sacrifice is not one of exclusion, but of an infinite and endless and joyous inclusion. And I thank God for it."

Julia Ward Howe, 1819 – 1910
Speech, "What is Religion?" World's Parliament of Religions, Chicago World's Fair, 1893

"The glory of Christianity is to conquer by forgiveness."

William Blake, 1757 – 1827
Poem, "Jerusalem" (1804)

"I have found that lived out, the hardest place to be a Christian is to be in a nice prosperous country with a lot of entertainment options because there's so many distractions."

Philip Yancey, born 1949
Article, "Faith That Matters," *Christian Post,* October 2, 2010

"Alexander, Caesar, Charlemagne, and I have founded empires. But on what did we rest the creations of our genius? Upon force. Jesus Christ founded his empire upon love; and at this hour millions of men would die for him."

Napoleon Bonaparte, 1769 – 1821
Attributed

"A perfect practice of Christianity would, of course, consist in a perfect imitation of the life of Christ—I mean, in so far as it was applicable in one's own particular circumstance. Not in an idiotic sense—it doesn't mean that every Christian should grow a beard, or be a bachelor, or become a traveling preacher. It means that every single act and feeling, every experience, whether pleasant or unpleasant, must be referred to God."

C. S. Lewis, 1898 – 1952
God in the Dock (1970)

"Jesus Christ: The meeting place of eternity and time, the blending of deity and humanity, the junction of heaven and earth."

Oswald Sanders, 1902 – 1992
Christ Incomparable (1952)

"I do not separate Christ from God more than a voice from the speaker or a beam from the sun. Christ is the voice of the speaker. He and the Father are the same thing, as the beam and the light, are the same light."

Michael Servetus, died 1553
On the Errors of the Trinity (1531)

"Jesus never pussyfooted."

Elizabeth Elliot, 1926 – 2015
The Mark of a Man (1981)

"Jesus is the God whom we can approach without pride and before whom we can humble ourselves without despair."

Blaise Pascal, 1623 – 1662
No. 528, *Pensées* (1670)

"The Lord ate from a common bowl, and asked the disciples to sit on the grass. He washed their feet, with a towel wrapped around His waist—He, who is the Lord of the universe!"

Clement of Alexandria, 150 – 215
"On Costly Vessels," *The Paedagogus, Bk I* (198)

"If I were not a Jew, I would be a Quaker."

Albert Einstein, 1879 – 1955
A.V. Douglas, "40 Minutes with Einstein,"
Journal of Royal Astronomical Society of Canada, Vol. 50 (1956)

"It is refreshing, and salutary, to study the poise and quietness of Christ. His task and responsibility might well have driven a man out of his mind. But He was never in a hurry, never impressed by numbers, never a slave of the clock."

J. B. Phillips, 1906 – 1982
Your God is Too Small (1952)

"For those who love, nothing is too difficult, especially when it is done for the love of our Lord Jesus Christ."

Saint Ignatius of Loyola, 1491 – 1556

"I am an historian, I am not a believer, but I must confess as a historian that this penniless preacher from Nazareth is irrevocably the very center of history. Jesus Christ is easily the most dominant figure in all history."

H. G. Wells, 1866 – 1946
Attributed

"The name Emmanuel takes in the whole mystery. Jesus is 'God with us.' He had a nature like our own in all things,

sin only excepted. But though Jesus was 'with us' in human flesh and blood, He was at the same time very God."

John Charles Ryle, 1816 – 1900
Expository Thoughts on the Gospels: St. Matthew (1856)

"In Christ was united the human and the divine. His mission was to reconcile God to man, and man to God; to unite the finite with the infinite."

Ellen G. White, 1827 – 1915
Testimonies for the Church, Vol. 2 (1871)

"A man who was completely innocent, offered himself as a sacrifice for the good of others, including his enemies, and became the ransom of the world. It was a perfect act."

Mahatma Gandhi, 1869 – 1948
Non-Violence in Peace and War, Vol. II (1949)

"The resurrection is the linchpin of Christianity."

Lee Strobel, 1952
The Case For Christ (1998)

"The gospel is not speculation but fact. It is truth, because it is the record of a Person who is the Truth."

Alexander Maclaren, 1826 – 1910
"The Epistles of St. Paul to the Colossians and Philemon"
The Expositor's Bible (1900)

"People talk about imitating Christ, and imitate Him in the little trifling formal things, such as washing the feet, saying His prayer, and so on; but if anyone attempts the real imitation of Him,

there are no bounds to the outcry with which the presumption of that person is condemned."

Florence Nightingale, 1820 – 1910
Essay, "Cassandra" (1860)

"I believe in Christianity as I believe that the sun has risen: not only I see it, but because by it I see everything else."

C. S. Lewis, 1898 – 1963
Essay, "Is Theology Poetry?" (1945)
First presented to the Oxford Socratic Club, November 6, 1944

"It is Christ Himself, not the Bible, who is the true Word of God. The Bible, read in the right spirit and with the guidance of good teachers, will bring us to Him."

C. S. Lewis, 1898 – 1963
Excerpt from a letter to Mrs. Johnson, November 8, 1952
Eds., W.H. Lewis and Walter Hooper;
The Collected Letters of C. S. Lewis, Vol. 3 (1966)

"I have read in Plato and Cicero sayings that are very wise and very beautiful; but I never read in either of them: 'Come unto me all ye that labour and are heavy laden.'"

Augustine, 354 – 430

"My Master has riches beyond the count of arithmetic, the measurement of reason, the dream of imagination or the eloquence of words. They are unsearchable!"

Charles H. Spurgeon, 1834 – 1892
Evening Devotional, August 22; *Morning and Evening* (1868)

"A man who was merely a man and said the sort of things Jesus said would not be a great moral teacher. He would either be a lunatic—on a level with the man who says he is a poached egg—or else he would be the Devil of Hell. You must make your choice. Either this man was, and is, the Son of God; or else a madman or something worse. You can shut Him up for a fool, you can spit at Him and kill him as a demon; or you can fall at His feet and call Him Lord and God. But let us not come with any patronizing nonsense about His being a great human teacher. He has not left that open to us. He did not intend to."

C. S. Lewis, 1898 – 1963
Mere Christianity (1952)

"I am no friend of present-day Christianity, though its Founder was sublime."

Vincent Van Gogh, 1853 – 1890
Letter to Theo van Gogh, October, 1884

"I wish not merely to be called Christian, but also to be Christian."

Saint Ignatius of Antioch, died 108
"Epistle to the Romans"
Written during his transport from Antioch to Rome for his execution

"To have Faith in Christ means, of course, trying to do all that He says. There would be no sense in saying you trusted a person if you would not take his advice. Thus, if you have really handed yourself over to Him, it must follow that you are trying to obey Him. But trying in a new way, a less worried way. Not doing these things in order to be saved, but because He has begun to save you already. Not hoping to get to Heaven as a reward for your actions, but inevitably wanting to act in a certain way because a first faint gleam of Heaven is already inside you."

C. S. Lewis, 1898 – 1963
Mere Christianity (1952)

"The nearer to Jesus, the nearer to the perfect calm of heaven; the nearer to Him, the fuller the heart is, not only of peace, but of life, and vigor, and joy, for these all depend on constant communion with Him. What the sun is to the day, what the moon is to the night, what the dew is to the flower, such is Jesus Christ to us. What bread is to the hungry, clothing to the naked, the shadow of a great rock to the traveler in a weary land, such is Jesus Christ to us."

Charles Spurgeon, 1834 – 1892
Morning Devotional, August 22; *Morning and Evening* (1865)

"Socrates taught for 40 years, Plato for 50, Aristotle for 40, and Jesus for only 3. Yet the influence of Christ's 3-year ministry infinitely transcends the impact left by the combined 130 years of teaching from these men who were among the greatest philosophers of all antiquity."

"Jesus painted no pictures; yet, some of the finest paintings of Raphael, Michelangelo, and Leonardo da Vinci received their inspiration from Him."

"Jesus wrote no poetry; but Dante, Milton, and scores of the world's greatest poets were inspired by Him. Jesus composed no music; still Haydn, Handel, Beethoven, Bach, and Mendelssohn reached their highest perfection of melody in the hymns, symphonies, and oratories they composed in His praise.

"Every sphere of human greatness has been enriched by this humble Carpenter of Nazareth."

Henry G. Bosch, 1914 – 1995
Founder of the Devotional, "Our Daily Bread" (1938)

"The humble, simple souls, who are little enough to see the bigness of God in the littleness of a Babe, are therefore the only ones who will ever understand the reason of His visitation. He came to this poor

earth of ours to carry on an exchange; to say to us, as only the Good God could say: 'you give me your humanity, and I will give you my Divinity; you give me your time, and I will give you My eternity; you give me your broken heart, and I will give you Love; you give me your nothingness, and I will give you My all.'"

Fulton J. Sheen, 1895 – 1979
The Eternal Galilean (1934)

"A Christian is one who points at Christ and says, 'I can't prove a thing, but there's something about his eyes and his voice. There's something about the way he carries his head, his hands, the way he carries his cross—the way he carries me.'"

Frederick Buechner. 1926
Wishful Thinking (1973)

"To know Jesus Christ for ourselves is to make Him a consolation, delight, strength, righteousness, companion, and end."

Richard Cecil, 1495 – 1553
J.H. Gilbert; *Dictionary of Burning Words of Brilliant Writer* (1895)

"All that I am I owe to Jesus Christ, revealed to me in His divine Book."

David Livingstone, 1813 – 1873
William Federer, *America's God and Country: Encyclopedia of Quotations* (2000)

"I am not engaged to Christianity by decent forms, or saving ordinances; it is not usage, it is not what I do not understand, that binds me to it—let these be the sandy foundations of falsehoods. What I revere and obey in it is its reality, its boundless charity, its deep interior life, the rest it gives to my mind, the echo it returns to my thoughts, the perfect accord it makes with my reason through

all its representation of God and His Providence; and the persuasion and courage that come out thence to lead me upward and onward."

Ralph Waldo Emerson, 1803 – 1882
Sermon, Second Church of Boston, September 9, 1832

"It is no slight testimonial, both to the merit and worth of Christianity, that in all ages since its promulgation the great mass of those who have risen to eminence by their profound wisdom and integrity have recognized and reverenced Jesus of Nazareth as the Son of the living God."

John Quincy Adams, 1767 – 1848
Letters of John Quincy Adams, To his Son, On the Bible and Its Teachings (1848)

"As a child I received instruction both in the Bible and in the Talmud. I am a Jew, but I am enthralled by the luminous figure of the Nazarene. . . ." Einstein was then asked if he accepted the historical existence of Jesus to which he replied, "Unquestionably! No one can read the Gospels without feeling the actual presence of Jesus. His personality pulsates in every word. No myth is filled with such life."

Albert Einstein, 1897 – 1955
"What Life Means to Einstein," Interview with George S. Viereck, Published in the "Saturday Evening Post," (October 26, 1929)

"Christianity wins more adherents by the life of the faithful than by long discussions of its merits."

Ignatius of Antioch, died 108
"Epistle of Ignatius to the Romans"

"In a profound way, Christianity without the resurrection is not simply Christianity without its final chapter. It is not Christianity at all."

Gerald O'Collins SJ, born 1932
Lecture, "The Resurrection of Jesus Christ," 1993

"It is the grandeur of Christ's character which constitutes the chief power of His ministry, not His miracles or teachings apart from his character. The greatest truth of the gospel is Christ Himself—a human body become the organ of the Divine nature, and revealing, under the conditions of an earthly life, the glory of God."

Horace Bushnell, 1802 – 1876
J.H. Gilbert; *Dictionary of Burning Words of Brilliant Writers* (1895)

"Out of love, God becomes man. He says: 'See, here is what it is to be a human being.'"

Søren Kierkegaard, 1813 – 1855
The Sickness unto Death (1849)

"If anyone could prove to me that Christ is outside the truth, and if the truth really did exclude Christ, I should prefer to stay with Christ and not with truth."

Fyodor Dostoevsky, 1821 – 1881
"Letter to Mme. N. D. Fonvisin," 1854
Letters of Fyodor Michailovich Dostoevsky to his Family and Friends (1914)

"The most pressing question on the problem of faith is whether a man as a civilized being can believe in the divinity of the Son of God, Jesus Christ, for therein rests the whole of our faith."

Fyodor Dostoevsky, 1821 – 1881, Attributed

"It is Jesus that you seek when you dream of happiness; He is waiting for you when nothing else you find satisfies you; He is the beauty to which you are so attracted; it is He who provoked you with that thirst for fullness that will not let you settle for compromise; it is He who urges you to shed the masks of a false life; it is He who reads in your heart your most genuine choices, the choices that others try to stifle. It is Jesus who stirs in you the desire to do something great with your

lives, the will to follow an ideal, the refusal to allow yourselves to be ground down by mediocrity, the courage to commit yourselves humbly and patiently to improving yourselves and society, making the world more human and more fraternal."

Pope John Paul II, 1920 – 2005
15th World Youth Day, Tor Vergata, August 19, 2000

One Solitary Life

– This is the original version of a popular poem about the life of Jesus Christ. Although the author is frequently cited as "unknown", the poem is actually attributed to James Allen Francis. –

Let us turn now to the story. A child is born in an obscure village. He is brought up in another obscure village. He works in a carpenter shop until he is thirty, and then for three brief years is an itinerant preacher, proclaiming a message and living a life. He never writes a book. He never holds an office. He never raises an army. He never has a family of his own. He never owns a home. He never goes to college. He never travels two hundred miles from the place where he was born. He gathers a little group of friends about him and teaches them his way of life. While still a young man, the tide of popular feeling turns against him. One denies him; another betrays him. He is turned over to his enemies. He goes through the mockery of a trial; he is nailed to a cross between two thieves, and when dead is laid in a borrowed grave by the kindness of a friend. Those are the facts of his human life. He rises from the dead.

Today we look back across nineteen hundred years and ask, What kind of trail has he left across the centuries? When we try to sum up his influence, all the armies that ever marched, all the parliaments that ever sat, all the kings that ever reigned are absolutely picayune in their influence on mankind compared with that of this one solitary life...

James Allan Francis, 1864 – 1928
The Real Jesus and Other Sermons (1926)

Fairest Lord Jesus

Fairest Lord Jesus,
ruler of all nature,
O thou of God and man the Son,
Thee will I cherish,
Thee will I honor,
thou, my soul's glory, joy, and crown.

Fair are the meadows,
fairer still the woodlands,
robed in the blooming garb of spring:
Jesus is fairer,
Jesus is purer
who makes the woeful heart to sing.

Fair is the sunshine,
fairer still the moonlight,
and all the twinkling starry host:
Jesus shines brighter,
Jesus shines purer
than all the angels heaven can boast.

Beautiful Savior!
Lord of all the nations!
Son of God and Son of Man!
Glory and honor,
praise, adoration,
now and forevermore be thine.

Anonymous
Hymn (1677)

Of the Father's Love Begotten

Of the Father's love begotten
ere the worlds began to be,

he is Alpha and Omega —
he the source, the ending he,
of the things that are, that have been,
and that future years shall see
evermore and evermore.

O that birth forever blessed,
when a virgin, blest with grace,
by the Holy Ghost conceiving,
bore the Savior of our race;
and the babe, the world's Redeemer,
first revealed his sacred face,
evermore and evermore.

This is he whom seers in old time
chanted of with one accord,
whom the voices of the prophets
promised in their faithful word;
now he shines, the long-expected;
let creation praise its Lord
evermore and evermore.

Let the heights of heaven adore him;
angel hosts, his praises sing:
powers, dominions, bow before him
and extol our God and King;
let no tongue on earth be silent,
every voice in concert ring
evermore and evermore.

Christ, to you, with God the Father
and the Spirit, there shall be
hymn and chant and high thanksgiving

and the shout of jubilee:
honor, glory, and dominion
and eternal victory
evermore and evermore.

Aurelius Clemens Prudentius, c. 346 – 413
Based on his Latin poem, "Corde natus," (1582)

Let All Mortal Flesh Keep Silence

Let all mortal flesh keep silence,
And with fear and trembling stand;
Ponder nothing earthly-minded,
For with blessing in His hand,
Christ our God to earth descending
Comes our homage to demand.

King of kings, yet born of Mary,
As of old on earth He stood,
Lord of lords, in human vesture,
In the body and the blood;
He will give to all the faithful
His own self for heavenly food.

Rank on rank the host of heaven
Spreads its vanguard on the way,
As the Light of light descendeth
From the realms of endless day,
Comes the powers of hell to vanquish
As the darkness clears away.

At His feet the six-winged seraph,
Cherubim with sleepless eye,
Veil their faces to the presence,
As with ceaseless voice they cry:

Alleluia, Alleluia
Alleluia, Lord Most High!

Gerard Moultrie, 1829 – 1885
Translation from the Greek
Divine Liturgy of Saint James (1864)

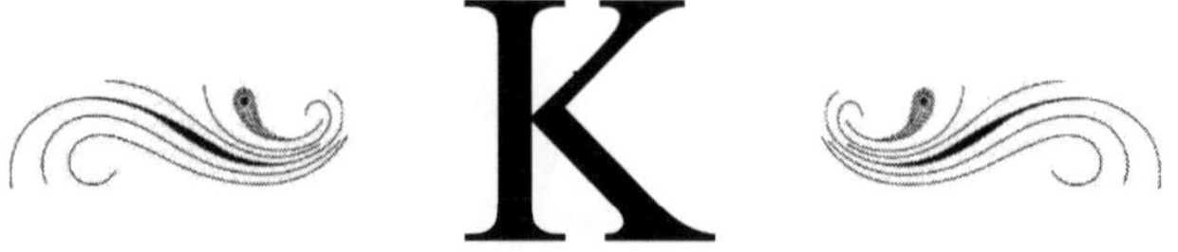

K

King of kings and Lord of lords, thine is the kingdom and the power and the glory forever.

David's Prayer

Yours, Lord, is the greatness and the power and the glory and the majesty and the splendor, for everything in heaven and earth is yours. Yours, O Lord, is the kingdom; you are exalted as head over all. Wealth and honor come from you; you are the ruler of all things. In your hands are strength and power to exalt and give strength to all. Now, our God, we give you thanks, and praise your glorious name.

1 Chronicles 29:11 – 13

Jesus taught the saying, "Thine is the kingdom, and the power, and the glory forever and ever. Amen."

Matthew 6:13

Now to the King Eternal, immortal, invisible, the only God, be honor and glory forever and ever. Amen

1 Timothy 1:17

DEUTERONOMY 10:17
For the Lord your God is God of gods and Lord of lords, the great, the mighty and the awesome God, who is not partial and takes no bribe.

PSALM 8:1
O Lord, our Lord, how majestic is your name in all the earth! You have set your glory above the heavens.

PSALM 19:1
The heavens declare the glory of God; the skies proclaim the work of his hands.

PSALM 24:7 - 8, 10
Lift up your heads, O gates! And be lifted up, O ancient doors, that the King of glory may come in. Who is this King of Glory? The Lord strong and mighty.... Who is he, this King of Glory? The Lord Almighty—he is the King of Glory.

PSALM 29:1 - 2
Ascribe to the Lord glory and strength. Ascribe to the Lord the glory due his name; worship the Lord in the splendor of his holiness.

PSALM 47:7
For God is the King of the earth; sing to him a song of praise.

PSALM 63:2
I have seen you in the sanctuary and beheld your power and your glory.

PSALM 136:3
Give thanks to the Lord of lords: His love endures forever.

PSALM 145:1
I will exalt you, my God the King; I will praise your name forever and ever.

PSALM 145:13
Your kingdom is an everlasting kingdom, and your dominion endures through all generations. The Lord is faithful to all his promises and loving toward all he has made.

ISAIAH 6:3
Holy, holy, holy is the Lord God Almighty; the whole earth of full of his glory.

ISAIAH 42:8
"I am the Lord; that is my name! I will not give my glory to another or my praise to idols."

ISAIAH 60:1
Arise, shine, for your light has come, and the glory of the Lord has risen upon you.

ISAIAH 60:19
No longer will you need the sun to shine by day, nor the moon to give its light by night, for the Lord your God will be your everlasting light, and your God will be your glory.

JEREMIAH 10:10
The Lord is the true God; he is the living God, the eternal King.

DANIEL 2:20
Praise be to the name of God for ever and ever; wisdom and power are his.

DANIEL 2:47
The king said to Daniel, "Surely your God is the God of gods and the Lord of kings and a revealer of mysteries, for you were able to reveal this mystery."

DANIEL 4:3
How great are his signs, how mighty his wonders! His kingdom is an eternal kingdom; his dominion endures from generation to generation.

DANIEL 7:14
And to Him was given dominion, glory and a kingdom, that all the peoples, nations and men of every language might serve Him. His dominion is an everlasting dominion which will not pass away; and His kingdom is one which will not be destroyed.

ZECHARIAH 14:9
The Lord will be king over the whole earth. On that day there will be one Lord, and his name the only name.

MATTHEW 5:3
Jesus went up on the mountainside and he began to teach them, "Blessed are the poor in spirit, for theirs is the kingdom of heaven."

MATTHEW 5:10
"Blessed are those who are persecuted because of righteousness, for theirs is the kingdom of heaven."

MATTHEW 6:10
Jesus prayed, "Thy kingdom come, thy will be done on earth as it is in heaven."

MATTHEW 6:31 – 33
He taught them, "So do not worry, saying, 'What shall we eat' or 'What shall we drink?' or 'What shall we wear?' But seek first his kingdom and his righteousness, and these things will be given to you as well."

MATTHEW 19:14
Jesus said, "Let the little children come to me, and do not hinder them, for the kingdom of heaven belongs to such as these."

MATTHEW 28:18
And Jesus came and said to them, "All authority in heaven and on earth has been given to me."

MARK 1:15
"The time has come," the Baptist said. "The kingdom of God has come near. Repent and believe the good news!"

LUKE 2:14
Glory to God in the highest, and on earth peace and goodwill toward men!

LUKE 12:27 – 32
Jesus said. "Consider the lilies how they grow: they toil not, they spin not; and yet I say unto you, that Solomon in all his glory was not arrayed like one of these. If then God so clothes the grass, which is today in the field, and tomorrow is cast into the oven; how much more will he clothe you, O ye of little faith? And seek not ye what ye shall eat, or what ye shall drink, neither be ye of doubtful mind. For all these things do the nations of the world seek after: and your Father knoweth that ye have need of these things. But rather seek ye the kingdom of God; and all these things shall be added unto you. Fear not,

little flock; for it is your Father's good pleasure to give you the kingdom."

LUKE 17:20 - 21
Once, on being asked by the Pharisees when the kingdom of God would some, Jesus replied, "The coming of the kingdom is not something that can be observed, nor will people say, 'Here it is,' or 'There it is,' because the kingdom of God is in your midst."

JOHN 1:14,16
The Word became flesh and made his dwelling among us. We have seen his glory, the glory of the One and Only who came down from the Father, full of grace and truth.... From the fullness of his grace we have received one blessing after another.

JOHN 3:3
Jesus replied, "Very truly I tell you, no one can see the kingdom of God unless they are born again."

JOHN 18:36 - 38
Jesus said, "My kingdom is not of this world. If it were, my servants would fight to prevent my arrest by the Jewish leaders. But now my kingdom is from another place." "You are a king, then!" said Pilate. Jesus answered, "You say that I am a king. In fact, the reason I was born and came into the world is to testify to the truth. Everyone on the side of truth listens to me." "What is truth?" retorted Pilate.

EPHESIANS 3:20 - 21
Now to him who is able to do immeasurably more than all that we ask or think, according to the power at work within us, to him be glory in the church and in Christ Jesus throughout all generations, forever and ever. Amen.

PHILIPPIANS 4:19
And my God will supply your every need according to his riches in glory in Christ Jesus.

1 TIMOTHY 6:15 - 16
God, the blessed and only Ruler, the King of kings and Lord of lords, who alone is immortal and lives in unapproachable light, whom no one has seen or can see. To him be honor and might forever. Amen.

HEBREWS 1:3
The Son is the radiance of God's glory, and the exact representation of his being.

2 PETER 3:18
Grow in the grace and knowledge of our Lord and Savior Jesus Christ. To him be the glory both now and forever. Amen.

JUDE 24 - 25
To him who is able to keep you from falling, and to present you faultless before his glorious presence with great joy—to the only God, our Savior, be glory and majesty, dominion and power both now and ever. Amen

REVELATION 4:11
You are worthy, O Lord, to receive glory and honor and power, for You created all things. And by Your will they exist and were created.

REVELATION 15:3 - 4
Great and marvelous are your deeds, Lord God Almighty. Just and true are your ways, King of the ages. Who will not fear you, O Lord, and bring glory to your name? For you alone are holy.

REVELATION 19:16
On his robe and on his thigh he has a name written, King of kings and Lord of lords.

"Joy to the World! The Lord is come!
Let earth receive her King!"

Isaac Watts, 1674 – 1748
From the hymn, "Joy to the World the Lord is Come" (1719)

"A man can no more diminish God's glory by refusing to worship Him than a lunatic can put out the sun by scribbling the word, 'darkness' on the walls of his cell."

C. S. Lewis, 1898 – 1963
The Problem of Pain (1940)

"The Kingdom of God is within you."

Leo Tolstoy, 1828 – 1910
The Kingdom of God is Within You (1894)

"There can be no Kingdom of God in the world without the Kingdom of God in our hearts."

Albert Schweitzer, 1875 – 1965
Ed., Charles R Joy; *Albert Schweitzer: An Anthology* (1956)

"The only significance of life consists in helping to establish the kingdom of God."

Leo Tolstoy, 1828 – 1910
The Kingdom of God is Within You (1894)

"There is a signature of wisdom and power impressed on the works of God, which evidently distinguishes them from the feeble imitations of men. Not only the splendor of the sun, but the glimmering light of the glowworm, proclaims his glory."

John Newton, 1725 – 1807
Newton's "Messiah Sermon Series",
Sermon No. 5 (circa 1785 – 1786)

"Heaven is not here, it's There. If we were given all we wanted here, our hearts would settle for this world rather than the next. God is forever luring us up and away from this one, wooing us to Himself and His still invisible Kingdom, where we will certainly find what we so keenly long for."

Elisabeth Elliot, 1926 – 2015
Keep a Quiet Heart (1995)

"How many prodigals are kept out of the Kingdom of God by the unlovely character of those who profess to be inside!"

Henry Drummond, 1851 – 1897
The Greatest Thing in the World (1880)

"O, Thou precious Lord Jesus Christ, we do adore Thee with all our hearts. Thou art Lord of all."

Charles Spurgeon, 1834 – 1892
Prayer No. 2, "Thanks Be Unto God,"
C. H. Spurgeon's Prayers (1905)
Introduction by Dinsdale T. Young

"It is not what we do that matters, but what a sovereign God chooses to do through us. God doesn't want our success; He wants us. He doesn't demand our achievements, He demands our obedience.

The Kingdom of God is a kingdom of paradox where through the ugly defeat of a cross, a holy God is utterly glorified. Victory comes through defeat; healing through brokenness; finding self through losing self."

Charles Colson, 1931 – 2012
Loving God (1983)

"Sacramental listening reminds us that current suffering isn't the end of the story. God loves us deeply, and the vision for the future is vaster and more magnificent than we could ever imagine. In these moments of profound human presence, we are awakened to the divine presence and see that the kingdom of God is coming and yet is already here".

Richard Rohr, 1943
Article, "Listening Well,"
The Christian Century Magazine, May 20, 2014

"If we only had eyes to see and ears to hear and wits to understand, we would know that the Kingdom of God in the sense of holiness, goodness, beauty is as close as breathing and is crying out to be born both within ourselves and within the world; we would know that the Kingdom of God is what we all of us hunger for above all other things even when we don't know its name or realize that it's what we're starving to death for. The Kingdom of God is where our best dreams come from and our truest prayers. We glimpse it at those moments when we find ourselves being better than we are and wiser than we know. We catch sight of it when at some moment of crisis a strength seems to come to us that is greater than our own strength. The Kingdom of God is where we belong. It is home, and whether we realize it or not, I think we are all of us homesick for it."

Frederick Buechner, 1926
Secrets in the Dark (2006)

"The devil can quote Scripture for his purpose; and the text of Scripture which he now most commonly quotes is, 'The Kingdom of heaven is within you.' That text has been the stay and support of more Pharisees and prigs and self-righteous spiritual bullies than all the dogmas in creation; it has served to identify self-satisfaction with the peace that passes all understanding. And the text to be quoted in answer to it is that which declares that no man can receive the kingdom except as a little child. What we are to have inside is a childlike spirit; but the childlike spirit is not entirely concerned about what is inside. It is the first mark of possessing it that one is interested in what is outside. The most childlike thing about a child is his curiosity and his appetite and his power of wonder at the world. We might almost say that the whole advantage of having the kingdom within is that we look for it somewhere else."

G. K. Chesterton, 1874 – 1936
What I Saw in America (1923)

"The Kingdom of God is not a matter of getting individuals to heaven, but of transforming the life on earth into the harmony of heaven."

Walter Rauschenbusch, 1861 – 1918
A Theology for the Social Gospel (1917)

"To will everything that God wills, and to will it always, in all circumstances and without reservations: that is the kingdom of God which is entirely within."

François Fénelon, 1651 – 1715
Christian Counsel on Divers Matters Pertaining to the Inner Life (1853)

"Jesus has many who love the kingdom of God, but few who bear a cross. He has many who desire His comfort, but few who desire his suffering. All want to rejoice with him, but few are willing suffer

for him. He writes: there are many who admire his miracles, but there are few who follow in the humiliation of the cross."

Thomas à Kempis, 1380 – 1471
Imitation of Christ (1418 – 1427)

"The kingdom that Jesus preached and lived was all about a glorious, uproarious, absurd generosity."

N. T. Wright, 1948
Luke for Everyone (2001)

"I will place no value on anything I have or may possess, except in relation to the kingdom of God. If anything will advance the interests of the kingdom, it shall be given away or kept, only as by giving or keeping it I shall most promote the glory of Him to whom I owe all my hopes in time or eternity."

David Livingstone, 1813 – 1873
Ed., David Chamberlin; *Some Letters from Livingstone, 1840 – 1872* (1940)

"The seeking of the kingdom of God is the chief business of the Christian life."

Jonathan Edwards, 1703 – 1758

"I'm fairly convinced that the Kingdom of God is for the broken-hearted. You write of 'powerlessness.' Join the club. We are not in control. God is."

Fred Rogers, 1928 – 2003
Tim Madigan, "Letter to Tim Madigan," *I'm Proud of You: Life Lessons from My Friend Fred Roger* (2007)

"What you do in the present—by painting, preaching, singing, sewing, praying, teaching, building hospitals, digging wells,

campaigning for justice, writing poems, caring for the needy, loving your neighbor as yourself—will last into God's future. These activities are not simply ways of making the present life a little less beastly, a little more bearable, until the day when we leave it behind altogether. They are part of what we may call building for God's kingdom."

N.T. Wright, 1948
Surprised by Hope (2007)

"Modern prophets say that our economics have failed us. No! It is not our economics which have failed; it is man who has failed—man who has forgotten God. Hence no manner of economic or political readjustment can possibly save our civilization; we can be saved only by a renovation of the inner man, only by a purging of our hearts and souls; for only by seeking first the Kingdom of God and His Justice will all these other things be added unto us."

Fulton J. Sheen, 1895 – 1979
The Prodigal World (1936)

"The soul rules over matter. Matter may pass away like a mote in the sunbeam, may be absorbed into the immensity of God, as a mystic absorbed into the heat of the Sun—but the soul is the kingdom of God, the abode of love, of truth, of virtue."

Ralph Waldo Emerson, 1803 – 1882
Miscellanies "Notes on the Lord's Supper"
The Complete Works of Ralph Waldo Emerson, Vol. 11 (1878)

"The kingdom of heaven was never intended to indulge the ease of triflers, but to the rest of them that labor. "

Matthew Henry, 1662 – 1714
Matthew, Chapter 11, *Matthew Henry's Commentary on the Whole Bible* (1710)

"Praise, my soul, the King of heaven;
to his feet your tribute bring.
Ransomed, healed, restored, forgiven,
evermore his praises sing.
Alleluia, alleluia!
Praise the everlasting King!"

Henry Francis Lyte, 1793 – 1847
From the Hymn, "Praise My Soul, the King of Heaven" (1834)

O Worship the King All Glorious Above

O worship the King all-glorious above,
O gratefully sing his power and his love:
our shield and defender, the Ancient of Days,
pavilioned in splendor and girded with praise.

O tell of his might and sing of his grace,
whose robe is the light, whose canopy space.
His chariots of wrath the deep thunderclouds form,
and dark is his path on the wings of the storm.

Your bountiful care, what tongue can recite?
It breathes in the air, it shines in the light;
it streams from the hills, it descends to the plain,
and sweetly distills in the dew and the rain.

Frail children of dust, and feeble as frail,
in you do we trust, nor find you to fail.
Your mercies, how tender, how firm to the end,
our Maker, Defender, Redeemer, and Friend!

O measureless Might, unchangeable Love,
whom angels delight to worship above!
Your ransomed creation, with glory ablaze,
in true adoration shall sing to your praise!

Robert Grant, 1779 – 1838
Hymn (1833)

You have loved me with an everlasting love.

"I have loved you with an everlasting love;
I have drawn you with loving-kindness."

Jeremiah 31:3

God is love. Whoever lives in love lives in God, and God in them.

1 John 4:16

The Ways of Love

Though I speak with the tongues of men and of angels, and have not love, I am become as sounding brass, or a tinkling cymbal.

And though I have the gift of prophecy, and understand all mysteries, and all knowledge; and though I have all faith, so that I could remove mountains, and have not love, I am nothing.

And though I bestow all my goods to feed the poor, and though I give my body to be burned, and have not love, it profiteth me nothing.

Love suffereth long, and is kind; love envieth not; love vaunteth not itself, is not puffed up,

Doth not behave itself unseemly, seeketh not her own,

is not easily provoked, thinketh no evil;

Rejoiceth not in iniquity, but rejoiceth in the truth;

Beareth all things, believeth all things, hopeth all things,
endureth all things.

Love never faileth: but whether there be prophecies, they shall fail;
whether there be tongues, they shall cease;
whether there be knowledge, it shall vanish away.

For we know in part, and we prophesy in part.

But when that which is perfect is come,

then that which is in part shall be done away.

When I was a child, I spake as a child, I understood as a child,
I thought as a child: but when I became a man, I put away
childish things.

For now we see through a glass, darkly; but then face to face:
now I know in part; but then shall I know even as also I am known.

And now abideth faith, hope, love, these three;
but the greatest of these is love.

The Thirteenth Chapter of First Corinthians

The Demands of Love

Love must be sincere. Hate what is evil; cling to what is good.
Be devoted to one another in love.
Honor one another above yourselves.
Never be lacking in zeal, but keep your spiritual fervor, serving the Lord.
Be joyful in hope, patient in affliction, faithful in prayer.
Share with the Lord's people who are in need.
Practice hospitality,
Bless those who persecute you; bless and do not curse.

Rejoice with those who rejoice; mourn with those who mourn.
Live in harmony with one another.
Do not be proud, but be willing to associate with people of low position.
Do not be conceited.
Do not repay anyone evil for evil.
Be careful to do what is right in the eyes of everyone.
If it is possible, as far as it depends on you, live at peace with everyone.
Do not take revenge my dear friends, but leave room for God's wrath,
for it is written: "It is mine to avenge; I will repay, says the Lord."
On the contrary:
if your enemy is hungry, feed him;
if he is thirsty, give him something to drink.
In doing this, you will heap burning coals on his head.
Do not be overcome by evil, but overcome evil with good.

Romans 12:9 – 21

EXODUS 15:13
In unfailing love you will lead the people you have redeemed. In your strength you will guide them to your holy dwelling.

1 CHRONICLES 16:34
O give thanks to the Lord, for he is good; for his steadfast love endures forever!

PSALM 13:5
But I trust in your unfailing love; my heart rejoices in your salvation.

PSALM 25:6 – 7
Remember, O Lord, your great mercy and love, for they are from old. Remember not the sins of my youth and my rebellious ways; according to your love remember me, for you are good, O Lord.

PSALM 25:10
All the ways of the Lord are loving and faithful for those who keep the demands of his covenant.

PSALM 33:22
May your unfailing love rest upon us, O Lord, even as we put our hope in you.

PSALM 36:7
How priceless is your unfailing love!

PSALM 62:11 - 12
One thing God has spoken, two things I have heard: "Power belongs to you, God, and with you, Lord, is unfailing love...."

PSALM 63:3
Because your steadfast love is better than life, my lips will praise you.

PSALM 86:5
You are forgiving and good, O Lord, abounding in love to all who call on you.

PSALM 86:15
But you, O Lord, are a compassionate and gracious God, slow to anger, abounding in love and faithfulness.

PSALM 89:1 - 2
I will sing of the Lord's great love forever; with my mouth I will make your faithfulness known through all generations. Your unfailing love will last forever. Your faithfulness is as enduring as the heavens.

PSALM 100:4 - 5
Enter his gates with thanksgiving and his courts with praise!

Give thanks to the Lord; bless his name! For the Lord is good; his steadfast love endures forever, and his faithfulness to all generations.

PSALM 103:11
For as high as the heavens are above the earth, so great is His love toward those who fear Him.

PSALM 103:17
But from everlasting to everlasting the Lord's love is with those who fear him, and his righteousness with their children's children.

PSALM 107:1
Give thanks to the Lord for he is good; his love endures forever.

PSALM 107:8 – 9
Let them give thanks to the Lord for his unfailing love and his wonderful deeds for men, for he satisfies the thirsty and fills the hungry with good things.

PSALM 138:2, 8
I will praise thy name for thy loving-kindness and for thy truth. . . . The Lord will perfect that which concerneth me: thy mercy O Lord, endureth forever: forsake not the works of thine own hands.

PSALM 145:13
Your kingdom is an everlasting kingdom and your dominion endures through all generations. The Lord is faithful to all his promises and loving toward all he has made.

LAMENTATIONS 3:22 – 23
Because of the Lord's great love we are not consumed, for his

compassions never fail. They are new every morning. Great is your faithfulness.

JOHN 3:16 - 17
For God so loved the world, that he gave his only begotten Son, that whosoever believeth in him should not perish, but have everlasting life. For God sent not his Son into the world to condemn the world; but that the world through him might be saved.

JOHN 13:34
A new command I give you: "Love one another. As I have loved you, so you must love one another. By this all men will know that you are my disciples, if you love one another."

JOHN 15:12
Jesus said, "My command is this: Love one another as I have loved you."

ROMANS 5:1, 8
Therefore, since we have been declared righteous by faith, we have peace with God through our Lord Jesus Christ.... God demonstrates his own love for us in this: While we were yet sinners, Christ died for us.

EPHESIANS 2:4 - 5
Because of this great love for us, God who is rich in mercy, made us alive in Christ even when we were dead in our transgressions—it is by grace you have been saved.

EPHESIANS 3:14 - 19
For this reason I bow my knees before the Father, from whom every family in heaven and on earth derives its name. I pray that out of his glorious riches he may strengthen you with

power through his Spirit in your inner being, so that Christ may dwell in your hearts through faith. And I pray that you, being rooted and established in love, may have power, together with all the Lord's holy people, to grasp how wide and long and high and deep is the love of Christ, and to know this love that surpasses knowledge—that you may be filled to the measure of all the fullness of God.

COLOSSIANS 3:12 - 14
Holy and dearly loved children, clothe yourselves with compassion, kindness, humility, gentleness and patience. Bear with each other and forgive whatever grievances you may have against one another. Forgive as the Lord forgave you. And over all these virtues put on love, which binds them all together in perfect unity.

1 PETER 4:8
Above all, love each other deeply, because love covers a multitude of sins.

1 JOHN 4 **Selected Verses**
Dear friends, let us love one another, for love comes from God. Everyone who loves has been born of God and knows God.... This is how God showed his love among us: He sent his one and only Son into the world that we might live through him. This is love: not that we loved God, but that he loved us and sent his Son as an atoning sacrifice for our sins. Dear friends, since God so loved us, we also ought to love one another. No one has seen God; but if we love one another, God lives in us and his love is made complete in us.... And so we know and rely on the love God has for us. God is love. Whoever lives in love lives in God, and God in them. There is no fear in love. But perfect love drives out fear.... We love because he first loved us.... And he has given us this command: Whoever loves God must also love his brother and sister.

JUDE 21
Keep yourselves in God's love as you wait for the mercy of our Lord Jesus Christ to bring you to eternal life. Be merciful to those who doubt.

"Though our feelings come and go, God's love does not."

C. S. Lewis, 1898 – 1963
Mere Christianity (1952)

"Love is not love which alters when it alteration finds."

William Shakespeare, 1564 – 1616
Sonnet 116 (1609)

"God, the Eternal God, is Love. Covet therefore that everlasting gift, that one thing which it is certain is going to stand, that one coinage which will be current in the universe when all other coinage of all the nations of the world shall be useless and unhonored."

Henry Drummond, 1851 – 1897
The Greatest Thing in the World and Other Writings (1870)

"God loves each of us as if there were only one of us."

Augustine of Hippo, 354 – 430
Confessions (397 – 400)
The above is a paraphrase of: *"O thou omnipotent God, thou carest for everyone of us as if thou didst care for him only, and so for all as if they were but one."*

"May the perfect grace and eternal love of Christ our Lord be our never-failing protection and help."

Ignatius of Loyola, 1491 – 1556
Letter 38, "Letter to Father Simon Rodrigues,"
Rome, March 8, 1542,
Translated by William J. Young, S. J.;
The Letters of Saint Ignatius of Loyola (1959)

"I have found that the paradox of love is to love until it hurts, then there is no hurt, but only love."

Mother Teresa, 1910 – 1997
The Simple Path (1995)

"The measure of love is to love without measure."

Saint Francis de Sales, 1567 – 1622

"Bitterness imprisons life; love releases it. Bitterness paralyzes life; love empowers it. Bitterness sours life; love sweetens it. Bitterness sickens life; love heals it. Bitterness blinds life; love anoints its eyes."

Harry Emerson Fosdick, 1878 – 1969
Riverside Sermons (1958)

"Don't get upset with your imperfections. Surrender to the power of God's love, which is greater than our weaknesses."

Saint Francis de Sales, 1567 – 1622

"By the cross we know the gravity of sin and the greatness of God's love toward us."

John Chrysostom, 349 – 407

"The supreme happiness of life is the conviction that we are loved."

Victor Hugo, 1802 – 1885
Les Misérables (1862)

"God is love. Therefore love. Without distinction, without calculation, without procrastination, love."

Henry Drummond, 1851 – 1897
The Greatest Thing in the World (1884)

"The greatest honor we can give Almighty God is to live gladly because of the knowledge of his love."

Julian of Norwich, born 1342

"The sin underneath all our sins is to trust the lie of the serpent that we cannot trust the love and grace of Christ and must take matters into our own hands."

Martin Luther, 1483 – 1546

"Where there is the greatest love, there are always miracles."

Willa Cather, 1873 – 1847
Death Comes for the Archbishop (1927)

"The many troubles in your household will tend to your edification if you strive to bear them in all gentleness, patience, and kindness. Keep this ever before you, and remember constantly that God's loving eyes are upon you amid all these little worries and vexations, watching whether you take them as He would desire. Offer up all such occasions to Him, and if sometimes you are put out, and give way to impatience, do not be discouraged, but make haste to regain your lost composure."

Saint Francis de Sales, 1567 – 1622

"He [Jesus] said, 'Love as I have loved you.' We cannot love too much."

Amy Carmichael, 1867 – 1951
Elisabeth Elliot, *A Chance to Die: The Life and Legacy of Amy Carmichael* (1987)

"Never doubt this, whatever may happen to you in life, at every moment you are loved."

Pope Francis, 1936

"There is tremendous relief in knowing His love to me is utterly realistic, based at every point on prior knowledge of the worst about me, so that no discovery can disillusion him about me, in the way I am so often disillusioned about myself, and quench his determination to bless me."

J.I. Packer, 1926 – 2020
Knowing God (1973)

"Death and love are the two wings that bear the good man to heaven."

Michelangelo, 1475 – 1564

"Go forth today, by the help of God's Spirit, vowing and declaring that in life—come poverty, come wealth, in death—come pain or come what may, you are and ever must be the Lord's. For this is written on your heart, 'We love Him because He first loved us.'"

Charles H. Spurgeon, 1834 – 1892
"Sermon No. 229," December 19, 1858

"All things that are on earth shall wholly pass away,
Except the love of God, which shall live and last for aye."

William Cullen Bryant, 1794 – 1878
Poem, "The Love of God," 1836;
Poetical Works of Wm. Cullen Bryant (1876)

"Riches take wings, comforts vanish, hope withers away, but love stays with us. Love is God."

Lew Wallace, 1827 – 1905
Ben-Hur: A Tale of the Christ (1880)

"Joy is love exalted; peace is love in repose; long-suffering is love enduring; gentleness is love in society; goodness is love in action;

faith is love on the battlefield; meekness is love in school; and temperance is love in training."

D. L. Moody, 1837 – 1899
Attributed

"There is no sin and there can be no sin on all the earth, which the Lord will not forgive to the truly repentant! Man cannot commit a sin so great as to exhaust the infinite love of God. Can there be a sin which could exceed the love of God?"

Fyodor Dostoyevsky, 1821 – 1881
The Brothers Karamazov (1880)

Love Divine, All Loves Excelling

Love divine, all loves excelling,
Joy of heav'n to earth come down:
fix in us thy humble dwelling,
all thy faithful mercies crown:
Jesus, thou art all compassion,
pure, unbounded love thou art;
visit us with thy salvation,
enter ev'ry trembling heart.

Breathe, O breathe thy loving Spirit
into ev'ry troubled breast;
let us all in thee inherit,
let us find the promised rest:
take away the love of sinning;
Alpha and Omega be;
End of faith, as its Beginning,
set our hearts at liberty.

Come, Almighty to deliver,
let us all thy life receive;

suddenly return, and never,
nevermore thy temples leave.
Thee we would be always blessing,
serve thee as thy hosts above,
pray and praise thee without ceasing,
glory in thy perfect love.

Finish, then, thy new creation;
pure and spotless let us be:
let us see thy great salvation
perfectly restored in thee;
changed from glory into glory,
'til in heav'n we take our place,
'til we cast our crowns before thee,
lost in wonder, love, and praise.

Charles Wesley, 1707 – 1788
Hymn (1747)

Thy mercies are new each morning. Thy mercies never cease; Thy mercies never fail.

Surely goodness and mercy shall follow me all the days of my life,
and I shall dwell in the house of the Lord forever.

Psalm 23:6

The steadfast love of the Lord never ceases; his mercies never come to an end; they are new every morning; great is your faithfulness.

Lamentations 3:22 – 23

PSALM 5:7
By your great mercy, I will come into your house; in reverence I will bow down before your holy temple.

PSALM 25:6 – 7
Remember, O Lord, your great mercy and love, for they are from old. Remember not the sins of my youth and my rebellious ways; according to your love remember me, for you are good, O Lord.

PSALM 40:11
Do not withhold your mercy from me, O Lord; may your love and your truth always protect me.

PSALM 51:1
Have mercy on me, O God, according to your great compassion blot out my transgressions. According to the multitude of thy tender mercies, blot out my transgressions.

PSALM 68:19
Praise be to the Lord, to God, our Savior who daily bears our burdens.

PSALM 86:6 – 7
Hear my prayer, O Lord; listen to my cry for mercy. In the days of my trouble, I call to you, for you will answer me.

PSALM 100:4 – 5
Enter into his gates with thanksgiving, and into his courts with praise: be thankful unto him, and bless his name. For the Lord is good; his mercy is everlasting; and his truth endures to all generations.

PSALM 103:10
He does not treat us as our sins deserve or repay us according to our iniquities.

PSALM 138:8
The Lord will perfect that which concerns me: thy mercy, O Lord, endures forever: forsake not the works of your own hands.

PSALM 145:18 – 19
The Lord is near to all who call on him, to all who call on him

in truth. He fulfills the desires of those who fear him; he hears their cry and saves them.

ISAIAH 55:6 – 7
Seek the Lord while he may be found; call on him while he is near. Let the wicked forsake his way and the evil man his thoughts. Let him turn to the Lord, and he will have mercy on him, and to our God for he will freely pardon.

HABAKKUK 3:1 – 2
Lord, I have heard of your fame; I stand in awe of your deeds, O Lord. Renew them in our day, in our time make them known; in wrath remember mercy.

MICAH 6:8
He has shown you, O man, what is good. And what does the Lord require of you? To act justly and to love mercy and to walk humbly with your God.

MICAH 7:18
Who is a God like you, who pardons sin and forgives transgressions? You do not stay angry forever but delight to show mercy.

ZECHARIAH 7:9
This is what the Lord Almighty says: "Administer justice; show mercy and compassion to one another."

MATTHEW 5:7
Jesus said to them, "Blessed are the merciful for they shall obtain mercy."

LUKE 1:50
His mercy extends to those who fear him from generation to generation.

EPHESIANS 2:4 - 5
Because of this great love for us, God who is rich in mercy, made us alive in Christ even when we were dead in our transgressions—it is by grace that you have been saved.

HEBREWS 4:16
Let us approach the throne of grace with confidence, so that we may receive mercy, and receive grace in our time of need.

1 PETER 1:3
Blessed be the God and Father of our Lord Jesus Christ! By his great mercy he gave us new birth into a living hope through the resurrection of Jesus Christ from the dead, that is, into an inheritance imperishable, undefiled, and unfading. It is reserved in heaven for you,

JUDE 2
Mercy unto you, and peace, and love, be multiplied. Mercy, peace and love be yours in abundance.

JUDE 21
Keep yourselves in God's love as you wait for the mercy of our Lord Jesus Christ to bring you to eternal life. Be merciful to those who doubt.

"Jesus, Son of the Eternal God, have mercy on me."

Michael Servetus, died 1553
(Last words before being burned alive for "heresy"
upon a pyre of his own books)

Fatherlike he tends and spares us
Well our feeble frame he knows

In his hand he gently bears us
Rescues us from all our foes.

Henry Francis Lyte,1793 – 1847
From the Hymn, "Praise My Soul, the King of Heaven" (1834)

"'God is glorious in all his works, but most glorious in his works of mercy."

Thomas Adams, (1583 – 1652)
Works of Thomas Adams Volume I (1860)
Thomas Southey described Adams as "Shakespeare of the Puritans"

"God's mercy is so great that you may sooner drain the sea of its water, or deprive the sun of its light, or make space too narrow, than diminish the great mercy of God."

Charles Spurgeon, 1834 – 1892
Sermon, "From Death to Life," July 26, 1863

"Embrace in one act the two truths—thine own sin, and God's infinite mercy in Jesus Christ."

Alexander Maclaren, 1826 – 1910
J. H. Gilbert, *Dictionary of Burning Words of Brilliant Writers* (1895)

"God is more willing to pardon than to punish. Mercy does more multiply in Him than sin in us. Mercy is His nature. He shows mercy, not because we deserve mercy, but because He delights in mercy."

Thomas Watson, 1620 – 1686
A Divine Cordial: An Exposition on Romans 8:28 (1663)

"A dark cloud is no sign that the sun has lost his light; and dark black convictions are no arguments that God has laid aside His mercy."

Charles Spurgeon, 1834 – 1892
The Saint and His Savior (1857)

"When our needs are permitted to grow to an extremity, and all visible hopes fail, then to have relief given wonderfully enhances the price of such a mercy."

John Flavel, died 1691
The Mystery of Providence (1677)

"Mercy sweetens all God's other attributes. God's holiness without mercy, and his justice without mercy were terrible.... Mercy sets God's power on work to help us; it makes his justice become our friend; it shall avenge our quarrels. God's mercy is one of the most orient pearls of his crown—God's mercy is his glory. His holiness makes him illustrious; his mercy makes him propitious."

Thomas Watson, 1620 – 1686
A Body of Practical Divinity (1692)

"The mercies of God make a sinner proud, but a saint humble."

Thomas Watson, 1620 – 1686
A Divine Cordial: An Exposition on Romans 8:28 (1663)

"The Gospel is good news of mercy to the undeserving. The symbol of the religion of Jesus is the cross, not the scales."

John Stott, 1921 – 2011
Christian Mission in the Modern World (1975)

"Kings in this world should imitate God; their mercy should be above their works."

William Penn, 1644 – 1718

"There is not a flower that opens, not a seed that falls into the ground and not an ear of wheat that nods on the end of its stalk in the wind

that does not preach and proclaim the greatness and the mercy of God to the whole world."

Thomas Merton, 1915 – 1968
The Seven Story Mountain (1948)

"The first fresh hour of every morning should be dedicated to the Lord, whose mercy gladdens it with golden light."

Charles Spurgeon, 1834 – 1892

"Mercy, detached from Justice, grows unmerciful."

C. S. Lewis, 1898 – 1963
Essay, "The Humanitarian Theory of Punishment," 1949

"Never despair of a child. The one you weep most for at the mercy seat may fill your heart with the greatest joys."

T. L. Cuyler, 1822 – 1909
Comp.; C. N. Douglas, *Forty Thousand Quotations, Prose and Poetical* (1917)

"God's mercy is a holy mercy; where it pardons, it heals."

Thomas Watson, 1620 – 1686
A Body of Practical Divinity (1692)

"God never withholds from his children that which his love and wisdom call good.

God's refusals are always merciful — 'severe mercies' at times but mercies all the same.

God never denies our heart's desire except to give us something better."

Elisabeth Elliot, 1926 – 2015
Attributed

"I seem forsaken and alone,
I hear the lion roar,
And every door is shut but one,
And that is Mercy's door."

William Cowper, 1731 – 1800
Poem, "The Waiting Soul"
The Works of William Cowper: His Life, Letters, and Poems (1854)

"May God in his mercy enable us without obstinacy
to perceive our errors."

Michael Servetus, died 1553

"Peace on earth and mercy mild
God and sinners reconciled."

Charles Wesley, 1707 – 1788
From the Hymn, "Hark, the Herald Angels Sing" (1739)

"May the Father of all mercies scatter light, and not darkness, upon our paths, and make us all in our several vocations useful here, and in His own due time and way, everlastingly happy."

George Washington, 1732 – 1799
"Letter to the Hebrew Congregation,"
Newport, R. I., August 18, 1790

"The quality of mercy is not strain'd,
It droppeth like the gentle rain from heaven
Upon the place beneath: it is twice blest;
It blesseth him that gives and him that takes:
'Tis mightiest in the mightiest: it becomes
The throned monarch better than his crown;
His sceptre shows the force of temporal power,

The attribute to awe and majesty,
Wherein doth sit the dread and fear of kings;
But mercy is above this sceptred sway;
It is enthroned in the hearts of kings,
It is an attribute to God himself;
And earthly power doth then show likest God's
When mercy seasons justice."

William Shakespeare, 1564 – 1616
The Merchant of Venice, written circa 1596 – 1599
Originally published (1600)

Nothing, O Lord, can take me from your grasp; nothing can separate me from your love in Christ Jesus. Never will you leave or forsake me.

Who shall separate us from the love of Christ? Shall tribulation, or distress, or persecution, or famine, or nakedness, or peril, or sword?... No, in all these things we are more than conquerors through him that loved us. For I am persuaded, that neither death, nor life, nor angels, nor principalities, nor powers, nor things present, nor things to come, nor height, nor depth, nor any other creature, shall be able to separate us from the love of God, which is in Christ Jesus our Lord.

Romans 8:35, 37 – 39

I will lift up mine eyes unto the hills, from whence cometh my help. My help cometh from the Lord, which made heaven and earth. He will not suffer thy foot to be moved: he that keepeth thee will not slumber. Behold, he that keepeth Israel shall neither slumber nor sleep. The Lord is thy keeper: the Lord is thy shade upon thy right hand. The sun shall not smite thee by day, nor the moon by night. The Lord shall preserve thee from all evil: he shall preserve thy soul. The Lord shall preserve thy going out and thy coming in from this time forth, and even for evermore.

Psalm 121

GENESIS 28:15
I am with you and will watch over you wherever you go, and I will bring you back to this land. I will not leave you until I have done what I have promised you.

EXODUS 34:14
The Lord replied, "My Presence will go with you, and I will give you rest."

DEUTERONOMY 4:31
For the Lord your God is a merciful God; he will not abandon or destroy you or forget the covenant with your ancestors, which he confirmed to them by oath.

DEUTERONOMY 20:3 - 4
Do not be fainthearted or afraid; do not panic or be terrified by them. For the Lord your God is the one who goes with you to fight for you against your enemies to give you victory.

DEUTERONOMY 31:6
Be strong and courageous. Do not be afraid or terrified—for the Lord your God goes with you; he will never leave you or forsake you. The Lord himself goes with you; do not be afraid; do not be discouraged.

JOSHUA 1:5
No one will be able to stand against you all the days of your life. As I was with Moses, so I will be with you; I will never leave you nor forsake you.

JOSHUA 1:9
Have I not commanded you? Be strong and courageous. Do not be frightened, and do not be dismayed, for the Lord your God is with you wherever you go.

1 SAMUEL 12:22
For the sake of his great name the Lord will not reject his people, because the Lord was pleased to make you his own.

1 CHRONICLES 28:20
And David said to Solomon his son, "Be strong and courageous, and do the work: fear not, nor be dismayed: for the Lord God, my God, is with you. He will not fail you, or forsake you, until all the work for the service of the house of the Lord is finished."

PSALM 9:10
Those who know your name will trust in you, for you have never forsaken those who seek you.

PSALM 11:4
The Lord is in his holy temple; the Lord is on his heavenly throne. He observes everyone on earth; his eyes examine them.

PSALM 16:11
You make known to me the path of life; in your presence there is fullness of joy; at your right hand are pleasures forevermore.

PSALM 23:6
Surely goodness and mercy shall follow me all the days of my life, and I will dwell in the house of the Lord forever.

PSALM 27:4
One thing have I asked of the Lord, that will I seek after: that I may dwell in the house of the Lord all the days of my life, to gaze upon the beauty of the Lord and to inquire in his temple.

PSALM 27:10
For my father and my mother have forsaken me, but the Lord will take me in.

PSALM 55:22
Cast thy burden upon the Lord, and he shall sustain thee; he shall never suffer the righteous to be moved.

PSALM 71:9, 18
Do not cast me off in the time of old age; do not forsake me when my strength fails.... Even when I am old and gray, do not forsake me, O God, until I declare your power to the next generation, your might to all who are to come.

PSALM 73:23 - 26
Yet I am always with you; you hold me by my right hand. You guide me with your counsel and afterward you will take me into glory. Whom have I in heaven but you? And earth has nothing I desire besides you. My flesh and my heart may fail, but God is the strength of my heart and my portion forever.

PSALM 91:2
He who dwells in the shelter of the Most High will rest in the shadow of the Almighty. I will say to the Lord, "My refuge and my fortress, my God, in whom I trust."

PSALM 91:14 - 16
"Because he loves me," says the Lord, "I will rescue him; I will protect him, for he acknowledges my name. He will call on me,

and I will answer him; I will be with him in trouble, I will deliver him and honor him. With long life I will satisfy him and show him my salvation."

PSALM 94:14
For the Lord will not reject his people; he will never forsake his inheritance.

PSALM 139:7 – 12
Where can I go from your Spirit? Where can I flee from your presence? If I go up to the heavens, you are there. If I make my bed in the depths, you are there. If I rise on the wings of the dawn, if I settle on the far side of the sea, even there your hand will guide me, your right hand will hold me fast. If I say, "Surely the darkness will hide me, and the light become night around me," even the darkness will not be dark to you; the night will shine like day, for darkness is as light to you.

PSALM 145:18
The Lord is near to all who call on him, to all who call on him in truth.

ISAIAH 41:10, 13 – 14
"So do not fear, for I am with you; do not be dismayed, for I am your God. I will strengthen you and help you; I will uphold you with my righteous right hand.... For I am the Lord your God who takes hold of your right hand and says to you, "Do not fear; I will help you. Do not be afraid.... for I myself will help you," declares the Lord, your Redeemer, the Holy One of Israel.

ISAIAH 42:16
I will lead the blind by ways they have not known, along unfamiliar paths I will guide them; I will turn the darkness

into light before them and make the rough places smooth. These are the things I will do; I will not forsake them.

ISAIAH 43:1 - 3, 5
But now, this is what the Lord says, "Do not fear for I have redeemed you; I have summoned you by name; you are mine. When you pass through the waters, I will be with you; when you pass through the rivers they will not sweep over you. When you walk through the fire, you will not be burned; the flames will not set you ablaze. For I am the Lord your God, the Holy One of Israel, your Savior.... Do not be afraid, for I am with you."

ISAIAH 46:3 - 4
"Listen to me... you whom I have upheld since your birth and have carried since you were born. Even to your old age and gray hairs I am he, I am he who will sustain you. I have made you and I will carry you; I will sustain you and I will rescue you."

JEREMIAH 23:24
"Who can hide in secret places so that I cannot see them?" declares the Lord. "Do not I fill heaven and earth?" declares the Lord.

JEREMIAH 29:11
"For I know the plans I have for you," declares the Lord, "plans to prosper you and not to harm you, plans to give you hope and a future."

ZEPHANIAH 3:17
The Lord your God is in your midst, a mighty one who will save; he will rejoice over you with gladness; he will quiet you by his love; he will exult over you with loud singing.

MICAH 7:7 - 8
But as for me, I watch in hope for the Lord, I wait for God my Savior; my God will hear me. Do not gloat over me, my enemy! Though I have fallen, I will rise. Though I sit in darkness, the Lord will be my light.

MATTHEW 28:20
Jesus said, "And surely I am with you always, to the very end of the age."

JOHN 6:37
Jesus said, "All that the Father gives me will come to me, and whoever comes to me I will never drive away."

JOHN 10: 27 - 30
Jesus said, "My sheep listen to my voice: I know them, and they follow me. I give them eternal life, and they shall never perish. No one shall snatch them out of my hand. My Father, who has given them to me, is greater than all; no one can snatch them out of my Father's hand. I and the Father are one."

JOHN 14:1 - 3; 15 - 18
Jesus said to his disciples, "Let not your heart be troubled; you believe in God, believe also in Me. In My Father's house are many mansions; if it were not so, I would have told you. I go to prepare a place for you. And if I go and prepare a place for you, I will come again and receive you to Myself; that where I am, there you may be also.... If you love Me, keep My commandments. And I will ask the Father, and He will give you another Helper, that He may abide with you forever—the Spirit of truth, whom the world cannot receive, because it neither sees Him nor knows Him; but you know Him, for He dwells with you and will be in you. I will not leave you orphans; I will come to you."

ACTS 17:27 - 28
He is not far from any one of us. 'For in him we live and move and have our being,' as some of your own poets have said.

ROMANS 8:28
And we know that all things work together for good to them that love God, to them who are the called according to his purpose.

PHILIPPIANS 4:6 - 7
Do not be anxious about anything, but in every situation, by prayer and petition, with thanksgiving, present your requests to God. And the peace of God, which transcends all understanding, will guard your hearts and your minds in Christ Jesus.

HEBREWS 4:16
Let us therefore come boldly unto the throne of grace, that we may obtain mercy, and find grace to help in time of need.

HEBREWS 13:5 - 6
Let your conversation be without covetousness; and be content with such things as ye have: for he hath said, "I will never leave thee, nor forsake thee." So that we may boldly say, "The Lord is my helper, and I will not fear what man shall do unto me."

1 PETER 5:7
Cast all your care upon him, for he cares for you.

"Do not look forward to the changes and chances of this life in fear; rather look to them with full hope that, as they arise, God, whose you are, will deliver you out of them. He is your keeper.

He has kept you hitherto. Do you but hold fast to his dear hand, and he will lead you safely through all things; and, when you cannot stand, he will bear you in his arms. Do not look forward to what may happen tomorrow. Our Father will either shield you from suffering, or he will give you strength to bear it."

Saint Francis de Sales, 1567 – 1622
Prayer, "Be at Peace"

"If the Lord be with us, we have no cause of fear. His eye is upon us, His arm over us, His ear open to our prayer— His grace sufficient, His promise unchangeable."

John Newton, 1725 – 1807
"Letter to the Rev. William Rose," April 15, 1776
The Works of the Reverend John Newton (1822)

"There are times when I feel that he has withdrawn from me, and I have often given him cause, but Easter is always the answer to My God, my God, why hast thou forsaken me!"

Madeleine L'Engle, 1918 – 2007
Madeleine L'Engle Herself: Reflections on a Writing Life (2001)

"Only he knew that to be left alone is not always to be forsaken."

George MacDonald, 1804 – 1905
At the Back of the North Wind (1871)

"However softly we speak, God is so close to us that he can hear us; nor do we need wings to go in search of him, but merely to seek solitude and contemplate him within ourselves, without being surprised to find such a good Guest there."

John of the Cross, 1542 – 1591

"However weak we are, however poor, however little our faith, or however small our grace may be, our names are still written on His heart; nor shall we lose our share in Jesus' love."

Charles Spurgeon, 1834 – 1892
Sermon No. 47, "Christ's Prayer for His People,"
October 21, 1885 *New Street Pulpit Vol. 1* (1855)

"Nothing can separate you from God's love; absolutely nothing. God is enough for time. God is enough for eternity. God is enough!"

Hannah Whitall Smith, 1832 – 1911

"How sweet it is to learn the Savior's love when nobody else loves us! When friends flee, what a blessed thing it is to see that the Savior does not forsake us but still keeps us and holds us fast and clings to us and will not let us go!"

Charles Spurgeon, 1834 – 1892
Sermon No. 47, "Christ's Prayer for His People," October 21, 1885
New Street Pulpit Vol. 1 (1855)

"Nothing so demoralizes the soul as fear. Only when we realize the presence of the Lord does fear give place to faith."

Sarah Frances Smiley, circa 1830 – 1917
The Fullness of Blessing; or the Gospel of Christ (1876)

"The proud man is forsaken of God."

Plato, born circa 428 BC
C.N. Douglas, comp.; *Forty Thousand Quotes: Prose and Poetical* (1917)

"Through the clouds of midnight, this bright promise shone, I will never leave thee, never leave thee alone."

Eliza E. Hewitt, 1851 – 1920
From the Hymn, "Fear Not, I Am With Thee," 1898

"When the time comes for you to die, you need not be afraid, because death cannot separate you from God's love."

Charles Spurgeon, 1834 – 1892
Sermon, Dec. 19, 1858; Royal Surrey Gardens;
Spurgeon's Sermons Vol. 5 (1859)

"My Lord God, I have no idea where I am going. I do not see the road ahead of me… you will lead me by the right road, though I may know nothing about it. Therefore, I will trust you always though I may seem to be lost and in the shadow of death. I will not fear, for you are ever with me, and you will never leave me to face my perils alone."

Thomas Merton, 1915 – 1968
"The Merton Prayer," *Reflections, A Magazine of Yale Divinity School* (2012)

"As I stood alone and forsaken, and the power of the sea and the battle of the elements reminded me of my own nothingness, and on the other hand, the sure flight of the birds recalled the words spoken by Christ: 'Not a sparrow shall fall on the ground without your Father.' Then, all at once, I felt how great and how small I was; then did those two mighty forces, pride and humility, happily unite in friendship."

Søren Kierkegaard, 1813 – 1855
Journal (1835)

"We need never shout across the spaces to an absent God. He is nearer than our own soul, closer than our most secret thoughts."

A.W. Tozer, 1897 – 1963
The Pursuit of God (1948)

"The light of God surrounds me; The love of God enfolds me;
The power of God protects me; The presence of God watches over me;
Wherever I am, God is."

James Dillet Freeman, 1912 – 2003
"The Prayer of Protection," First appeared in the Silent Unity
Christmas Service during World War II (1940)

"Does God seem far away? Guess who moved."

Author Unknown

"Teach me to feel that thou art always nigh;
teach me the struggles of the soul to bear.
To check the rising doubt, the rebel sigh,
teach me the patience of unanswered prayer."

George Croly, 1780 – 1860
Stanza 5, Hymn, "Spirit of God, Descend Upon My Heart" (1854)

"Let the world turn upside down, let everything be in darkness,
in smoke, in uproar – God is with us."

Saint Francis de Sales, 1567 – 1622)
Letters to Persons in the World (1883)

"Nothing has separated us from God but our own will, or rather
our own will is our separation from God."

William Law, 1686 – 1761
The Grounds and Reasons of Christian Regeneration
or Christian Rebirth (1739)

"Your faith will not fail while God sustains it; you are not strong
enough to fall away while God is resolved to hold you."

J.I. Packer, 1926 – 2020
Knowing God (1973)

"It is God to whom and with whom we travel, and while He is the end of our journey, He is also at every stopping place."

Elisabeth Elliot, 1926 – 2015
All That Was Ever Ours (1982)

"We believe that the divine presence is everywhere."

Saint Benedict, circa 480 – 547
Rule of Benedict (516)

"Your God is ever beside you—indeed, He is even within you."

St. Alphonsus Maria de Ligouri, 1696 – 1787
Booklet, "How to Converse with God" (1753)

"In me there is darkness, But with You there is light;
I am lonely, but You do not leave me;
I am feeble in heart, but with You there is help;
I am restless, but with You there is peace.
In me there is bitterness, but with You there is patience;
I do not understand Your ways, But You know the way for me.
Lord Jesus Christ, You were poor And in distress, a captive and forsaken as I am.
You know all man's troubles; You abide with me When all men fail me;
You remember and seek me; It is your will that I should know you and turn to You.
Lord, I hear Your call and follow; Help me."

Dietrich Bonhoeffer, 1906 – 1945
From "Morning Prayer for Fellow Prisoners," Christmas, 1943
Prisoner for God: Letters and Papers from Prison (1951)

"The earth shall soon dissolve like snow,
The sun forbear to shine;
But God, who call'd me here below,
Will be forever mine."

John Newton, 1725 – 1807
From the Hymn, "Amazing Grace," (1772)

"Deep, solemn optimism, it seems to me, should spring from this firm belief in the presence of God in the individual; not a remote, unapproachable governor of the universe, but a God who is very near every one of us, who is present not only in earth, sea and sky, but also in every pure and noble impulse of our hearts, the source and center of all minds, their only point of rest."

Helen Keller, 1880 – 1968
Essay, "Optimism," (1903)

"May not a single moment of my life be lived outside the light and love of God's presence and not a single minute without the entire surrender of myself as a vessel for Him to fill full of His Spirit and His love."

Andrew Murray, 1825 – 1917
Murray's prayer
Lena Choy; *Andrew Murray: The Authorized Biography* (2004)

"Courage for the great sorrows of life, and patience for the small ones, and when you have laboriously accomplished your daily task, go to sleep in peace. God is awake."

Victor Hugo, 1802 – 1885
From the Preface of the play, *Cromwell* (1827)

"In solitude we are least alone."

Lord Byron, 1788 – 1824
Childe Harold's Pilgrimage (1812)

I will lift up mine eyes to the hills—
From whence comes my help?
My help comes from the Lord,
Who made heaven and earth.
He will not allow your foot to be moved;
He who keeps you will not slumber,
Behold He who keeps Israel
shall neither slumber nor sleep.
The Lord is your keeper;
The Lord is your shade at your right hand
The sun shall not strike you by day,
Nor the moon by night.
The Lord shall preserve you from all evil;
He shall preserve your soul.
The Lord shall preserve your going out and your coming in
From this time forth, and even forevermore.

Psalm 121

How Firm a Foundation

"How firm a foundation, ye saints of the Lord,
Is laid for your faith in His excellent word!
What more can He say than to you He hath said—
To you who for refuge to Jesus have fled?"

"Fear not, I am with thee, oh, be not dismayed,
For I am thy God, and will still give thee aid;
I'll strengthen thee, help thee, and cause thee to stand,
Upheld by My gracious, omnipotent hand."

"When through the deep waters I call thee to go,
The rivers of sorrow shall not overflow;
For I will be with thee thy trouble to bless,
And sanctify to thee thy deepest distress".

"When through fiery trials thy pathway shall lie,
My grace, all-sufficient, shall be thy supply;
The flame shall not harm thee; I only design
Thy dross to consume and thy gold to refine."

"The soul that on Jesus doth lean for repose,
I will not, I will not, desert to his foes;
That soul, though all hell should endeavor to shake,
I'll never, no never, no never forsake."

Unknown
Hymn (1787)

Abide With Me

Abide with me; fast falls the eventide;
The darkness deepens; Lord with me abide.
When other helpers fail and comforts flee,
Help of the helpless, O abide with me.

Swift to its close ebbs out life's little day;
Earth's joys grow dim; its glories pass away;
Change and decay in all around I see;
O Thou who changest not, abide with me.

Not a brief glance I beg, a passing word,
But as Thou dwell'st with Thy disciples, Lord,
Familiar, condescending, patient, free.
Come not to sojourn, but abide with me.

Come not in terror, as the King of kings,
But kind and good, with healing in Thy wings;
Tears for all woes, a heart for every plea.
Come, Friend of sinners, thus abide with me.

Thou on my head in early youth didst smile,
And though rebellious and perverse meanwhile,
Thou hast not left me, oft as I left Thee.
On to the close, O Lord, abide with me.

I need Thy presence every passing hour.
What but Thy grace can foil the tempter's power?
Who, like Thyself, my guide and stay can be?
Through cloud and sunshine, Lord, abide with me.

I fear no foe, with Thee at hand to bless;
Ills have no weight, and tears no bitterness.
Where is death's sting? Where, grave, thy victory?
I triumph still, if Thou abide with me.

Hold Thou Thy cross before my closing eyes;
Shine through the gloom and point me to the skies.
Heaven's morning breaks, and earth's vain shadows flee;
In life, in death, O Lord, abide with me.

Reverend Henry Francis Lyte, 1793 – 1877
Hymn (1847)

God of Abraham, Isaac, and Jacob; Holy One of Israel; Father, Son, Holy Spirit; Thou, O God, art One. Only thou art God—there is no other.

"I am the Lord and there is no other; apart from me there is no God. I will strengthen you though you have not acknowledged me, so that from the rising of the sun to the place of its setting men may know that there is none besides me. I am the Lord and there is no other. And there is no God apart from me, a righteous God and a Savior; there is none but me. Turn to me and be saved, all you ends of the earth; for I am God, and there is no other."

Isaiah 45:5 – 6; 21 – 22

"Remember this, keep it in mind, take it to heart. Remember the former things, those of long ago; I am God, and there is no other. I am God, and there is none like me. I make known the end from the beginning from ancient times, what is still to come. I say, 'My purpose will stand, and I will do all that I please. What I have said, that I will bring about; what I have planned, that I will do.'"

Isaiah 46: 8 – 11

To Him who is able to keep you from falling, and to present you faultless before the presence of his glory with exceeding joy— to the only wise God our Savior, be glory and majesty, dominion and power, both now and ever. Amen.

Jude 24 – 25

EXODUS 3:5 - 6
"Do not come any closer," God said to Moses. "Take off your sandals, for the place where you are standing is holy ground." Then he said, "I am the God of your father, I am the God of Abraham, the God of Isaac, the God of Jacob." At this, Moses hid his face because he was afraid to look at God.

EXODUS 15:11
Who among the gods is like you, Lord? Who is like you– majestic in holiness, awesome in glory, working wonders?

DEUTERONOMY 4:35, 39
To you it was shown that you might know that the Lord, He is God; there is no other besides Him.... Acknowledge and take to heart this day that the Lord is God in heaven above and on the earth below. There is no other.

DEUTERONOMY 6:4 - 5
Hear, O Israel: The Lord our God, the Lord is one. Love the Lord with all your heart and with all your soul and with all your strength

DEUTERONOMY 30:19 - 20
"I call heaven and earth to witness against you today, that I have set before you life and death, blessing and curse. Therefore, choose life, that you and your offspring may live, loving the Lord your God, obeying his voice and holding fast to him,

for he is your life and the length of your days, that you may dwell in the land that the Lord swore to your fathers, to Abraham, to Isaac, and to Jacob, to give them."

1 SAMUEL 2:2
There is none holy like the Lord: for there is none besides you; there is no rock like our God.

2 SAMUEL 7:22
How great you are, O Sovereign Lord! There is none like you, and there is no God but you, as we have heard with our own ears.

2 SAMUEL 22:32
For who is God besides the Lord? And who is the Rock except our God?

1 KINGS 8:60
So that all the world may know that the Lord is God and that there is no other.

2 KINGS 19:15
And Hezekiah prayed to the Lord: "O Lord God of Israel, enthroned between the cherubim, you alone are God over all the kingdoms of the earth. You have made the heavens and the earth."

1 CHRONICLES 17:20
There is no one like you, O Lord God, and there is no God but you, as we have heard with our own ears.

NEHEMIAH 9:6
You are the Lord, you alone. You have made the heavens, the heaven of heavens, and all their starry host, the earth and all

that is on it, the seas and all that is in them; and you preserve all of them: and the host of heaven worships you.

PSALM 68:19
Praise be to the Lord, to God our Savior, who daily bears our burdens.

PSALM 83:18
Let them know that you, whose name is the Lord—that you alone are the Most High over all the earth.

PSALM 86:10
For you are great and do marvelous deeds; you alone are God.

PSALM 144:15
Blessed are the people whose God is the Lord.

PSALM 146:5 - 6
Blessed is he whose help is the God of Jacob, whose hope is in the Lord his God, the Maker of heaven and earth, the sea and everything in them—the Lord who remains faithful forever.

ISAIAH 41:14
"Do not be afraid, for I myself will help you," declares the Lord, your Redeemer, the Holy One of Israel.

ISAIAH 43:1 - 3, 5
But now, this is what the Lord says.... "Fear not, for I have redeemed you; I have summoned you by name; you are mine. When you pass through the waters, I will be with you; when you pass through the rivers they will not sweep over you. When you walk through the fire, you will not be burned; the flames will not set you ablaze. For I am the Lord your God, the Holy One of Israel, your Savior.... Do not be afraid, for I am with you."

ISAIAH 43:10 – 11, 25
"You are my witnesses," declares the Lord, "and my servant whom I have chosen, that you may know and believe me and understand that I am he. Before me there was no god formed, and there will be none after me. I, even I, am the Lord, and apart from me there is no savior.... I, even I, am he who blots out your transgressions, for my own sake, and remembers your sins no more."

ISAIAH 44:6, 8
This is what the Lord says, Israel's King and Redeemer, the Lord Almighty: "I am the first and the last; and there is no God besides me.... Do not tremble, do not be afraid. Did I not proclaim this and foretell it long ago? You are my witnesses. Is there any God besides me? No, there is no other Rock; I know not one."

ISAIAH 46:9 – 11
"Remember the former things of old; for I am God, and there is no other; I am God, and there is none like me, declaring the end from the beginning and from ancient times things not yet done, saying, 'My counsel shall stand, and I will accomplish all my purpose.' What I have said, that I will bring about; what I have planned, that I will do."

ISAIAH 47:4
Our Redeemer—the Lord Almighty is his name— is the Holy One of Israel.

ISAIAH 48:17
This is what the Lord says, your Redeemer, the Holy One of Israel: "I am the Lord your God, who teaches you what is best for you, who directs you in the way you should go. If only you had paid attention to my commands, your peace would have been like a river."

ISAIAH 64:4
Since ancient times no one has heard, no ear has perceived, no eye has seen any God besides you, who acts on behalf of those who wait for him.

HOSEA 13:4
"But I have been the Lord your God ever since you came out of Egypt. You shall acknowledge no God but me, no Savior except me."

ZECHARIAH 14:9
The Lord will be king over the whole earth. On that day there will be one Lord, and his name the only name.

MARK 12:28 - 34
One of the scribes asked Jesus, "Of all the commandments, which is the most important?" "The most important one," answered Jesus, "is this: 'Hear, O Israel, the Lord our God, the Lord is one. And you shall love the Lord your God with all your heart and with all your soul and with all your mind and with all your strength.' The second is this: 'You shall love your neighbor as yourself.' There is no commandment greater than these." And the scribe said to him, "You are right, Teacher, in saying that God is one and there is no other but him. And to love him with all the heart and with all the understanding and with all the strength, and to love one's neighbor as oneself is more important than all burnt offerings and sacrifices." And when Jesus saw that he answered wisely, he said to him, "You are not far from the kingdom of God."

JOHN 6:68 - 69
Simon Peter answered him, "Lord, to whom shall we go? You have the words of eternal life. We believe and we know that you are the Holy One of God."

JOHN 10:30
Jesus declared, "I and the Father are one."

JOHN 14:1
Jesus said to his disciples, "Let not your hearts be troubled. Believe in God; believe also in me."

JOHN 14:9
Jesus said to them, "Anyone who has seen me has seen the Father."

JOHN 17:3
Jesus prayed, "Now this is eternal life: that they may know you, the only true God, and Jesus Christ whom you have sent."

1 CORINTHIANS 8:6
Yet for us there is but one God, the Father, from whom all things came and for whom we live; and there is but one Lord, Jesus Christ, through whom all things came and through whom we live.

EPHESIANS 4:4 - 6
There is one body and one Spirit—just as you were called to one hope when you were called—one Lord, one faith, one baptism; one God and Father of all who is over all and through all and in all.

1 TIMOTHY 1:17
Now to the King eternal, immortal, invisible, the only God, be honor and glory forever and ever. Amen.

1 TIMOTHY 2:3 - 5
God our Savior wants all to be saved and to come to a know-ledge of the truth. For there is one God and one mediator

between God and men, the man Jesus Christ, who gave himself as a ransom for all.

"Bring me a worm that can comprehend a man, and then I will show you a man that can comprehend the Triune God."

John Wesley, 1703 – 1791
Quoted by Henry in *The Life of Mrs. Fletcher: Consort and Relict of The Reverend John Fletcher, Vicar of Madely* (1824)

'There is but one only, living, and true God, who is infinite in being and perfection, a most pure spirit, invisible, without body, parts, or passions; immutable, immense, eternal, incomprehensible, almighty, most wise, most holy, most free, most absolute...."

Chapter 2, "Of God, and the Holy Trinity,"
Westminster Confession of Faith (1646)

"The Trinity is revealed to us only in the Bible. God has revealed some things to us through nature and through conscience. But the Trinity is not among them. This He has revealed to us by supernatural revelation and by supernatural revelation alone."

Gresham Machen, 1881 – 1937
The Christian Faith in the Modern World (1936)

"To meditate on the three Persons of the Godhead is to walk in thought through the garden eastward in Eden and to tread on holy ground. Our sincerest effort to grasp the incomprehensible mystery of the Trinity must remain forever futile, and only by deepest reverence can it be saved from actual presumption."

A.W. Tozer, 1897 – 1963
Knowledge of the Holy (1961)

"I tell you the solemn truth that the doctrine of the Trinity is not so difficult to accept for a working proposition as any one of the axioms of physics."

Henry Brooks Adams, 1838 – 1918
Esther (1884)

"The Universal Presence of God is a fact. God is here. The whole universe is alive with his life. And he is no strange or foreign God, but the Father of our Lord Jesus Christ...."

A.W. Tozer, 1897 – 1963
The Pursuit of God (1948)

"Father, Son, and Holy Spirit mean that the mystery beyond us, the mystery among us, and the mystery within us are all the same mystery."

Frederick Buechner, 1926
Beyond Words: Daily Readings in the ABC's of Faith (2004)

"I gave in, and admitted that God was God, and knelt and prayed: perhaps, that night, the most dejected and reluctant convert in all England."

C. S. Lewis, 1898 – 1963
Surprised by Joy (1955)

"The great act of faith is when a man decides that he is not God."

Oliver Wendell Holmes, Jr., 1841 – 1935
"Letter to William James," March 24, 1907

"The love of a mother is the veil of a softer light between the heart and the heavenly Father."

Samuel Taylor Coleridge, 1772 – 1834
Thomas Allsop, Ed.; *Letters, conversations, and recollections of S. T. Coleridge* (1836)

"Praise, praise the Father, praise the Son
And praise the Spirit, Three in One!
O praise Him! O praise Him!
Alleluia! Alleluia! Alleluia!"

Saint Francis of Assisi, died 1226
"Canticle of Brother Sun and Sister Moon," ca. 1226

The Prayer of Saint Dominic

"May God the Father who made us, bless us.
May God the Son send his healing among us.
May God the Holy Spirit move within us,
and give us eyes to see with, ears to hear with,
and hands that your work may be done.
May we walk and preach the word of God to all.
May the angel of peace watch over us
and lead us at last by God's grace to the Kingdom.
Amen."

Dominic, 1170 – 1221

"It is not easy to find a name that will suitably express so great an excellence, unless it is better to speak in this way: the Trinity, one God, of whom are all things, through whom are all things, in whom are all things.

Thus, the Father and the Son and the Holy Spirit, and each of these by Himself, is God, and at the same time they are all one God; and each of them by Himself is a complete substance, and yet they are all one substance.

The Father is not the Son nor the Holy Spirit; the Son is not the Father nor the Holy Spirit; the Holy Spirit is not the Father nor the Son: but the Father is only Father, the Son is only Son, and the Holy Spirit is only Holy Spirit. To all Three belong the same eternity, the same unchangeableness, the same majesty, the same power. In the Father is unity, in the Son equality, in the Holy Spirit the harmony of unity and equality.

And these three attributes are all one because of the Father,

all equal because of the Son, and all harmonious because of the Holy Spirit."

Saint Augustine, 354 – 430
On Christian Doctrine (426)

The Nicene Creed

We believe in one God, the Father, the Almighty,
maker of heaven and earth, of all that is, seen and unseen.
We believe in one Lord, Jesus Christ, the only Son of God,
eternally begotten of the Father,
God from God, Light from Light, true God from true God,
begotten, not made, of one Being with the Father.
Through him all things were made.
For us and for our salvation he came down from heaven:
by the power of the Holy Spirit
he became incarnate from the Virgin Mary,
and was made man.
For our sake he was crucified under Pontius Pilate;
he suffered death and was buried.
On the third day he rose again in accordance with the Scriptures;
he ascended into heaven and is seated at the right hand of the Father.
He will come again in glory to judge the living and the dead,
and his kingdom will have no end.
We believe in the Holy Spirit, the Lord, the giver of life,
who proceeds from the Father and the Son.
With the Father and the Son he is worshiped and glorified.
He has spoken through the Prophets.
We believe in one holy catholic and apostolic Church.
We acknowledge one baptism for the forgiveness of sins.

We look for the resurrection of the dead,
and the life of the world to come. Amen.

First Council of Nicaea, June 19, 325
Original form of the creed adopted by this council

Apostles' Creed

I believe in God, the Father Almighty, maker of heaven and earth; And in Jesus Christ his only Son, our Lord; who was conceived by the Holy Spirit, born of the Virgin Mary, suffered under Pontius Pilate, was crucified, dead, and buried; the third day he rose from the dead; he ascended into heaven, and sitteth at the right hand of God the Father Almighty; from thence he shall come to judge the quick and the dead. I believe in the Holy Spirit, the holy catholic church, the communion of saints, the forgiveness of sins, the resurrection of the body, and the life everlasting. Amen.

Date of writing is uncertain.
Referenced in a letter written by the Council of Milan in 390

Now Thank We All Our God

All praise and thanks to God
the Father now be given,
the Son and Spirit blest,
who reign in highest heaven
the one eternal God,
whom heaven and earth adore;
for thus it was, is now,
and shall be evermore.

Martin Rinckart, 1586 – 1649
Stanza 3, Hymn (1636)

The God of Abraham Praise

The God of Abraham praise,
who reigns enthroned above;

Ancient of Everlasting Days,
and God of Love;
Jehovah, great I AM!
by earth and heaven confessed;
I bow and bless the sacred name
forever blest.
The great I AM has sworn;
I on this oath depend.
I shall, on eagle wings upborne,
to heaven ascend.
I shall behold God's face;
I shall God's power adore,
and sing the wonders of God's grace
forevermore.
The heavenly land I see,
with peace and plenty blest;
a land of sacred liberty,
and endless rest.
There milk and honey flow,
and oil and wine abound,
and trees of life forever grow
with mercy crowned.
The God who reigns on high
the great archangels sing,
and "Holy, holy, holy!" cry
"Almighty King!
Who was, and is, the same,
and evermore shall be:
Jehovah, Lord, the great I AM,
we worship thee!"

Attributed, Daniel ben Judah, circa Mid-14th Century
Christian adaptation of an Ancient Jewish hymn,
"Yigdal Elohim Hai" (1770)
Paraphraser, Thomas Olivers, 1725 – 1799

The Navy Hymn
Eternal Father, Strong to Save

Eternal Father, strong to save
Whose arm hath bound the restless wave,
Who bidd'st the mighty ocean deep
Its own appointed limits keep;
Oh, hear us when we cry to Thee,
For those in peril on the sea!

O Christ! *Whose voice the waters heard*
And hushed their raging at Thy word,
Who walked'st on the foaming deep,
And calm amidst its rage didst sleep;
Oh, hear us when we cry to Thee,
For those in peril on the sea!

Most Holy Spirit! *Who didst brood*
Upon the chaos dark and rude,
And bid its angry tumult cease,
And give, for wild confusion, peace;
Oh, hear us when we cry to Thee,
For those in peril on the sea!

O Trinity *of love and power!*
Our brethren shield in danger's hour;
From rock and tempest, fire and foe,
Protect them wheresoe'er they go;
Thus evermore shall rise to Thee
Glad hymns of praise from land and sea.

William Whiting, 1825 – 1878
Hymn (1860)

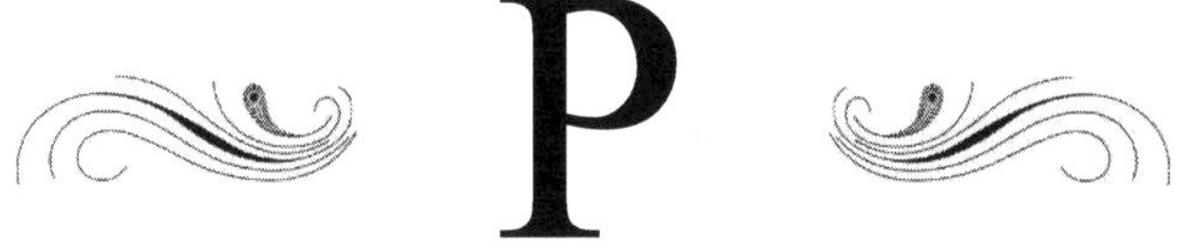

Thou will keep him in perfect peace whose mind is stayed on Thee.

The Lord bless you and keep you;
the Lord make His face shine upon you and be gracious to you;
The Lord lift up His countenance upon you,
and give you peace.

Numbers 6:24 – 26

Rejoice in the Lord always. I will say it again: Rejoice! Let your gentleness be evident to all. The Lord is near. Do not be anxious about anything, but in everything by prayer and petition, with thanksgiving, present your requests to God. And the peace that passes understanding will guard your hearts and your minds in Christ Jesus.

Philippians 4:4 – 7

Jesus said to his disciples, "Peace I leave with you, my peace I give you. I do not give to you as the world gives. Do not let your heart be troubled and do not be afraid."

John 14:27

But the fruit of the Spirit is love, joy, peace, patience, kindness, goodness, faithfulness, gentleness and self-control.

Galatians 5:22

PSALM 4:8
I will lie down and sleep in peace, for you alone, O Lord, make me dwell in safety.

PSALM 29:11
The Lord gives strength to his people; the Lord blesses his people with peace.

PSALM 34:14
Turn from evil and do good; seek peace and pursue it.

PSALM 37:11
But the meek will inherit the land and enjoy great peace.

PROVERBS 14:30
A heart at peace gives life to the body; but envy rots the bones.

PROVERBS 16:7
When a man's ways are pleasing to the Lord, he makes even his enemies live at peace with him.

PROVERBS 17:1
Better a dry crust with peace than a house full of feasting with strife.

ISAIAH 9:6
For unto us a child is born, a son is given, and the government shall be upon his shoulders. And he will be called Wonderful Counselor, Mighty God, Everlasting Father, the Prince of Peace.

ISAIAH 11:6
The wolf shall also dwell with the lamb, and the leopard shall lie down with the kid; and the calf and the young lion and the fatling together; and a little child shall lead them.

ISAIAH 26:3
Thou will keep in perfect peace him whose mind is stayed on Thee, because he trusts Thee.

ISAIAH 32:17
The fruit of righteousness will be peace; the effect of righteousness will be quietness and confidence forever.

ISAIAH 48:17
This is what the Lord says, your Redeemer, the Holy One of Israel: "I am the Lord your God, who teaches you what is best for you, who directs you in the way you should go. If only you had paid attention to my commands, your peace would have been like a river.

ISAIAH 53:4 - 5
Surely he has borne our griefs and carried our sorrows; yet we esteemed him stricken, smitten by God, and afflicted. But he was pierced for our transgressions; he was crushed for our iniquities; the punishment that brought us peace was on him, and by his wounds we are healed.

MICAH 5:4 - 5
He will stand and shepherd his flock in the strength of the Lord, in the majesty of the name of the Lord his God. And they will live securely, for then his greatness will reach to the ends of the earth. And he will be their peace.

LUKE 2:14
Glory to God in the highest, and on earth peace, and goodwill toward men.

JOHN 16:33
Jesus said to his disciples, "These things I have spoken unto you, that in me ye might have peace. In the world ye shall have tribulation: but be of good cheer; I have overcome the world."

ACTS 10:36
You know the message God sent to the people of Israel, telling the good news of peace through Jesus Christ, who is Lord of all.

ROMANS 5:1 - 2
Therefore, since we have been justified through faith, we have peace with God through our Lord Jesus Christ, through whom we have gained access by faith into this grace in which we now stand.

ROMANS 12:18
If possible, so far as it depends on you, live peaceably with all.

ROMANS 15:13
May the God of hope fill you with all joy and peace as you trust in him, so that you may overflow with hope by the power of the Holy Spirit.

1 CORINTHIANS 14:33
God is not a God of disorder, but of peace.

2 CORINTHIANS 13:11
Finally, brothers, be of one mind, live in peace. And the God of peace will be with you.

EPHESIANS 2:14
For he himself is our peace.

COLOSSIANS 3:15
Let the peace of Christ rule in your hearts—and be thankful.

PHILIPPIANS 4:8
Finally brothers, whatever is true, whatever is noble, whatever is right, whatever is pure, whatever is lovely, whatever is admirable—if anything is excellent or praiseworthy—think about such things. Whatever you have learned or received or heard from me—put it into practice. And the God of peace will be with you.

1 THESSALONIANS 5:23 - 24
May God himself, the God of peace, sanctify you through and through. May your whole spirit, soul and body be kept blameless at the coming of our Lord Jesus Christ. The one who called you is faithful and he will do it.

2 THESSALONIANS 3:19
Now may the Lord of peace himself give you peace at all times and in every way. The Lord be with all of you.

JUDE 2
Mercy unto you, and peace, and love, be multiplied. Mercy, peace and love be yours in abundance.

"Who except God can give you peace?
Has the world ever been able to satisfy the heart?"

Saint Gerard Majella, 1725 – 1755

"Restlessness and impatience change nothing except our peace and joy. Peace does not dwell in outward things, but in the heart prepared to wait trustfully and quietly on Him who has all things safely in His hands."

Elisabeth Elliot, 1926 – 2015
Keep a Quiet Heart (1995)

"Peace is the beauty of life. It is sunshine. It is the smile of a child, the love of a mother, the joy of a father, the togetherness of a family. It is the advancement of man, the victory of a just cause, the triumph of truth."

Menachem Begin, 1913 – 1992
Nobel Lecture, Oslo, Norway, December 10, 1978

"I feel within me a peace above all earthly dignities, a still and quiet conscience."

William Shakespeare, 1564 – 1616
Cardinal Woolsey speaking, Act 3, Scene 2, *Henry VIII* (1613)

"Peace on earth, and mercy mild,
God and sinners reconciled."

Charles Wesley, 1707 – 1788
From the Hymn, "Hark the Herald Angels Sing" (1739)

"First keep peace with yourself then you can also bring peace to others."

Thomas à Kempis, 1380 – 1471
Imitation of Christ (c.1418)

"Let your door stand open to receive Him, offer Him welcome in your mind, and then you will see the riches of simplicity, the treasures

of peace, the joy of grace. Throw wide the gate of your heart, stand before the sun of the everlasting light."

Saint Ambrose, Bishop of Milan, born circa 340 – died 397
Exposition on Psalm 118 (c. 386 – 390)

"Do not look forward in fear to the changes and chances of this life; rather, look to them with full confidence that, as they arise, God, to whom you belong will in His love enable you to profit by them. He has guided you thus far in life, and He will lead you safely through all trials, and when you cannot stand it, God will bury you in His arms.

Do not fear what may happen tomorrow: the same everlasting Father who cares for you today

will take care of you then and every day. He will either shield you from suffering, or will give you unfailing strength to bear it. Be at peace, then, and put aside all anxious thoughts and imaginations. Amen."

Francis de Sales, 1567 – 1622
Prayer, "Be at Peace"

"Did I offer peace today? Did I bring a smile to someone's face? Did I say words of healing? Did I let go of my anger and resentment? Did I forgive? Did I love? These are the real questions. I must trust that the little bit of love that I sow now will bear many fruits, here in this world and the life to come."

Henri Nouwen, 1932 – 1996
From a journal entry written during his later years

"Peace begins with a smile. Smile five times a day at someone you don't really want to smile at; do it for peace."

Mother Teresa, 1910 – 1997
Quoted by Michael Collopy, photographer and personal friend
Ed., Michael Collopy; *Architects of Peace: Visions of Hope in Words and Images* (2000)

"God cannot give us a happiness and peace apart from Himself, because it is not there. There is no such thing."

C. S. Lewis, 1898 – 1963
Mere Christianity (1952)

"Mankind must remember that peace is not God's gift to his creatures; peace is our gift to each other."

Elie Wiesel, 1928 – 2016
Nobel Lecture, Oslo University, December 12, 1986

*"You may say I'm a dreamer, but I'm not the only one.
I hope someday you'll join us. And the world will live as one."*

John Lennon, 1940 – 1980
From the song, "Imagine," Released October 11, 1971

"Peace is an awareness of reserves from beyond ourselves, so that our power is not so much in us as through us."

Harry Emerson Fosdick, 1878 – 1969
On Being Fit to Live With: Sermons on Post-War Christianity (1946)

"In His will is our peace,"

Dante Alighieri, 1265 – 1321
The Divine Comedy 1308 – 1320
(T.S. Eliot said that this is the most profound line in literature.)

"Thou hast made us for thyself, O Lord, and our heart is restless until it finds its rest in thee."

Saint Augustine, 354 – 430
Confessions 397 – 400

"True peace consists in not separating ourselves from the will of God."

Thomas Aquinas, 1225 – 1274
Attributed

"When I lay these questions before God, I get no answer. But a rather special sort of 'No answer.' It is not the locked door. It is more like a silent, certainly not uncompassionate, gaze. As though He shook His head not in refusal but waiving the question. Like, 'Peace, child, you don't understand.'"

C. S. Lewis, 1898 – 1963
A Grief Observed (1961)

"Peace hath her victories no less renowned than war."

John Milton, 1608 – 1674
"Sonnet XVI To the Lord General Cromwell," Composed 1652

*"If God be our God, He will give us peace in trouble.
When there is a storm without, He will make peace within.
The world can create trouble in peace, but God can create
peace in trouble."*

Thomas Watson, c. 1620 – 1686
"The Ten Commandments," A Body of Practical Divinity (1692)

*"In Him alone lie our security, our confidence, our trust.
A spirit of restlessness and resistance can never wait,
but one who believes he is loved with an everlasting love,
and knows that underneath are the everlasting arms,
will find strength and peace."*

Elisabeth Elliot, 1926 – 2015
Quest for Love: True Stories of Passion and Purity (1984)

"Peace comes when there is no earth-born cloud between us and God. Peace is the consequence of forgiveness, God's removal of that which hides or obscures His face and so breaks union with Him."

Charles H. Brent, 1862 – 1929
"In the Evening," *With God in Prayer* (1907)

"Happiness is the soul in peace."

Edward Counsel, 1849 – 1939
Maxims (1889)

"Have courage for the great sorrows of life, and patience for the small ones, and when you have laboriously accomplished your daily task, go to sleep in peace. God is awake."

Victor Hugo, 1802 – 1885
From the Preface to his play, "Cromwell" (1827)

"Strive to preserve your heart in peace; let no event of this world disturb it; reflect that all must come to an end."

John of the Cross, 1542 – 1591
"Sayings of Light and Love"

*"Lord, make me an instrument of thy peace.
Where there is hatred, let me sow love."*

Saint Francis of Assisi, died 1226
Attributed

"Don't lose your inner peace for anything whatsoever, even if your whole world seems upset."

Saint Francis de Sales, 1567 – 1622
Introduction to the Devout Life (1609)

"Rest and peace will only be satiated in God."

Saint Augustine, 354 – 430
Confessions (397 – 400)

"There is only one way of victory over the bitterness and rage that comes naturally to us— To will what God wills brings peace."

Amy Carmichael, 1867 – 1951
Attributed

"Do everything calmly and peacefully. Do as much as you can as well as you can. Strive to see God in all things without exception, and consent to His will joyously. Do everything for God, uniting yourself to him in word and deed. Walk very simply with the Cross of the Lord and be at peace with yourself."

Saint Francis de Sales, 1567 – 1622

"You may either win your peace or buy it. Win it by resistance to evil, or buy it by compromise with evil."

John Ruskin, 1819 – 1900
The Two Paths (1859)

"As on the Sea of Galilee,
The Christ is whispering Peace."

John Greenleaf Whittier, 1807 – 1892
"The Cable Hymn," 1858
The Tent on the Beach and Other Poems (1867)

"Avoid popularity if you would have peace."

Abraham Lincoln, 1809 – 1865
Attributed

"You called and cried out loud and shattered my deafness.
You were radiant and resplendent, you put to flight my blindness.
You were fragrant and I drew in my breath, and now I pant
after you. I tasted you, and I feel but hunger and thirst for you.
You touched me and I set on fire to attain the peace which is yours."

Saint Augustine, 354 – 430
Confessions (397 – 400)

"Peace is better than fortune."

Saint Francis de Sales, 1567 – 1622
Introduction to the Devout Life (1609)

"O Lord, support us all the day long until the shadows lengthen, and the evening comes, and the busy world is hushed, and the fever of life is over, and our work is done. Then, Lord, in your mercy, grant us a safe lodging, a holy rest, and peace at the last."

John Henry Cardinal Newman, 1801 – 1890
"Prayer for a Happy Death"

Veni, veni Emmanuel
"O come, Desire of nations, bind
All peoples in one heart and mind
Bid envy, strife, and quarrels cease,
Fill the whole world with heaven's peace."

From the Hymn, "O Come, O Come Emmanuel"
Latin *(Veni, veni Emmanuel)* 12th century
Translated, J.M. Neale (1851)

I Heard the Bells on Christmas Day

I heard the bells on Christmas day
Their old familiar carols play
And mild and sweet their songs repeat
Of peace on earth good will to men

And in despair I bowed my head
There is no peace on earth I said
For hate is strong and mocks the song
Of peace on earth, good will to men

Then rang the bells, more loud and deep
God is not dead, nor does he sleep
The wrong shall fail, the right prevail
With peace on earth, good will to men

Henry Wadsworth Longfellow, 1807 – 1882
Christmas Carol based on the Civil War Era poem, "Christmas Bells,"
Written Christmas Day, 1863

It is Well with My Soul

When peace, like a river, attendeth my way,
When sorrows like sea billows roll;
Whatever my lot, Thou hast taught me to say,
It is well, it is well with my soul.

Refrain:
It is well with my soul,
It is well, it is well with my soul.

Though Satan should buffet, though trials should come,
Let this blest assurance control,
That Christ hath regarded my helpless estate,
And hath shed His own blood for my soul.

My sin—oh, the bliss of this glorious thought!—
My sin, not in part but the whole,
Is nailed to the cross, and I bear it no more,
Praise the Lord, praise the Lord, O my soul!

For me, be it Christ, be it Christ hence to live:
If Jordan above me shall roll,
No pang shall be mine, for in death as in life
Thou wilt whisper Thy peace to my soul.

But, Lord, 'tis for Thee, for Thy coming we wait,
The sky, not the grave, is our goal;
Oh, trump of the angel! Oh, voice of the Lord!
Blessed hope, blessed rest of my soul!

And Lord, haste the day when the faith shall be sight,
The clouds be rolled back as a scroll;
The trump shall resound, and the Lord shall descend,
Even so, it is well with my soul.

Horatio G. Spafford, 1828 – 1888
Hymn (1873)

In quietness and trust is my strength, O Lord.

You will keep in perfect peace him whose mind is stayed on you, because he trusts you. Trust in the Lord forever, for the Lord, the Lord is the Rock eternal.

Isaiah 26:3 – 4

This is what the Sovereign Lord says, "... in quietness and trust is your strength."

Isaiah 30:15

Jesus said to his disciples, "Let not your hearts be troubled. Trust in God; trust also in me.... Let not your hearts be troubled and do not be afraid."

John 14:1,27

1 CHRONICLES 16:11
Look to the Lord and his strength; seek his face always.

2 CHRONICLES 16:9
The eyes of the Lord search the whole earth in order to strengthen those whose hearts are fully committed to him.

JOB 13:15
Though he slay me, yet will I trust in him.

JOB 19:25
I know that my redeemer lives, and that in the end he will stand upon the earth. And after my skin has been destroyed, yet in my flesh I will see God; I myself will see him with my own eyes—I, and not another. How my heart yearns within me!

PSALM 4:5
Offer right sacrifices and trust in the Lord.

PSALM 9:10
Those who know your name trust in you, for you, Lord, have never forsaken those who seek you.

PSALM 18:30
God is a shield to all who trust in him.

PSALM 25:1
To you, O Lord, I lift up my soul; in you I trust, O my God.

PSALM 27:1
The Lord is my light and my salvation; whom shall I fear? The Lord is the strength of my life; of whom shall I be afraid?

PSALM 31:14 - 15
But in you, I trust, O Lord; I say, "You are my God." My times are in your hands.

PSALM 33:20 – 21
We wait in hope for the Lord; he is our help and shield. In him our hearts rejoice, for we trust in his holy name. May your unfailing love rest upon us, O Lord, even as we put our hope in you.

PSALM 37:3 – 4
Trust in the Lord and do good; dwell in the land and enjoy safe pasture. Delight yourself in the Lord and he will give you the desire of your heart.

PSALM 37:5,7
Commit your way to the Lord; trust in him and he will act.... Be still before the Lord and wait patiently for him, do not fret....

PSALM 42:5
Why are you downcast, O my soul? Why so disturbed within me? Put your hope in God, for I will yet praise him, my Savior and my God.

PSALM 46:1 – 2
God is our refuge and strength, a very present help in trouble. Therefore, we will not fear, though the earth be removed, and though the mountains be carried into the midst of the sea.

PSALM 56:3 – 4
When I am afraid, I will trust in you. In God, whose word I praise—in God I trust and I am not afraid.

PSALM 62:5
Let all that I am wait quietly before God, for my hope is in him.

PSALM 62:8
Trust in him at all times, O people; pour out your hearts to him, for he is our refuge.

PSALM 84:12
O Lord Almighty, blessed is the man who trusts in you.

PSALM 91:2
He who dwells in the shelter of the Most High will rest in the shadow of the Almighty. I will say to the Lord, "My refuge and my fortress, my God, in whom I trust."

PSALM 112:1,7
Blessed is the man who fears the Lord, who finds great delight in his commands.... He will have no fear of bad news; his heart is steadfast, trusting in the Lord.

PSALM 118:6
The Lord is with me; I will not be afraid. What can man do to me?

PSALM 121:1 – 2
I will lift up mine eyes unto the hills, from whence cometh my help. My help cometh from the Lord, which made heaven and earth.

PSALM 130:5 – 6
I wait for the Lord, my soul waits, and in his word I put my hope.

PSALM 131:2
Surely I have stilled and quieted my soul; like a weaned child with his mother, like a weaned child is my soul within me.

PSALM 138:8
The Lord will perfect that which concerns me; Your mercy, O Lord, endures forever; Do not forsake the works of Your hands.

PSALM 143:8
Let the morning bring me word of your unfailing love, for I have put my trust in you.

PSALM 146:3
Put not your trust in princes.

PROVERBS 3:5 - 6
Trust in the Lord with all your heart and lean not to your own understanding; in all thy ways acknowledge him, and he shall direct thy paths.

PROVERBS 17:1
Better a dry crust with peace and quiet than a house full of feasting with strife.

PROVERBS 17:28
Even a fool, when he holdeth his peace, is counted wise: and he that shutteth his lips is esteemed a man of understanding.

ECCLESIASTES 3:7
... a time to tear and a time to mend, a time to be silent and a time to speak,

ECCLESIASTES 4:6
Better is a handful with quietness, than both hands full with toil and grasping for the wind.

ISAIAH 25:9
In that day they will say, "Surely this is our God; we trusted in him, and he saved us. This is the Lord, we trusted in him; let us rejoice and be glad in his salvation."

ISAIAH 32:17 - 18
The fruit of righteousness will be peace; the effect of righteousness will be quietness and confidence forever. My people will live in peaceful dwelling places, in secure homes, in undisturbed places of rest.

ISAIAH 40:31
But they that wait upon the Lord shall renew their strength; they shall mount up with wings as eagles; they shall run and not be weary; they shall walk and not faint.

ISAIAH 50:10
Let him who walks in the dark, who has no light, trust in the name of the Lord and rely on his God.

JEREMIAH 17:7
Blessed is the man who trusts in the Lord, whose confidence is in him.

LAMENTATIONS 3:26
It is good to wait quietly for the salvation of the Lord.

NAHUM 1:7
The Lord is good, a refuge in times of trouble. He cares for those who trust in him.

HABAKKUK 3:17 - 18
Though the fig tree does not bud and there are no grapes on the vines, though the olive crop fails and the fields produce no food, though there are no sheep in the pen and no cattle in the stalls, yet I will rejoice in the Lord, I will be joyful in God my Savior.

ZEPHANIAH 3:17
The Lord your God is with you, he is mighty to save. He will take great delight in you, he will quiet you with his love, he will rejoice over you with singing.

LUKE 1:45
Blessed is she who has believed that what the Lord has said to her will be accomplished.

ROMANS 15:13
May the God of hope fill you with all joy and peace as you trust in him, so that you may overflow with hope by the power of the Holy Spirit.

PHILIPPIANS 4:19
But my God shall supply all your need according to his riches in glory by Christ Jesus.

1 THESSALONIANS 4:11 – 12
Make it your ambition to lead a quiet life, to mind your own business and to work with your hands, just as we told you, so that your daily life may win the respect of others and so that you will not be dependent on anyone.

JAMES 1:19
Know this, my beloved brothers: let every person be quick to hear, slow to speak, slow to anger.

1 PETER 3:4
... A gentle and quiet spirit is of great worth in God's sight.

"Do not look forward to what may happen tomorrow; the same everlasting Father who cares for you today will take care of you

tomorrow and every day. Either He will shield you from suffering, or He will give you unfailing strength to bear it. Be at peace, then, put aside all anxious thoughts and imaginations, and say continually: 'The Lord is my strength and my shield; my heart has trusted in Him and I am helped. He is not only with me but in me and I in Him.'"

Saint Francis de Sales, 1566 – 1622

"Humility is perfect quietness of heart. It is to expect nothing, to wonder at nothing that is done to me, to feel nothing done against me. It is to be at rest when nobody praises me, and when I am blamed or despised. It is to have a blessed home in the Lord, where I can go in and shut the door, and kneel to my Father in secret, and am at peace as in a deep sea of calmness, when all around and above is trouble."

Andrew Murray, 1828 – 1917
Humility (1884)

"It is neither wealth nor splendor but tranquility and occupation which give you happiness."

Thomas Jefferson, 1743 – 1806
Letter From Thomas Jefferson to his sister
Anna Jefferson Marks, July 12, 1788

"Never be hurried in anything. Do all things calmly and in a spirit of repose. Do not lose your inward peace even if everything seems to be going wrong. What is anything in life compared to peace of soul?"

Saint Francis de Sales, 1566 – 1622
Introduction to the Devout Life (1609)

"The serene, silent beauty of a holy life is the most powerful influence in the world, next to the might of God."

Blaise Pascal, 1623 – 1662

"In Him alone lie our security, our confidence, our trust. A spirit of restlessness and resistance can never wait, but one who believes he is loved with an everlasting love, and knows that underneath are the everlasting arms, will find strength and peace."

Elisabeth Elliot, 1926 – 2015
Quest for Love: True Stories of Passion and Purity (1996)

"Peace does not dwell in outward things, but in the heart prepared to wait trustfully and quietly on Him who has all things safely in His hands."

Elisabeth Elliot, 1926 – 2015
Keep a Quiet Heart (1995)

"… the deepest communion with God is beyond words, on the other side of silence."

Madeleine L'Engle, 1918 – 2007
Walking on Water (1972)

"A quiet conscience makes one strong!"

Anne Frank, 1929 – 1945
The Diary of a Young Girl (1947)

"Humility is simply the disposition which prepares the soul for living on trust."

Andrew Murray, 1828 – 1917
Humility (1884)

"Leave it all in the Hands that were wounded for you."

Elisabeth Elliot, 1926 – 2015
Keep a Quiet Heart (1995)

"Trust the past to God's mercy,
the present to God's love,
and the future to God's providence."

Saint Augustine, 354 – 430

"We shall steer safely through every storm, so long as our heart is right, our intention fervent, our courage steadfast, and our trust fixed on God."

Saint Francis De Sales, 1567 – 1622
The Spiritual Letters of Saint Francis De Sales (1871)

"He that takes truth for his guide, and duty for his end, may safely trust God's providence to lead him aright."

Blaise Pascal, 1623 – 1662

"Quietness of soul is the fruit of seeking God."

A.Z. Tozer, 1897 – 1963
The Pursuit of God (1948)

"Never be afraid to trust an unknown future to a known God."

Corrie ten Boom, 1892 – 1983
The Hiding Place (1971)

"Trust is the antidote to a troubled heart."

Dr. Bob Wenz, 1949 – 2012
Navigating Your Perfect Storm (2010)

"The sin underneath all our sins is to trust the lie of the serpent that we cannot trust the love and grace of Christ and must take matters into our own hands."

Martin Luther, 1483 – 1546
Commentary on the Book of Genesis (1545)
Written over the span of the last ten years of his life

"If you believe in a God who controls the big things,
you have to believe in a God who controls the little things.
It is we, of course, to whom things look 'little' or 'big'."

Elisabeth Elliot, 1926 – 2015
Let Me Be a Woman (1976)

"Day by day, morning by morning, begin your walk with Him in the calm trust that God is at work in everything…. It is your personal business, as a discipline of your heart, to learn to be peaceful and safe in God in every situation…. Remember, friend, where your real living is going on. In your thinking, in your reacting, in your heart of hearts—here is where your walk with God begins and continues. So when you start to move into trusting Him, stay there. Don't wander out again into worry and doubt."

Anne Ortlund, 1923 – 2013
My Sacrifice His Fire: Weekday Readings for Women (1999)

"All I have seen teaches me to trust the creator for all I have not seen."

Ralph Waldo Emerson, 1803 – 1882
"Immortality," *Letters and Social Aims XI* (1883)

"In God we trust."

Motto, United States of America

"Trust God and live a day at a time."

Norman Vincent Peale, 1898 – 1993
Stay Alive All Your Life (1957)

"I believe the promises of God enough to venture an eternity on them."

Isaac Watts, 1674 – 1748

"When I try, I fail. When I trust, He succeeds."

Corrie ten Boom, 1892 – 1983
The Hiding Place (1971)

"You do not need to know precisely what is happening, or exactly where it is all going. What you need is to recognize the possibilities and challenges offered by the present moment, and to embrace them with courage, faith and hope."

Thomas Merton, 1915 – 1968
Conjectures of a Guilty Bystander (1966)

"Why is fear part of earth life? Perhaps our Heavenly Father's greatest hope is that through our fears we may choose to turn to Him. The uncertainties of earth life can help to remind each of us that we are dependent on Him. But that reminder is not automatic. It involves our agency. We must choose to take our fears to Him, and choose to allow him to direct us. We must make these choices when what we feel most inclined to do is to rely more and more on our own frantic and distorted thinking."

Virginia H. Pearce, 1945,
Speech, "Fear," October 1992

"God is God. Because he is God, He is worthy of my trust and obedience. I will find rest nowhere but in His holy will that is unspeakably beyond my largest notions of what he is up to."

Elisabeth Elliot, 1926 – 2015
Through Gates of Splendor (1957)

"Merciful Lord,
grant to your faithful people pardon and peace,
that they may be cleansed from all their sins,

and serve you with a quiet mind;
through Jesus Christ our Lord. Amen."

An Australian Prayer Book

"Anxiety is a temptation in itself and also the source from which and by which other temptations come.
Therefore, above all else, calm and compose your mind.
Gently and quietly pursue your aim."

Saint Francis De Sales, 1567 – 1622
"Anxiety of Mind," *Introduction to a Devout Life* (1609)

"Worry does not empty tomorrow of its sorrows;
it empties today of its strength."

Corrie ten Boom, 1892 – 1983
Clippings From My Notebook (1983)

"The greatest lesson a soul has to learn is that God, and God alone, is enough for all its needs. This is the lesson that all God's dealings with us are meant to teach, and this is the crowning discovery of our entire Christian life."

Hannah Whitall Smith, 1832 – 1911
The God of All Comfort (1906)

"The right word may be effective, but no word was ever as effective as a rightly timed pause."

Mark Twain, 1835 – 1910

"There is nothing great, there is nothing holy, there is nothing wise,
there is nothing fair, but to depend wholly upon God,
like a child does and can do only what is bidden...."

Jeanne-Marie Guyon, 1648 – 1717
Andy Zubko; *A Treasury of Spiritual Wisdom* (1996)

"Beware of despairing about yourself: you are commanded to put your trust in God, not in yourself."

Saint Augustine, 354 – 430

"Trust God for greater things; with your five loaves and two fishes. He will show you a way to feed thousands."

Horace Bushnell, 1802 – 1876
J.H. Gilbert; *Dictionary of Burning Words of Brilliant Writers* (1895)

". . . . sustained and soothed,
By an unfaltering trust, approach thy grave,
Like one that wraps the drapery of his couch
About him, and lies down to pleasant dreams."

William Cullen Bryant, 1794 – 1878
From the poem, "Thanatopsis" (1817)

"As prayer without faith is but a beating of the air, so trust without prayer [is] but a presumptuous bravado. He that promises to give, and bids us trust His promises, commands us to pray, and expects obedience to his commands. He will give, but not without our asking."

Thomas Lye, 1621 – 1684
Sermons of the Great Ejection (1662)

"Nothing strengthens authority so much as silence."

Leonardo da Vinci, 1452 – 1519

"There are three great truths,
1st, That there is a God;
2nd, That He has spoken to us in the Bible;

3rd, That He means what He says.
Oh, the joy of trusting Him!"

Hudson Taylor, 1802 – 1935
A.J. Broomhall; *Hudson Taylor and China's Open Century, Book VI: Assault on the Nine* (1988)

"Blessed are they who have nothing to say,
and who cannot be persuaded to say it."

James Russell Lowell, 1819 – 1891
Speech, Banquet for Grand Duke Alexis, Revere House Hotel, Boston, November 11, 1871

"Restlessness and impatience change nothing except our peace and joy. Peace does not dwell in outward things, but in the heart prepared to wait trustfully and quietly on Him who has all things safely in His hands."

Elisabeth Elliott, 1926 – 2015
"Waiting," *Keep a Quiet Heart* (1995)

"Christ chargeth me to believe his daylight at midnight."

Samuel Rutherford, 1600 – 1661
Attributed

Place all your trust in God and God will Himself do battle for you against the enemy.

Saint Francis de Sales, 1567 – 1622
Paraphrase, "Sermon on Temptation", 1st Sunday of Lent, 1622
Translator, Elizabeth Stopp; *Saint Francis de Sales: Selected Letters* (1960)

"First keep peace within yourself, then you can bring peace to others."

Thomas à Kempis, 1380 – 1471
Imitation of Christ (ca.1418 – 1427)

"Learning to trust is one of life's most difficult tasks."

Isaac Watts, 1674 – 1748

"Go courageously to do whatever you are called to do. If you have any fears, say to your soul: 'The Lord will provide for us.' If your weakness troubles you, cast yourselves on God, and trust in him. The apostles were mostly unlearned fishermen, but God gave them learning enough for the work they had to do. Trust in him, depend on his providence; fear nothing."

St. Francis de Sales, 1557 – 1622
Hoagland and Angelini, *The Book of Saints* (1986)

"We thank you also for those disappointments and failures that lead us to acknowledge our dependence on you alone."

A General Thanksgiving
Book of Common Prayer (1979)

"Assurance grows by repeated conflict, by our repeated experimental proof of the Lord's power and goodness to save: when we have been brought very low and helped, sorely wounded and healed, cast down and raised again, have given up all hope— and been suddenly snatched from danger, and placed in safety; and when these things have been repeated to us and in us a thousand times over, we begin to learn to trust simply to the word and power of God, beyond and against appearances."

John Newton, 1725 – 1807
"Letter II to Mrs. ____," September, 1764
Cardiphonia (1780)

Near to the Heart of God

There is a place of quiet rest,
Near to the heart of God,
A place where sin cannot molest,
Near to the heart of God.

Refrain:
O Jesus, blest Redeemer,
Sent from the heart of God,
Hold us, who wait before Thee,
Near to the heart of God.

There is a place of comfort sweet,
Near to the heart of God.
A place where we our Savior meet,
Near to the heart of God.

There is a place of full released
Near to the heart of God
A place where all is joy and peace
Near to the heart of God.

Cleland Boyd McAfee, 1866 – 1944
Hymn, 1903

If Thou but Suffer God to Guide Thee

If thou but suffer God to guide thee
And hope in Him through all thy ways,
He'll give thee strength, whate'er betide thee,
And bear thee through the evil days.
Who trusts in God's unchanging love
Builds on the Rock that naught can move.

What can these anxious cares avail thee,
These never-ceasing moans and sighs?
What can it help if thou bewail thee
O'er each dark moment as it flies?
Our cross and trials do but press
The heavier for our bitterness.

Be patient and await His leisure
In cheerful hope, with heart content
To take whate'er thy Father's pleasure
And His discerning love hath sent,
Nor doubt our inmost wants are known
To Him who chose us for His own.

God knows full well when times of gladness
Shall be the needful thing for thee.
When He has tried thy soul with sadness
And from all guile has found thee free,
He comes to thee all unaware
And makes thee own His loving care.

Nor think amid the fiery trial
That God hath cast thee off unheard,
That he whose hopes meet no denial
Must surely be of God preferred.
Time passes and much change doth bring
And sets a bound to everything.

All are alike before the Highest;
'Tis easy to our God, we know,
To raise thee up, though low thou liest,
To make the rich man poor and low.
True wonders still by Him are wrought
Who setteth up and brings to naught.

Sing, pray, and keep His ways unswerving,
Perform thy duties faithfully,
And trust His Word, though undeserving,
Thou yet shalt find it true for thee.
God never yet forsook in need
The soul that trusted Him indeed.

Georg Neumark,1621 – 1681
Hymn (1641)

R

In repentance and rest is salvation. Hold my sins before me, Lord, so that I may turn from them and be forgiven.

This is what the Sovereign Lord, the Holy One of Israel, says: "In repentance and rest is your salvation, in quietness and trust is your strength."

Isaiah 30:15

Jesus said, "Come unto me, all you who are weary and heavy-laden, and I will give you rest. Take my yoke upon you and learn from me, for I am gentle and humble in heart, and you will find rest for your souls. For my yoke is easy and my burden is light."

Matthew 11:28 – 30

If we confess our sins, he is faithful and just to forgive us our sins and to cleanse us from all unrighteousness.

1 John 1:9

GENESIS 2:2 – 3

And on the seventh day God finished his work that he had done, and he rested on the seventh day from all his work that he had done. So God blessed the seventh day and made it holy, because on it God rested from all his work that he had done in creation.

EXODUS 33:14

The Lord said to Moses, "My Presence will go with you, and I will give you rest."

DEUTERONOMY 33:12

Let the beloved of the Lord rest secure in him, for he shields him all day long, and the one the Lord loves rests between his shoulders.

2 CHRONICLES 7:14

If my people who are called by my name will humble themselves, and pray and seek my face and turn from their wicked ways, then I will hear from heaven and will forgive their sin and heal their land.

JOB 42:1 – 6

Then Job replied to the Lord: "I know that you can do all things; no plan of yours can be thwarted." You asked, 'Who is this that obscures my counsel without knowledge?' Surely I spoke of things I did not understand, things too wonderful for me to know.

"You said, 'Listen now, and I will speak; I will question you, and you shall answer me.'

My ears had heard of you but now my eyes have seen you. Therefore, I despise myself and repent in dust and ashes."

PSALM 4:8
I will lie down and sleep in peace, for you alone, O Lord, make me dwell in safety.

PSALM 23:2 – 3
He maketh me to lie down in green pastures, he leadeth me beside still waters, he restoreth my soul.

PSALM 27:14
Wait for the Lord; be strong and take heart and wait for the Lord.

PSALM 38:18
But I confess my sins; I am deeply sorry for what I have done.

PSALM 55:6
I said, "Oh, that I had the wings of a dove! I would fly away and be at rest."

PSALM 62:1 – 2, 5
My soul finds rest in God alone; my salvation comes from him.... he is my fortress; I will never be shaken.... Find rest, O my soul, in God alone; my hope comes from him.

PSALM 91:1
He who dwells in the shelter of the Most High, will rest in the shadow of the Almighty.

PSALM 103:2 – 5
Praise the Lord, O my soul, and forget not all his benefits—who forgives all your sins and heals all your diseases, who redeems your life from the pit and crowns you with love and compassion, who satisfies your desires with good things so that your youth is renewed like the eagle's.

PSALM 103:12
As far as the east is from the west, so far does he remove our transgressions from us.

PSALM 116:7
Be at rest once more, O my soul, for the Lord has been good to you.

PROVERB 19:23
The fear of the Lord leads to life: Then one rests content, untouched by trouble.

PROVERBS 28:13
Whoever conceals his transgressions will not prosper, but he who confesses and forsakes them will obtain mercy.

ISAIAH 43:25
"I, yes I, am He who blots out your transgressions for my own sake and remembers your sins no more."

ISAIAH 55:6 – 7
Seek the Lord while he may be found; call upon him while he is near; let the wicked forsake his way, and the unrighteous man his thoughts; let him return to the Lord, that he may have compassion on him, and to our God, for he will abundantly pardon.

JEREMIAH 6:16
This is what the Lord says: "Stand at the crossroads and look; ask for the ancient paths, ask where the good way is, and walk in it, and you will find rest for your souls."

JEREMIAH 31:34
This is what the Lord says, "For I will forgive their wickedness and will remember their sins no more."

LAMENTATIONS 3:40
Let us test and examine our ways, and return to the Lord!

EZEKIEL 18:32
"For I take no pleasure in the death of anyone," declares the Sovereign Lord. "Repent and live!"

JOEL 2:13
And rend your hearts and not your garments. Return to the Lord your God, for he is gracious and merciful, slow to anger, and abounding in steadfast love; and he relents over disaster.

MICAH 7:19
You will again have compassion on us; you will tread our sins underfoot and hurl all our iniquities into the depths of the sea.

MATTHEW 3:8
Produce fruit in keeping with repentance.

MATTHEW 4:17
From that time Jesus began to preach, saying, "Repent, for the kingdom of heaven is at hand."

MATTHEW 6:12
Jesus taught them, saying, "Forgive us our trespasses as we forgive those who trespass against us."

MATT 6:14
Jesus said, "For if you forgive others their trespasses, your heavenly Father will also forgive you."

MATT 9:13
Jesus said, "Go and learn what this means, 'I desire mercy, and not sacrifice.' For I came not to call the righteous, but sinners."

MATTHEW 18:21 - 22

Then Peter came up and said to him, "Lord, how often will my brother sin against me, and I forgive him? As many as seven times?" Jesus said to him, "I do not say to you seven times, but seventy times seven."

MARK 6:31

The apostles gathered around Jesus and reported to him all they had done and taught. Then because so many people were coming and going that they did not even have a chance to eat, he said to them, "Come with me by yourselves to a quiet place and get some rest."

LUKE 5:32

Jesus said, "I have not come to call the righteous but sinners to repentance."

LUKE 6:37

Jesus said, "Do not judge, and you will not be judged. Do not condemn, and you will not be condemned. Forgive, and you will be forgiven."

LUKE 15:7

Jesus said, "Just so I tell you that there will be more joy in heaven over one sinner who repents than over ninety-nine righteous persons who need no repentance."

LUKE 24:46 - 47

He told them, "This is what is written: The Christ will suffer and rise from the dead on the third day, and the repentance and forgiveness of sins will be preached in his name to all nations, beginning at Jerusalem."

ACTS 3:19
Repent therefore, and turn again, that your sins may be blotted out.

ROMANS 2:4
Or do you presume on the riches of his kindness and forbearance and patience, not realizing that God's kindness is meant to lead you to repentance?

EPHESIANS 1:7
In him we have redemption through his blood, the forgiveness of our trespasses, according to the riches of his grace.

EPHESIANS 4:32
Be kind and tender-hearted to one another, forgiving each other just as in Christ God forgave you.

COLOSSIANS 1:13 - 14
For God has rescued us from the dominion of darkness and brought us into the kingdom of the Son he loves, in whom we have redemption, and the forgiveness of sins.

COLOSSIANS 3:13
Bear with each other and forgive any complaint you may have against one another. Forgive as the Lord forgave you.

HEBREWS 3:15
Today, if you hear his voice, do not harden your hearts...

HEBREWS 8:12
God said to his people, "For I will forgive their wickedness and will remember their sins no more."

JAMES 4:8 - 10
Draw near to God, and he will draw near to you. Cleanse your

hands, you sinners, and purify your hearts. Humble yourselves before the Lord, and he will exalt you.

1 PETER 5:7
Cast all your anxiety on Him, because He cares for you.

2 PETER 3:9
The Lord is not slow to fulfill his promise as some count slowness, but is patient toward you, not wishing that any should perish, but that all should reach repentance.

REVELATION 3:14, 19
The words of the Amen, the faithful and true witness, the beginning of God's creation, "Those whom I love, I reprove and discipline, so be zealous and repent."

"You have made us for yourself, O Lord, and our heart is restless until it rests in you."

Augustine, 354 – 430
Confessions (397 – 400)

"Sweet shall be your rest if your heart does not reproach you."

Thomas à Kempis, 1380 – 1471
The Imitation of Christ (circa 1418 – 1427)

"If we forgive other people, our hearts are made fit to receive forgiveness."

Corrie ten Boom, 1892 – 1983
Tramp For the Lord (1974)

"Jesus calls us to his rest, and meekness is His method. The meek man cares not at all who is greater than he, for he has long ago decided that the esteem of the world is not worth the effort."

A.W. Tozer, 1897 – 1963
Pursuit of God (1948)

"As long as I am content to know that He is infinitely greater than I, and that I cannot know Him unless He shows Himself to me, I will have Peace, and He will be near me and in me, and I will rest in Him."

Thomas Merton, 1915 – 1968
Thoughts in Solitude (1958)

"God has promised forgiveness to your repentance, but He has not promised tomorrow to your procrastination."

Augustine, 354 – 430
Confessions (397 – 400)

"The lilies grow, Christ says, of themselves; they toil not, neither do they spin. They grow, that is, automatically, spontaneously, without trying, without fretting, without thinking."

Henry Drummond, 1851 – 1897
Beautiful Thoughts (1892)

"Once I knew what it was to rest upon the rock of God's promises, and it was indeed a precious resting place, but now I rest in His grace. He is teaching me that the bosom of His love is a far sweeter resting-place than even the rock of His promises."

Hannah Whitall Smith, 1842 – 1911
The Christian's Secret of a Holy Life
Ed., Melvin Dieter; *The Unpublished Personal Writings of Hannah Whitall Smith* (1994)

"Through the dark and stormy night
Faith beholds a feeble light
Up the blackness streaking;
Knowing God's own time is best,

In a patient hope I rest
For the full day-breaking!"

John Greenleaf Whittier, 1807 – 1892
Poem, "Barclay of Ury" (1847)

"I have read in Plato and Cicero sayings that are very wise and very beautiful; but I never read in either of them: 'Come unto me all ye that labor and are heavy laden.'"

Augustine, 354 – 430
Attributed

"Forgiveness is the fragrance the violet sheds on the heel that has crushed it."

Mark Twain, 1835 – 1910
Attributed

"No soul can be really at rest until it has given up all dependence on everything else and has been forced to depend on the Lord alone. As long as our expectation is from other things, nothing but disappointment awaits us."

Hannah Whitall Smith, 1832 – 1911
The God of All Comfort (1906)

"Rest time is not waste time.
It is economy to gather fresh strength.
It is wisdom to take occasional furlough.
In the long run, we shall do more by sometimes doing less."

Charles Spurgeon, 1834 – 1892
Lectures to My Students, Volume 1 (1875)

"Rest is not idleness, and to lie sometimes on the grass under trees on a summer's day, listening to the murmur of the water, or watching the clouds float across the sky, is by no means a waste of time."

John Lubbock, 1834 – 1913
The Use of Life (1894)

"True repentance is no light matter. It is a thorough change of heart about sin, a change showing itself in godly sorrow and humiliation—in heartfelt confession before the throne of grace—in a complete breaking off from sinful habits, and an abiding hatred of all sin. Such repentance is the inseparable companion of saving faith in Christ."

J. C. Ryle, 1816 – 1900
Expository Thoughts on the Gospels (1856)

"Sins are remitted as if they had never been committed."

Thomas Adams, 1583 – 1652
Adams has been called "The Shakespeare of the Puritans"
Ed., I. E. D. Thomas; *A Puritan Golden Treasury* (1977)

"I can forgive, but I cannot forget, is only another way of saying, I will not forgive. Forgiveness ought to be like a cancelled note—torn in two and burned up, so that it can never be shown against one."

Henry Ward Beecher, 1813 – 1871
Life Thoughts (1858)

"To be a Christian means to forgive the inexcusable, because God has forgiven the inexcusable in you."

C. S. Lewis, 1898 – 1963
Sermon, "The Weight of Glory," Church of St. Mary the Virgin, Oxford, June 8, 1941

"The recognition of sin is the beginning of salvation."

Martin Luther, 1483 – 1546
Translator, C.M. Jacobs; *The Collected Works of Martin Luther* (2018)

"Repentance, not proper behavior or even holiness, is the doorway to grace. And the opposite of sin is grace, not virtue."

Philip Yancey, 1949
What's So Amazing About Grace (1997)

"A great many people want to bring their faith, their works, their good deeds to Him for salvation. Bring your sins, and He will bear them away into the wilderness of forgetfulness, and you will never see them again."

Dwight L. Moody, 1837 – 1899
Ed., Rev. J. B. McClure, *Moody's Anecdotes and Illustrations* (1899)

"He that cannot forgive others, breaks the bridge over which he himself must pass if he would ever reach heaven; for everyone has need to be forgiven."

Edward Herbert, 1583 – 1648,
The Autobiography of Edward, Lord Herbert of Cherburg (1719)

"To love means loving the unlovable. To forgive means pardoning the unpardonable. Faith means believing the unbelievable. Hope means hoping when everything seems hopeless."

G.K. Chesterton, 1874 – 1936
Attributed
Perhaps a paraphrase from *Orthodoxy* (1908)

"Repentance is the turning of the soul from the way of midnight to the point of the coming sun."

Henry Ward Beecher, 1813 – 1887
Life Thoughts (1858)

"After grief for sin there should be joy for forgiveness."

A.W. Pink, 1886 – 1952
A. W. Pink's Studies in the Scriptures, Volume 7 (1934-35)

"He that confesses his sin, begins his journey toward salvation. He that is sorry for it, mends his pace. He that forsakes it, is at his journey's end."

Francis Quarles, 1592 – 1644
Enchiridion Containing Institutions Divine and Moral (1640 – 41)

"Many think they repent when it is not the offense but the penalty that troubles them."

Thomas Watson, 1620 – 1686
Attributed
Ed., I.E.D; Thomas, *A Puritan Golden Treasury* (1975)

"We are today accepted in the Beloved, today absolved from sin, today acquitted at the bar of God.... We are now pardoned; even now are our sins put away; even now we stand in the sight of God accepted, as though we had never been guilty. 'There is therefore now no condemnation to them which are in Christ Jesus.' There is not a sin in the Book of God, even now, against one of His people. Who dares to lay anything to their charge? There is neither speck, nor spot, nor wrinkle, nor any such thing remaining upon any one believer in the matter of justification in the sight of the Judge of all the earth."

Charles Haddon Spurgeon, 1834 – 1892
Devotion, Morning May 15, *Morning and Evening* (1865)

"May a merciful God preserve me from a Christian Church in which everyone is a saint! I want to be and remain in the church and little flock of the fainthearted, the feeble and the ailing, who feel and recognize the wretchedness of their sins, who sigh and cry to God incessantly for comfort and help, who believe in the forgiveness of sins."

Martin Luther, 1483 – 1546
Luther's Works, Volume XXII (published 1900 – 1986) (1957)

"Forgiveness does not mean excusing."

C. S. Lewis, 1898 – 1963
Essay read to his students at Cambridge, May 11, 1959
Published in *Fern Seeds and Elephants* (1975)

"We need not climb up into heaven to see whether our sins are forgiven: let us look into our hearts, and see if we can forgive others. If we can, we need not doubt but God has forgiven us."

Thomas Watson, 1620 – 1686
Ed., I.E.D Thomas; *A Puritan Golden Treasury* (1975)

"We all want progress, but if you're on the wrong road, progress means doing an about-turn and walking back to the right road; in that case, the man who turns back soonest is the most progressive."

C. S. Lewis, 1898 – 1963
Mere Christianity (1952)

Repentance, as we know, is basically not moaning and remorse, but turning and change.

J.I. Packer, 1926 – 2020
Article, "Marks of Repentance," From the Booklet,
God in Our Midst, 1987

"Heaven finds an ear when sinners find a tongue."

Francis Quarles,1592 – 1644
"The Christian Ambassador," Vol. 1-11 (1863)

"It is better to be affected with a true penitent sorrow for sin than to be able to resolve the most difficult cases about it."

Thomas à Kempis, 1380 – 1471
Comp., C.N. Douglas; *Forty Thousand Quotations Prose and Poetical* (1917)

"Whatever weakens your reason, impairs the tenderness of your conscience, obscures your sense of God, or takes off the relish for spiritual things then it is sin for you, however innocent it may be in itself."

Suzanna Wesley, 1669 – 1742
Letter to son, John Wesley, June 8, 1725

"Remorse is the consciousness of doing wrong with no sense of love; penitence the same consciousness with the feeling of sorrow and tenderness added."

Frederick W. Robertson, 1816 – 1853
Sermon, "Triumph Over Hindrance," October 20, 1850

"When a child can be brought to tears, not from fear of punishment, but from repentance of his offense, he needs no chastisement. When the tears begin to flow from grief at one's own conduct, be sure there is an angel nestling in the bosom."

Horace Mann, 1796 – 1859
Thoughts Selected from the Writings of Horace Mann (1872)

"When we have heartily repented of a wrong, we should let all the waves of forgetfulness roll over it, and go forward unburdened to meet the future."

Henry Ward Beecher, 1815 – 1867
Life Thoughts (1860)

"But with the morning cool repentance came."

Sir Walter Scott, 1771 – 1832
Rob Roy (1817)

"Some often repent yet never reform; they resemble a man traveling a dangerous path who frequently starts and stops, but never turns back."

Bonnell Thornton, 1725 – 1768
Rev. John Thornton, Maxims and Directions for Youth, on a Variety of Important and Interesting Subjects (1811)

"Of all acts, is not, for a man, repentance the most divine?"

Thomas Carlyle, 1795 – 1881
Sartor Resartus (1834)

"The beginning of atonement is the sense of its necessity."

Lord Byron, 1788 – 1824
From the poem, "Manfred" (1817)

"Come home to Him who made thy heart,
Come weary and oppressed
To come to Jesus is thy part;
His part to give thee rest."

George MacDonald, 1824 – 1905
J.H. Gilbert; *Dictionary of Burning Words and Brilliant Writers* (1895)

"It is impossible for a man to be freed from the habit of sin before he hates it, just as it is impossible to receive forgiveness before confessing his trespasses."

Ignatius of Antioch, died 108

"He comes never late who comes repentant."

Juan de Horozco, 1559 – 1608
Attributed

"Men do not differ much about what things they call evils; they differ enormously about what evils they will call excusable."

G. K. Chesterton, 1874 – 1936
"Illustrated London News," October 23, 1909

"Jesus reserved his hardest words for the hidden sins of hypocrisy, pride, greed and legalism."

Philip Yancey, 1949
Rumors of Another World (2003)

"It is perilously easy to have amazing sympathy with God's truth and remain in sin."

Oswald Chambers, 1874 – 1917
Biddy Chambers, *God's Workmanship* (1953)

"Forgiveness does not mean ignoring what has been done or putting a false label on an evil act. It means, rather, that the evil act no longer remains as a barrier to the relationship. Forgiveness is a catalyst creating the atmosphere necessary for a fresh start and a new beginning."

Martin Luther King, Jr., 1929 – 1968
Christmas Sermon delivered at Dexter Avenue Baptist Church
Montgomery, Alabama, 1957

"To be humbly ashamed is to be plunged in the cleansing bath of truth."

George MacDonald, 1824 – 1905
Unspoken Sermons (1867)

"To err is human, to forgive, divine."

Alexander Pope, 1688 – 1744
"An Essay on Criticism," (1711)

"Heart-suffering because of sin is the best proof that the Holy Spirit dwells in your heart.

Johann Arndt, 1555 – 1621
True Christianity (1605 – 1610)

"How else but through a broken heart may Lord Christ enter in?"

Oscar Wilde, 1854 – 1900
Poem, "Ballad of Reading Gaol," (1898)

"Great is the difference betwixt a man's being frightened at, and humbled for his sins."

Thomas Fuller, 1608 – 1661
The Cause and Care of a Wounded Conscience (1647)

"True Repentance is that saving grace wrought in the soul by the spirit of God, whereby a sinner is made to see and be sensible of his sin, is grieved and humbled before God on account of it, not so much for the punishment to which sin has made him liable, as that thereby God is dishonored and offended, his laws violated, and his own soul polluted and defiled. This grief arises from love for God, and is accompanied with a hatred of sin, a fixed resolution to forsake it, and expectation of favor and forgiveness through the merits of Christ."

Wellins Calcott, 1726 – 1779
Thoughts Moral and Divine, IV (1761)

"To sin is a human business, to justify sins is a devilish business."

Leo Tolstoy, 1866 – 1933
Attributed

"Forgiveness is an act of the will, and the will can function regardless of the temperature of the heart.

Corrie ten Boom, 1892 – 1983
"Guidepost" article, "I'm Still Learning to Forgive", 1972

"Forgiveness is a strange thing. It can sometimes be easier to forgive our enemies than our friends. It can be hardest of all to forgive people we love. Like all of life's important coping skills, the ability to forgive and the capacity to let go of resentments most likely take root very early in our lives."

Fred Rogers, 1928 – 2003
The World According to Mister Rogers (2003)

"Genuine repentance must bear the seal of a corrected life."

Lewis F. Korns, 1856 – 1939
Thoughts (1915)

"Repentance is purgative; fear not the working of this pill."

Thomas Watson, 1620 – 1686
The Doctrine of Repentance (1668)

"Repentance was never yet produced in any man's heart apart from the grace of God."

Charles Haddon Spurgeon, 1834 – 1892
Spurgeon's Sermons Volume VI (1860)

"Repentance is a change of mind, or a conversion from sin to God; not some one bare act of change, but a lasting durable state of new life, which is called regeneration."

Henry Hammond, 1807 – 1864
Day's Collacon (1883)

"The glory of Christianity is to conquer by forgiveness."

William Blake, 1757 – 1827
"Jerusalem," (circa 1808)

"God's whole nature moves toward the man who wants to be free from sin, as broadly and irresistibly as the summer moves from the south toward the north."

Henry Ward Beecher, 1813 – 1887
Proverbs from Plymouth Pulpit (1887)

"There are only two kinds of men: the righteous who think they are sinners and sinners who think they are righteous."

Blaise Pascal, 1623 – 1662
Pensées (1670)

"It is a severe rebuke upon us, that God makes us so many allowances, and we make so few to our neighbor."

William Penn, 1644 – 1718
Fruits of Solitude (1682)

"He who is devoid of the power to forgive is devoid of the power to love."

Martin Luther King, Jr., 1929 – 1968
Christmas Sermon delivered at Dexter Avenue Baptist Church, Montgomery, Alabama, 1957

"In spiritual things, it is God who performs all things for you. Rest in Him then."

Charles Spurgeon, 1834 – 1893
Sermon, "Strong Faith is a Faithful God" (1915)

"Chronic remorse, as all the moralists are agreed, is a most undesirable sentiment. If you have behaved badly, repent, make what amends you can and address yourself to the task of behaving better next time. On no account brood over your wrongdoing. Rolling in the muck is not the best way of getting clean."

Aldous Huxley, 1894 – 1963
Brave New World (1932)

It may be an infinitely less evil act to murder a man than to refuse to forgive him. The former may be an act of a moment of passion; the latter is the heart's choice.

George MacDonald, 1824 – 1905
"It Shall Not Be Forgotten," *Unspoken Sermons, First Series* (1867)

"My sin—oh, the bliss of this glorious thought!
My sin, not in part but the whole,
Is nailed to the cross, and I bear it no more.
Praise the Lord, praise the Lord, O my soul!"

Horatio Spafford, 1828 – 1888
Hymn, "It is Well with My Soul," 1873 or 1876

"Repentance means turning away from one's own work to the mercy of God. The whole Bible calls to us and cheers us: Turn back, turn back. Return—where to? To the everlasting grace of God who does not leave us. God will be merciful....

Dietrich Bonhoeffer, 1906 – 1945
Sermon, November 19, 1933, *God is in the Manger* (2010)

Beneath the Cross of Jesus

Beneath the cross of Jesus
I fain would take my stand,
The shadow of a mighty rock within a weary land;
A home within the wilderness, a rest upon the way,
From the burning of the noontide heat, and the burden of the day.

Upon that cross of Jesus mine eye at times can see
The very dying form of One Who suffered there for me;
And from my stricken heart with tears two wonders I confess;
The wonders of redeeming love and my unworthiness.

I take, O cross, thy shadow for my abiding place;
I ask no other sunshine than the sunshine of His face;
Content to let the world go by to know no gain or loss,
My sinful self my only shame, my glory all the cross.

Elizabeth Cecilia Clephane, 1830 – 1869
Hymn (1868)

Psalm 51
David's Prayer of Confession and Repentance
Selected verses

Have mercy on me, O God, according to your steadfast love;
according to your abundant mercy blot out my transgressions.
Wash me thoroughly from my iniquity, and cleanse me from my sin!

For I know my transgressions, and my sin is ever before me.
Against you, you only, have I sinned and done what is evil
in your sight,
so that you may be justified in your words and blameless
in your judgment.

Purge me with hyssop, and I shall be clean; wash me, and I shall be
whiter than snow.

Let me hear joy and gladness; let the bones that you
have broken rejoice.
Hide your face from my sins, and blot out all my iniquities.
Create in me a clean heart, O God, and renew a right spirit
within me.

Cast me not away from your presence, and take not your
Holy Spirit from me.
Restore to me the joy of your salvation, and uphold me with
a willing spirit.
Then I will teach transgressors your ways, and sinners will return
to you.

Deliver me from bloodguiltiness, O God, O God of my salvation,
and my tongue will sing aloud of your righteousness.
O Lord, open my lips, and my mouth will declare your praise.

For you will not delight in sacrifice, or I would give it;
you will not be pleased with a burnt offering.
The sacrifices of God are a broken spirit;
a broken and contrite heart you will not despise.

S

You have said, "Be still, and know that I am God." Teach me, Father, to stop striving, to wait patiently, to be silent and still in my soul.

"Be still, and know that I am God; I will be exalted among the nations, I will be exalted in the earth."

Psalm 46:10

The Lord is in his holy temple; let all the earth be silent before him.

Habakkuk 2:20

Be silent, O all flesh, before the Lord

Zechariah 2:13

EXODUS 14:13 – 14
(Moses speaking to God's people) "Do not be afraid. Stand firm and you will see the deliverance the Lord will bring you today.... The Lord will fight for you; you need only to be still."

JOB 6:24
Teach me and I will be silent; make me understand how I have gone astray.

JOB 37:14
Stop and consider God's wonders.

PSALM 4:4
In your anger do not sin; when you are on your beds, search your hearts and be silent.

PSALM 27:14
Wait for the Lord; be strong and take heart and wait for the Lord.

PSALM 37:7 - 8
Be still before the Lord and wait patiently for him.... Refrain from anger and turn from wrath; do not fret—it only leads to evil.

PSALM 40:1
I waited patiently for the Lord's help; then he listened to me and heard my cry.

PSALM 89:9
You rule over the surging sea; when the waves mount up, you still them.

PSALM 130:5 - 6
I wait for the Lord, my soul waits, and in his word I put my hope. My soul waits for the Lord more than watchmen wait for the morning, more than watchmen wait for the morning.

PSALM 131:2
But I have calmed and quieted my soul, like a weaned child with its mother; like a weaned child is my soul within me.

PROVERBS 17:28
Even a fool is thought wise if he keeps silent, and discerning if he holds his tongue.

ECCLESIASTES 3:7
A time to tear and a time to mend, a time to be silent and a time to speak.

ISAIAH 30:18
Yet the Lord longs to be gracious to you; he rises to show you compassion. For the Lord is a God of justice. Blessed are all who wait for him.

MARK 4:39
And he arose, and rebuked the wind, and said unto the sea, "Peace, be still." And the wind ceased, and there was a great calm.

PHILIPPIANS 4:6
Do not be anxious about anything, but in everything by prayer and supplication with thanksgiving let your requests be made known to God.

". . . for the knowledge of God is received in divine silence."

John of the Cross, 1542 – 1591
Entry No. 26, "Sayings of Light and Love"

"The very best and utmost attainment in this life is to remain still and let God act and speak in thee."

Meister Eckhart, 1260 – 1328

"Be still. Stillness reveals the secrets of eternity."

Lao-Tzu, ca. 500 BC

"Silence is God's first language."

John of the Cross, 1542 – 1591

"Let us labor for an inward stillness—
An inward stillness and an inward healing.
That perfect silence where the lips and heart
Are still, and we no longer entertain
Our own imperfect thoughts and vain opinions,
But God alone speaks to us and we wait
In singleness of heart that we may know
His will, and in the silence of our spirits,
That we may do His will and do that only."

Henry Wadsworth Longfellow, 1807 – 1882
Christus: A Mystery (1872)

"Stillness of person and steadiness of features are signal marks of good breeding."

Oliver Wendell Holmes, Sr., 1809 – 1894
The Professor at the Breakfast-Table: With the Story of Iris (1860)

"In the name of God, stop a moment, cease your work, look around you."

Leo Tolstoy, 1828 – 1910
Essays, Letters and Miscellanies (1899)

"God speaks in the silence of the heart.
Listening is the beginning of prayer."

Mother Teresa, 1910 – 1997
In the Heart of the World (1997)

"We need to find God and he cannot be found in noise and restlessness. God is the friend of silence."

Mother Teresa, 1910 – 1997
A Gift of God (1975)

"Seek first God's Kingdom, that is, become like the lilies and the birds, become perfectly silent—then shall the rest be added unto you."

Søren Kierkegaard, 1813 – 1855
"The Lilies of the Field and the Birds of the Air," *Journals* (1849)

"Prayer begins by talking to God, but it ends by listening to him. In the face of Absolute Truth, silence is the soul's language."

Fulton J. Sheen, 1895 – 1975

"A judicious silence is always better than truth spoken without charity."

Saint Francis de Sales, 1557 – 1622

"In the inner stillness where meditation leads, the Spirit secretly anoints the soul and heals our deepest wounds."

John of the Cross, 1542 – 1591

"If God is spending work upon a Christian, let him be still and know that it is God. And if he wants work, he will find it there—in the being still."

Henry Drummond, 1851 – 1897
The Ideal Life (1897)

"In a world of noise, confusion, and conflict it is necessary that there be places of silence, inner discipline and peace. In such places love can blossom."

Thomas Merton, 1915 – 1968
New Seeds of Contemplation (1963)

"There is hardly ever a complete silence in our soul. God is whispering to us well-nigh incessantly. Whenever the sounds of the world die out of the soul, or sink low, Then we hear these whisperings of God."

Frederick William Faber, 1814 – 1863
Ed., Martin H. Manse; *The Westminster Collection of Christian Quotations* (2001)

"If we will only learn silence, we will learn two things: to pray and to be humble. You cannot love unless you have humility, and you cannot be humble if you do not love. From the silence of the heart God speaks."

Mother Teresa, 1910 – 1997
Come Be My Light: The Private Writings of the Saint of Calcutta (2003)

"In the rush and noise of life, as you have intervals, step home within yourselves and be still. Wait upon God, and feel His good presence; this will carry you evenly through your day's business."

William Penn, 1644 – 1718

"What is it that stands higher than words? Action. What is it that stands higher than action? Silence."

Saint Francis of Assisi, d.1226

"Within yourself is a stillness and a sanctuary to which you can retreat at any time and be yourself... to listen with a still heart, with a waiting, open soul, without passion, without desire, without judgment, without opinions."

Hermann Hesse, 1887 – 1962
Siddhartha (1922)

"One's action ought to come out of an achieved stillness: not to be a mere rushing on."

D. H. Lawrence, 1885 – 1930
Ed., J. T. Boulton, *The Letters of D. H. Lawrence Vol. 5, 1924 – 1927* (1989)

"Silence is wisdom's best reply."

Euripides, ca.480 – 406 BC

"The fruit of silence is prayer,
the fruit of prayer is faith,
the fruit of faith is love,
the fruit of love is service
and the fruit of service is peace."

Mother Teresa, 1910 – 1997
A Simple Path (1995)

"Too many words cause exhaustion. Better to abide in stillness... In stillness muddied water turns to clarity."

Lao Tzu, ca. 500 BC

"Stillness is our most intense mode of action. It is in our moments of deep quiet that is born every idea, emotion, and drive which we eventually honor with the name of action. We reach the highest in meditation, and farthest in prayer. In stillness every human being is great."

Leonard Bernstein, 1918 – 1990
D.J. Green, "Religion and Ethics"
Friends of Silence.net; Vol. XIV, No. 11 (December 2001)

"If I were a physician and I were allowed to prescribe one remedy for all the ills of the world, I would prescribe silence. For even if the word of God were proclaimed in the modern world, how could one hear it with so much noise? Therefore, create silence!"

Søren Kierkegaard, 1813 – 1855
The Essential Kierkegaard (1978)

"The mind does nothing but talk, ask questions, search for meaning; the heart does not talk, does not ask questions, does not search for meaning. Silently, it moves toward God and surrenders. The heart is God's servant."

Saint Francis of Assisi, died 1226

"The silence of prayer is the silence of listening."

Elizabeth O'Connor, 1928
Search for Silence (1972)

"Mere silence is not wisdom, for wisdom consists in knowing when and how to speak and when and where to keep silent."

Jean-Pierre Camus, 1584 – 1562
Ed., Martin Manser; *The Westminster Collection of Christian Quotations* (2001)

*"The highest virtue is to restrain the tongue.
He approaches nearest the gods who knows how to be silent, even though he is in the right...."*

Cato the Elder, 234 – 149 B.C.

"The most important thing is silence. We cannot place ourselves directly in God's presence without imposing upon ourselves interior

and exterior silence. That is why we must accustom ourselves to stillness of the soul, of the eyes, and of the tongue."

Mother Teresa, 1910 – 1997
Love, a Fruit Always in Season: Daily Meditations from the Words of Mother (1987)

"Rumors and slander are best answered with silence."

Ben Jonson, 1572 – 1637

"The highest thoughts are those least dependent on language."

John Ruskin, 1819 – 1900

"Power rests in tranquility."

Richard Cecil, 1495 – 1553
Andy Zubko; *Treasury of Spiritual Wisdom* (2000)

"Speech is silver,
Silence is golden;
Speech is human,
silence is divine."

German proverb

"Solitude shows us what should be; society shows us what we are."

Richard Cecil, 1748 – 1810
Ed., Josiah Pratt; *Remains of Mr. Cecil* (1836)

"The inner is foundation of the outer
The still is master of the restless
The Sage travels all day
yet never loses his inner treasure."

Lao-Tzu, ca. 500 BC

"What a strange power there is in silence...."

Ralph Waldo Emerson, 1803 – 1882
Andy Zubko; *Treasury of Spiritual Wisdom* (2000)

"The truest communication with God is absolute total silence; there is not a single word that can convey this communication."

Bernadette Roberts, 1931 – 2017
The Path to No-Self: Life at the Center (1985)

"Go placidly amid the noise and haste and remember what peace there may be in silence."

Max Ehrmann, 1872 – 1945
Poem, "Desiderata" (1927)

"Silence is the cornerstone of Character."

American Indian saying

"Silence is the mother of truth."

Benjamin Disraeli, 1804 – 1881
Tancred (1847)

"Silence is the language God speaks and everything else is a bad translation."

Thomas Keating, 1923 – 2018
Invitation to Love (1992)

"We all have within us a center of stillness surrounded by silence."

Dag Hammarskjol, 1905 – 1961
Text distributed to all visitors of The Meditation Room at the UN Headquarters

"True silence is the rest of the mind, and is to the spirit what sleep is to the body, nourishment and refreshment."

William Penn, 1644 – 1718
Advice to His Children (circa 1699)

"There are silent depths in the ocean which storms that lash the surface into fury never reach."

Orison S. Marden, 1848 – 1924
You Can, But Will You (1920)

"Blessed is the man who, having nothing to say, abstains from giving us wordy evidence of the fact."

George Eliot, 1819 – 1880
Impressions of Theophrastus Such (1879)

"Nothing in all creation is so like God as stillness."

Meister Eckhart, 1260 – 1328

"We live in an age of haste. Some people look at an egg and expect it to crow."

Orison S. Marden, 1848 – 1924
Forbes Book of Quotations: 10,000 Thoughts on the Business of Life (1997)

"He can never speak well who knows not how to hold his peace...."

Plutarch, born circa 46

"An inability to stay quiet, an irritable desire to act directly, is one of the most conspicuous failings of mankind...."

Walter Bagehot, 1826 – 1877
Physics and Politics (1869)

"Silently now, I wait for Thee,
Ready, my God, thy will to see;
Open my eyes, illumine me,
Spirit divine."

Clara H. Scott, 1841 – 1897
Hymn, "Open My Eyes, That I May See" (1895)

"The right word may be effective, but no word was ever as effective as a rightly timed pause."

Mark Twain, 1835 – 1910
Albert Bigelow Paine, *Mark Twain's Speeches* (1923)

"A fool cannot be silent."

Greek Proverb

"There are times when good words are to be left unsaid out of esteem for silence."

Saint Benedict, d. 547
Rule of Saint Benedict (516)

"The notion of silence appears to unsettle—or puzzle—no small number of people of all walks of life... Something as 'unproductive' as silence is not often taken seriously. The evaluation of silence differs from culture to culture. In the West, if you notice that someone is silent for a prolonged period of time, the tendency might be to ask, 'Are you all right?' Or the silence might be interpreted as a sign of unbalanced introversion or isolation or passive aggression. In India, they would say of the silent one, 'Ah muni!' (Ah, there is a holy soul!)"

Elias Marechal
Tears of an Innocent God (2015)

"Silence is the only real thing we can lay hold of in this world of passing dreams. Time is a shadow that will vanish with the twilight of humanity; but Silence is a part of the eternal. All things that are true and lasting have been taught to men's hearts by Silence."

Jerome K. Jerome, 1859 – 1927
The Selected Works of Jerome K. Jerome (2013)

"The grandest operations, both in nature and in grace, are the most silent and imperceptible. The shallow brook babbles on its passage, and is heard by every one; but the coming on of the seasons is silent and unseen. The storm rages and alarms; but its fury is soon exhausted, and its effects are partial and soon remedied; but the dew, though gentle and unheard, is immense in quantity, and the very life of large portions of the earth. And these are pictures of the operations of grace in the church and in the soul."

Richard Cecil, 1748 – 1810
John Bate, *A Cyclopædia of Illustrations of Moral and Religious Truths* (1866)

"A life with a peaceful center can weather all storms."

Norman Vincent Peale, 1898 – 1993
Stay Alive All Your Life (1957)

"Silence gives us a new outlook on everything. Jesus is always waiting for us in silence. In that silence he will listen to us, there he will speak to our soul, and there we will hear his voice."

Mother Teresa, 1910 – 1997
Love: A Fruit Always in Season (1987)

"In the silence of the heart God speaks. If you face God in prayer and silence, God will speak to you. Then you will know that you are nothing. It is only when you realize your nothingness, your emptiness, that God can fill you with Himself. Souls of prayer are souls of great silence."

Mother Teresa, 1910 – 1997
In the Heart of the World (1995)

"There are all kinds of silences and each of them means a different thing. There is the silence that comes with morning in a forest, and this is different from the silence of a sleeping city. There is silence after a rainstorm, and before a rainstorm, and these are not the same. There is the silence of emptiness, the silence of fear, the silence of doubt. There is a certain silence that can emanate from a lifeless object as from a chair lately used, or from a piano with old dust upon its keys, or from anything that has answered to the need of a man, for pleasure or for work. This kind of silence can speak. Its voice may be melancholy, but it is not always so; for the chair may have been left by a laughing child or the last notes of the piano may have been raucous and gay. Whatever the mood or the circumstance, the essence of its quality may linger in the silence that follows. It is a soundless echo."

Beryl Markham, 1902 – 1986
West with the Night (1942)

"Whenever there is stillness there is the still small voice, God's speaking from the whirlwind, nature's old song and dance…."

Annie Dillard, born 1945
Teaching a Stone to Talk: Expeditions and Encounters (1982)

"Seek first God's kingdom; that is, become like the lilies and the birds, become perfectly silent—then shall the rest be added to you."

Søren Kierkegaard, 1813 – 1845
Journals (1849)

"In stillness we are receiving the fullness of life."

Anonymous

Be Still My Soul

Be still, my soul: the Lord is on your side;
bear patiently the cross of grief or pain;
leave to your God to order and provide;
in ev'ry change he faithful will remain.
Be still, my soul: your best, your heav'nly Friend
through thorny ways leads to a joyful end.

Be still, my soul: your God will undertake
to guide the future as he has the past.
Your hope, your confidence let nothing shake;
all now mysterious shall be bright at last.
Be still, my soul: the waves and winds still know
his voice who ruled them while he dwelt below.

Be still, my soul: when dearest friends depart,
and all is darkened in the vale of tears,
then shall you better know his love, his heart,
who comes to soothe your sorrow and your fears.
Be still, my soul: your Jesus can repay
from his own fullness all he takes away.

Be still, my soul: the hour is hast'ning on
when we shall be forever with the Lord,
when disappointment, grief, and fear are gone,

sorrow forgot, love's purest joys restored.
Be still, my soul: when change and tears are past,
all safe and blessed we shall meet at last.

Katharina von Schlegel, born 1697;
Translated by Jane Borthwick, 1855

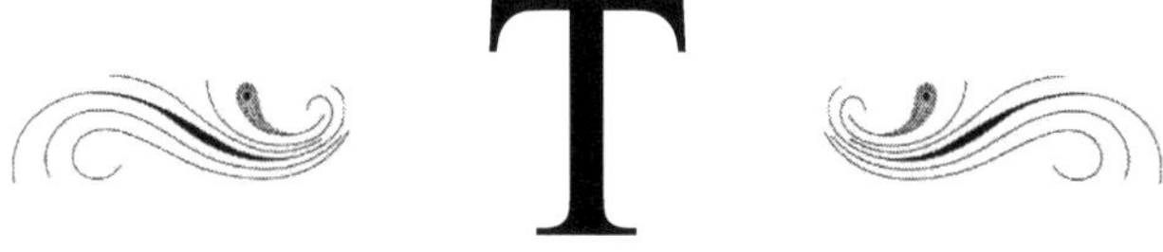

Thy eternal word, O God, is truth.

The grass withers and the flowers fade, but the Word of the Lord endures forever.

Isaiah 40:8

Jesus answered, "I am the way, the truth, and the life.
No one comes to the Father except through me."

John 14:6

DEUTERONOMY 8:3
Man does not live on bread alone but on every word that comes from the mouth of the Lord.

DEUTERONOMY 30:14
The word is very near you; it is in your mouth and in your heart so you may obey it.

2 SAMUEL 7:28
O Sovereign Lord, you are God! Your words are true.

PSALM 18:30
As for God, his way is perfect; the word of the Lord is flawless. He is a shield for all who take refuge in him.

PSALM 25:5
Guide me in your truth and teach me, for you are God my Savior, and my hope is in you all day long.

PSALM 33:4
For the word of the Lord is right and true; he is faithful in all he does.

PSALM 43:3
Send forth your light and your truth, let them guide me; let them bring me to your holy mountain, to the place where you dwell.

PSALM 84:11
Teach me your way, O Lord, and I will walk in your truth; give me an undivided heart that I may fear your name. (Note: "fear of the Lord" is often defined as reverential awe)

PSALM 100:4 - 5
Enter into his gates with thanksgiving, and into his courts with praise: be thankful unto him, and bless his name. For the Lord is good; his mercy is everlasting; and his truth endures to all generations.

PSALM 12:6
The words of the Lord are pure words, like silver refined in a furnace on the ground, purified seven times.

PSALM 118:89
Forever, O Lord, your word is firmly fixed in the heavens.

PSALM 119:89
Your word, O Lord, is eternal: it stands firm in the heavens.

PSALM 119:105
Your word is a lamp unto my feet and a light unto my path.

PSALM 130:30
The unfolding of your words gives light; it imparts understanding to the simple.

PSALM 119:142
Your righteousness is an everlasting righteousness. Your law is truth.

PSALM 119:160
All your words are true; all your righteous words are eternal.

PSALM 130:5 - 6
I wait for the Lord, my soul waits, and in his word I put my hope.

PROVERBS 30:5 - 6
Every word of God proves true; he is a shield to those who take refuge in him.

ISAIAH 45:19
"I, the Lord, speak the truth; I declare what is right."

ISAIAH 55:10 - 11
"As the rain and snow come down from heaven and do not return to it without watering the earth and making it bud and flourish, so that it yields seed for the sower and bread for the eater, so is my word that goes out from my mouth: It will not return to me empty, but will accomplish what I desire and achieve the purpose for which I sent it."

MATTHEW 4:4
Jesus answered, "It is written: 'Man does not live on bread alone, but on every word that comes from the mouth of God.'"

MATTHEW 24:35
Jesus said, "Heaven and earth will pass away, but my words will never pass away."

JOHN 1:1
In the beginning was the Word, and the Word was with God and the Word was God.

JOHN 1:14, 16 – 17
The Word became flesh and made his dwelling among us. We have seen his glory, the glory of the One and Only who came down from the Father, full of grace and truth. From the fullness of his grace we have received one blessing after another... grace and truth came through Jesus Christ.

JOHN 6:47
Jesus said, "I tell you the truth, he who believes has everlasting life."

JOHN 8:31 – 32
Jesus said, "If you hold to my teaching, you are really my disciples. Then you will know the truth and the truth will set you free."

JOHN 16:13
When the Spirit of truth comes, he will guide you into all the truth, for he will not speak on his own authority, but whatever he hears he will speak, and he will declare to you the things that are to come.

JOHN 17:17
Jesus prayed for his disciples, "Sanctify them by the truth; your word is truth."

JOHN 18:37
"You are a king, then!" said Pilate. Jesus answered, "You are right in saying that I am a king. In fact, for this reason I was born, and for this I came into the world, to testify to the truth. Everyone on the side of truth listens to me."

ROMANS 15:4
For whatever was written in former days was written for our instruction, that through endurance and through the encouragement of the scriptures we might have hope.

EPHESIANS 1:13
And you also were included in Christ when you heard the word of truth, the gospel of your salvation.

PHILIPPIANS 4:8
Finally brothers, whatever is true, whatever is noble, whatever is right, whatever is pure, whatever is lovely whatever is admirable—if anything is excellent or praiseworthy—think about such things. Whatever you have learned or received or heard from me—put it into practice. And the God of peace will be with you.

COLOSSIANS 3:16
Let the word of Christ dwell in you richly.

1 TIMOTHY 2:3 - 5
God our Savior wants all to be saved and to come to a knowledge of the truth. For there is one God and one mediator between God and men, the man Jesus Christ, who gave himself as a ransom for all.

2 TIMOTHY 2:15
Do your best to present yourself to God as one approved, a worker who has no need to be ashamed, rightly handling the word of truth.

2 TIMOTHY 3:16
All scripture is God-breathed and is useful for teaching, rebuking, correcting and training in righteousness.

HEBREWS 4:12
For the word of God is living and active. Sharper than any double-edge sword, it penetrates even to dividing soul and spirit, joints and marrow; it judges the thoughts and attitudes of the heart.

1 PETER 1:23 - 25
For you have been born again, not of perishable seed, but of imperishable, through the living and enduring word of God. For "All men are like grass, and their glory is like the flowers of the field; the grass withers and the flowers fade, but the word of the Lord endures forever."

1 JOHN 5:20
And we know that the Son of God has come and has given us understanding, so that we may know him who is true; and we are in him who is true, in his Son Jesus Christ. He is the true God and eternal life.

"Where I found truth, there I found my God who is truth himself."

Augustine, 354 – 430
Confessions (397-400)

"The Holy Scriptures are our letters from home."

Augustine, 354 – 430

"If there is something more excellent than the truth, then that is God; if not, then truth itself is God."

Augustine, 354 – 430
De Libero Arbitrio (387 – 395)

"The truth is incontrovertible. Malice may attack it, ignorance may deride it, but in the end, there it is."

Winston Churchill, 1874 – 1965
Speech in the House of Commons, May 17, 1916

"So great is my veneration for the Bible, and so strong my belief, that when duly read and meditated on, it is of all books in the world, that which contributes most to make men good, wise, and happy— that the earlier my children begin to read it, the more steadily they pursue the practice of reading it throughout their lives, the more lively and confident will be my hopes that they will prove useful citizens of their country, respectable members of society, and a real blessing to their parents...."

John Quincy Adams, 1767 – 1848
Letter to his son, George Washington Adams, 1811

"Holy Scripture is more than a watchword. It is also more than 'light for today.' It is God's revealed Word for all men, for all times. Holy Scripture does not consist of individual passages; it is a unit and is intended to be used as such."

Dietrich Bonhoeffer, 1906 – 1945
Life Together (1939)

"'What is truth?' said jesting Pilate; and would not stay for an answer."

Francis Bacon, 1561 – 1626
"Essays, Civil and Moral, Of Truth,"
The Harvard Classics (1909 – 1914)

"Our minds possess by nature an insatiable desire to know the truth."

Cicero, born January 3, 106 BC

"It is impossible to enslave mentally or socially a Bible-reading people. The principles of the Bible are the groundwork of human freedom."

Horace Greeley, 1811 – 1872
Ed., Tryon Edwards; *A Dictionary of Thoughts* (1897)

"'But what is truth?' 'T'was Pilate's question put to Truth itself, that deign'd him no reply."

William Cowper, 1731 – 1800
J. R. Boyd, *The Task, Table Talk, and Other Poems of William Cowper* (1857)

"In what light soever we regard the Bible, whether with reference to revelation, to history, or to morality, it is an invaluable and inexhaustible mine of knowledge and virtue."

John Quincy Adams, 1767 – 1848
Letters of John Quincy Adams, to His Son, on the Bible and Its Teachings (1848)

"Truth is as impossible to be soiled by any outward touch as the sunbeam."

John Milton, 1608 – 1674
Introduction, *The Doctrine and Discipline of Divorce* (1643)

"Men occasionally stumble over the truth, but most of them pick themselves up and hurry off as if nothing ever happened."

Winston S. Churchill, 1874 – 1965
Quoted in *Reader's Digest*, May 1947

"By reading the scriptures I am so renewed that all nature seems renewed around me and with me. The sky seems to be a pure, a cooler blue, the trees a deeper green. The whole world is charged with the glory of God and I feel fire and music under my feet."

Thomas Merton, 1915 – 1968
The Seven Story Mountain (1948)

"Nothing gives rest but the sincere search for truth."

Blaise Pascal, 1623 – 1662
Pensées (1670)

"I speak as a man of the world to men of the world; and I say to you, Search the Scriptures! The Bible is the book of all others, to be read at all ages, and in all conditions of human life; not to be read once or twice or thrice through, and then laid aside, but to be read in small portions of one or two chapters every day, and never to be intermitted, unless by some overruling necessity."

John Quincy Adams, 1767 – 1848
Letter to his son, George Washington Adams, 1811

"We search the world for truth;
We cull the good, the pure, the beautiful,
From graven scroll and written scroll,
From all old flower fields of the soul;

And, weary seekers of the best,
We come back laden from our quest,
To find that all the sages said
Is in the Book our mothers read."

John Greenleaf Whittier, 1807 – 1892
Poem, "The Book Our Mothers Read,"
Poems of John Greenleaf Whittier (1878)

"If you look for truth, you may find comfort in the end; if you look for comfort you will not get either comfort or truth, only soft soap and wishful thinking to begin, and in the end, despair."

C. S. Lewis, 1898 – 1963
Mere Christianity (1952)

"What are heavy? sea-sand and sorrow.
What are brief? today and tomorrow.
What are frail? spring blossoms and youth.
What are deep? the ocean and truth."

Christina Rossetti, 1830 – 1894
Christina Rossetti: The Complete Poems (1907)

"The gospel is not speculation but fact. It is truth, because it is the record of a Person who is the Truth."

Alexander Maclaren, 1826 – 1910
The Epistles of St. Paul to the Colossians and Philemon The Expositor's Bible (1866)

"Do the truth you know, and you shall learn the truth you need to know."

Louisa May Alcott, 1832 – 1888
Journal entry June, 1857; *Louisa May Alcott: Her Life Letters and Journals* (1889)

"Conquer the angry one by not getting angry; conquer the wicked by goodness; conquer the stingy by generosity, and the liar by speaking the truth."

Gautama Buddha, circa 5th – 4th century B.C.

"Beyond a doubt truth bears the same relation to falsehood as light to darkness."

Leonardo da Vinci, 1452 – 1519
Ed., Jean Paul Richeter; *The Notebooks of Leonardo Da Vinci* (1810)

"Truth, crushed to earth, shall rise again;
The eternal years of God are hers;
But Error, wounded, writhes with pain,
And dies among his worshippers."

William Cullen Bryant, 1794 – 1878
Poem, "The Battle-Field"
Signed and dated, New York, May 18th, 1878.

"Humility is truth."

Desiderius Erasmus, 1466 – 1536

"The truths that I know best I have learned on my knees.
I never know a thing well, till it is burned into my heart by prayer."

John Bunyan, 1628 – 1688
The Works of that Eminent Servant of Christ,
John Bunyan (1831)

"Truth is the substance of the soul."

Edward Counsel, 1849 – 1939
Maxims (1889)

"Let us never be guilty of sacrificing any portion of truth
on the altar of peace."

J. C. Ryle, 1816 – 1900
Knots Untied: Being Plain Statements on Disputed Points in Religion (1874)

"I have sometimes seen more in a line of the Bible that I could well
tell how to stand under, and yet at another time the whole Bible
hath been to me as dry as a stick."

John Bunyan, 1628 – 1688
Grace Abounding to the Chief of Sinners (1666)

"There is a book worth all other books which were ever printed."

Patrick Henry, 1736 – 1799
William Wirt, *Sketches of the Life and Character of Patrick Henry* (1817)

"As a matter of honor, one man owes it to another to manifest the truth."

Thomas Aquinas, 1225 – 1274
Summa Theologica (1485)

"Give me truths: for I am weary of the surfaces."

Ralph Waldo Emerson, 1803 – 1882
Poem, "Blight," *Early Poems of Ralph Waldo Emerson* (1899)

"England has two books, the Bible and Shakespeare.
England made Shakespeare, but the Bible made England."

Victor Hugo, 1802 – 1885
Preface to his Play, *Cromwell* (1827)

"I believe that in the end the truth will conquer."

John Wycliffe, 1320 – 1384
Wycliffe's statement to the Duke of Lancaster, 1831
Edward Galliat, *Champions of the Right* (1885)

"There is no middle ground. What is not true is false."

Henry Kletzing, 1850 – 1910
Traits of Character Illustrated in the Bible (1898)

"In all debates, let Truth be thy aim, not Victory."

William Penn, 1644 – 1718
Some Fruits of Solitude in Reflections and Maxims (1682)

"The Bible is a book in comparison with which all others in my eyes are of minor importance and which in all my perplexities and distresses, the Bible has never failed to give me light and strength."

Robert E. Lee, 1807 – 1870
Letter to the Hon. A. W. Beresford Hope, Kent, England, April 16, 1866, Lexington, Virginia
Robert Edward Lee, *Recollections and Letters of Robert E. Lee* (1904)

"Let us rejoice in the truth wherever we find its lamp burning."

Albert Schweitzer, 1875 – 1965
Ed., Charles R. Joy; *Albert Schweitzer: An Anthology* (1947).

"The study of God's word, for the purpose of discovering God's will is a secret discipline which has formed the great characters".

James W. Alexander, 1804 – 1859
Tryon Edwards, *A Dictionary of Thoughts* (1908)

"For to believe what you please, and not to believe what you please, is to believe yourselves, not the gospel."

Saint Augustine, 354 – 430
Contra Faustum (400)

"Hard are the ways of truth and rough to walk."

John Milton, 1608 – 1674
Paradise Regain'd (1671)

"Truth does not change because it is, or is not, believed by a majority of people."

Giordano Bruno, 1548 – 1600
C. Turnbull, *The Life and Teaching of Giordano Bruno: Philosopher, Martyr, Mystic* (1913)

"Truth will always be truth regardless of lack of understanding, disbelief, or ignorance."

W. Clement Stone, 1902 – 2002

"The greatest friend of truth is Time,
her greatest enemy is Prejudice,
and her constant is Humility."

Charles C. Colton, 1780 – 1832
Lacon, Or, Many Things in Few Words: Addressed to Those Who Think (1820)

"Without the Way there is no going;
without the Truth there is no knowing;
without the Life there is no living."

Thomas à Kempis, 1380 – 1471
The Imitation of Christ (c. 1418 – 1427)

"Truth and love are the two most powerful things in the world; and when they both go together they cannot easily be withstood."

Ralph Cudworth, 1617 – 1688
Article, "On Truth and Love," 1678

"Open my eyes that I may see
Glimpses of truth Thou hast for me;
Place in my hand the wonderful key
That shall unclasp and set me free.

Open my ears that may hear
Voices of truth Thou sendest clear;
And while the wave notes fall on my ear,
Everything false will disappear."

Clara H. Scott, 1841 – 1897
From the hymn, "Open My Eyes That I May See," 1895

"The truth does not change according to our ability to stomach it emotionally."

Flannery O'Connor, 1925 – 1964
From a letter to Betty Hester, September 6, 1955

"Everything we hear is an opinion, not a fact. Everything we see is a perspective, not the truth."

Marcus Aurelius, 121 – 180
Meditations (167)

"We know truth, not only by reason, but also by the heart, and it is from this last that we know first principles; and reason, which has nothing to do with it, tries in vain to combat them. The skeptics who desire truth alone labor in vain."

Blaise Pascal, 1623 – 1662
Pensées (1669)

"The Bible, as a revelation from God, was not designed to give us all the information we might desire, nor to solve all the questions about which the human soul is perplexed, but to impart enough to be a safe guide to the haven of eternal rest."

Albert Barnes, 1798 – 1870
J.H. Gilbert, *Dictionary of Burning Words and Brilliant Writers* (1895)

"Truth, like the sun, submits to be obscured, but like the sun, only for a time."

Christian Nestell Bovee, 1820 – 1904
Intuition and Summaries of Thought (1862)

"It is Christ Himself, not the Bible, who is the true Word of God. The Bible, read in the right spirit and with the guidance of good teachers, will bring us to Him."

C. S. Lewis, 1898 – 1963
Letter, November 8, 1952, *The Letters of C. S. Lewis* (1966)

"He is the free man whom the truth makes free,
And all are slaves besides."

William Cowper, 1731 – 1800
"The Task: A Poem in Six Books" (1785)

"Truth, in the end, shall shine divinely clear,
But sad the darkness till those times appear."

George Crabbe, 1754 – 1832
Poem, "The Borough," Letter IV (1810)

"It does not require great learning to be a Christian and be convinced of the truth of the Bible. It requires only an honest heart and a willingness to obey God."

Albert Barnes, 1798 – 1870
Notes Explanatory and Practical on the Gospels: Matthew and Mark (1853)

"The Bible is to us what the star was to the wise men; but if we spend all our time in gazing upon it, observing its motions, and admiring its splendor, without being led to Christ by it, the use of it will be lost to us."

Reverend Thomas Adam, (1701 – 1784)
Private Thoughts on Religion (1814)

"No educated man can afford to be ignorant of the Bible."

Theodore Roosevelt, 1858 – 1919
Realizable Ideals (1912)
"The Earl Lectures" of Pacific Theological Seminary,
delivered at Berkeley, California, 1911

"Do not try to make the Bible relevant: its relevance is axiomatic. Do not defend God's word but testify to it.... Trust the Word. It is a ship loaded to the very limits of its capacity."

Dietrich Bonhoeffer, 1906 – 1945
Eberhard Bethge, *Dietrich Bonhoeffer: A Biography* (1966)

"God suffers in the multitude of souls whom His word cannot reach. Religious truth is imprisoned in a small number of manuscript books, which confine instead of spread the public treasure. Let us break the seal which seals up holy things and give wings to Truth in order that she may win every soul that comes into the world by her word no longer written at great expense by hands easily palsied, but multiplied like the wind by an untiring machine. Yes, it is a press, certainly, but a press from which shall soon flow in inexhaustible streams the most abundant and most marvelous liquor that has ever flowed to relieve the thirst of man! Through it God will spread His Word. A spring of pure truth shall flow from it! Like a new star, it shall scatter the darkness of ignorance And cause a light heretofore unknown to shine among men."

Johannes Gutenberg, 1400 – 1468
Lines written in the *Gutenberg Bible* by Johannes Gutenberg

U

Of the riches of your wisdom and knowledge, Lord, impart to me, I pray, understanding of those things which are of you—the deep things of the Spirit.

This is what the Lord says:
"Let not the wise man boast of his wisdom
or the strong man boast of his strength,
or the rich man boast of his riches,
but let him who boasts boast about this:
that he understands and knows me, that I am the Lord,
who exercises kindness, justice and righteousness on earth,
for in these I delight," declares the Lord.

Jeremiah 9:23 – 24

Oh, the depth of the riches of the wisdom and knowledge of God! How unsearchable his judgments and his paths beyond tracing out! Who has known the mind of the Lord? Or who has been his counselor? Who has ever given to God, that God should repay him? For from him and through him and to him are all things. To him be the glory forever! Amen.

Romans 11:33 – 36

DEUTERONOMY 29:29
The secret things belong to the Lord our God, but the things revealed belong to us and to our children forever.

2 CHRONICLES 20:12
O God, we do not know what to do, but our eyes are on you.

JOB 6:24
Teach me and I will be silent; make me understand how I have gone astray.

JOB 12:12
Wisdom is found in the old, and discretion comes with great age.

JOB 12:13, 22
To God belong wisdom and power; counsel and understanding are his.... He reveals the deep things of darkness and brings deep shadows into the light.

JOB 28:20, 23 - 24
From where then does wisdom come? Where does understanding dwell?... God understands the way to it and he alone knows where it dwells, for he views the ends of the earth.

JOB 28:28
The fear of the Lord—that is wisdom—and to shun evil is understanding.
– (Note: "fear of the Lord" is often defined as reverential awe) –

JOB 32:7 - 8
I thought, "Age should speak; advanced years should teach wisdom." But it is the Spirit in a man, the breath of the Almighty, that gives him understanding.

JOB 36:26
How great is God—beyond our understanding! The number of his years is past finding out.

JOB 37:16
Do you know how the clouds hang poised, those wonders of him who is perfect in knowledge.

PSALM 14:1
The fool says in his heart, "There is no God."

PSALM 25:4 - 5
Show me your ways, O Lord, teach me your paths; guide me in your truth and teach me, for you are my God my Savior, and my hope is in you all day long.

PSALM 51:6
Surely you desire truth in the inner parts; you teach me wisdom in the inmost place.

PSALM 86:11
Teach me your way, O Lord, that I may walk in your truth.

PSALM 90:12
Teach us to realize the brevity of life, so that we may grow in wisdom.

PSALM 111:10
The fear of the Lord is the beginning of wisdom; all who follow his precepts have good understanding. To him belongs eternal praise.

PSALM 119:73
Your hands made me and formed me; give me understanding to learn your commands.

PSALM 119:130
The unfolding of your word gives light; it gives understanding to the simple.

PSALM 119:169
May my cry come before you, O Lord; give me understanding according to your word.

PSALM 147:5
Great is the Lord and mighty in power; his understanding is infinite.

PROVERBS 1:7
The fear of the Lord is the beginning of wisdom; fools despise wisdom and instruction.

PROVERBS 2:1 - 6
My son, if you accept my words and store up my commands within you, turning your ear to wisdom and your heart to understanding, and if you call out for insight and cry aloud for understanding, and if you look for it as if for silver and search for it as if for hidden treasure, then you will understand the fear of the Lord and find the knowledge of God. For the Lord gives wisdom, and from his mouth come knowledge and understanding.

PROVERBS 2:11
Discretion will protect you, and understanding will guard you.

PROVERBS 3:5 - 6
Trust in the Lord with all your heart and lean not to your own understanding; in all thy ways acknowledge him and he shall direct thy paths.

PROVERBS 3:7 - 8
Do not be wise in your own eyes; fear the Lord and turn away from evil. It will be healing to your body and refreshment to your bones.

PROVERBS 3:13
Blessed is the man who finds wisdom, the one who gains understanding.

PROVERBS 4:7
Wisdom is the principal thing; therefore get wisdom: and with all thy getting get understanding.

PROVERBS 9:10
The fear of the Lord is the beginning of wisdom, and knowledge of the Holy One is understanding.

PROVERBS 11:2
When pride comes, disgrace follows, but with humility comes wisdom.

PROVERBS 12:15
Fools think their own way is right, but the wise listen to others.

PROVERBS 14:12
There is a way that seems right to a man but in the end it leads to death.

PROVERBS 14:29
A patient man has great understanding, but a quick-tempered man displays folly.

PROVERBS 15:14
The discerning heart seeks knowledge, but the mouth of the fool feeds on folly.

PROVERBS 15:33
The fear of the Lord teaches a man wisdom, and humility comes before honor.

PROVERBS 17:27
A man of knowledge uses words with restraint, a man of understanding is even-tempered.

PROVERBS 18:2
A fool finds no pleasure in understanding but delights in airing his own opinions.

PROVERBS 20:5
The purposes of a man's heart are deep waters, but a man of understanding draws them out.

PROVERBS 24:3 - 4
By wisdom a house is built and through understanding it is established; through knowledge its rooms are filled with rare and beautiful treasures.

ECCLESIASTES 2:26
To the man who pleases him, God gives wisdom, knowledge and happiness, but to the sinner he gives the task of gathering and storing up wealth to hand it over to the one who pleases God. This too is meaningless, a chasing after the wind.

ISAIAH 40:12 - 14
Who has measured the waters in the hollow of his hand, or with the breadth of his hand marked off the heavens? Who has

held the dust of the earth in a basket, or weighed the mountains on the scales and the hills in a balance? Who has understood the mind of the Lord, or instructed him as counselor? Whom did the Lord consult to enlighten him, and who taught him the right way? Who was it that taught him knowledge or showed him the path of understanding?

ISAIAH 40:28
Do you not know? Have you not heard? The Lord is the everlasting God, the Creator of the ends of the earth. He will not grow weary, and his understanding no one can fathom.

ISAIAH 48:17
This is what the Lord says, your Redeemer, the Holy One of Israel: "I am the Lord your God, who teaches you what is best for you, who directs you in the way you should go. If only you had paid attention to my commands, your peace would have been like a river."

JEREMIAH 24:7
This is what the Lord says, "I will give them a heart to know me, that I am the Lord. They will be my people and I will be their God."

JEREMIAH 29:11 – 13
"For I know the plans I have for you," declares the Lord, "plans to prosper you and not to harm you, plans to give you hope and a future. Then you will call upon me and come and pray to me, and I will listen to you. You will seek me and find me when you seek me with all your heart."

JEREMIAH 33:2 – 3
This is what the Lord says, he who made the earth and established it—the Lord is his name. "Call to me and I will answer

you and tell you great and unsearchable things you do not know."

DANIEL 2:20 - 22
Daniel answered and said, "Blessed be the name of God for ever and ever: for wisdom and might are his: And he changeth the times and the seasons: he removeth kings, and setteth up kings: he giveth wisdom unto the wise, and knowledge to them that know understanding: He revealeth the deep and secret things: he knoweth what is in the darkness, and the light dwelleth with him."

LUKE 24:25 - 32 **Discourse on the Road to Emmaus**
Jesus said to them, "How foolish you are, and how slow to believe all that the prophets have spoken! Did not the Messiah have to suffer these things and then enter his glory?" And beginning with Moses and all the Prophets, he explained to them what was said in all the Scriptures concerning himself. As they approached the village to which they were going, Jesus continued on as if he were going farther. But they urged him strongly, "Stay with us, for it is nearly evening; the day is almost over." So he went in to stay with them. When he was at the table with them, he took bread, gave thanks, broke it and began to give it to them. Then their eyes were opened and they recognized him, and he disappeared from their sight. They asked each other, "Were not our hearts burning within us while he talked with us on the road and opened the Scriptures to us?"

ROMANS 11:33
Oh, the depth of the riches of the wisdom and knowledge of God! How unsearchable his judgments, and his paths beyond tracing out!

ROMANS 12:2

Do not conform any longer to the pattern of this world, but be transformed by the renewing of your mind. Then you will be able to test and approve what God's will is—his good, pleasing, and perfect will.

1 CORINTHIANS 1:20, 25 - 29, 31

Where is the wise man? Where is the scholar? Where is the philosopher of this age? Has God not made foolish the wisdom of this world?.... For the foolishness of God is wiser than man's wisdom, and the weakness of God is stronger than man's strength. Brothers and sisters, think of what you were when you were called. Not many among you were wise by human standards; not many were influential; not many were of noble birth. But God chose the foolish things of the world to shame the wise; God chose the weak things of the world to shame the strong. He chose the lowly things of the world and the despised things—and the things that are not— to nullify the things that are, so that no one may boast before him.... Therefore, let him who boasts, boast in the Lord.

1 CORINTHIANS 2:9 - 12

What no eye has seen, what no ear has heard, and what no human mind has conceived—the things God has prepared for those who love him—these are the things God has revealed to us by his Spirit. The Spirit searches all things, even the deep things of God. For who knows a person's thoughts except their own spirit within them? In the same way no one knows the thoughts of God except the Spirit of God. What we have received is not the spirit of the world, but the Spirit who is from God, so that we may understand what God has freely given us.

EPHESIANS 1:17 - 19

I keep asking that the God of our Lord Jesus Christ, the Glorious Father, may give you the Spirit of wisdom and revelation, so that you may know him better. I pray that the eyes of your heart may be enlightened in order that you may know the hope to which he has called you, the riches of his glorious inheritance in the saints, and his incomparably great power for us who believe.

EPHESIANS 5:2

Try to discern what is pleasing to the Lord.

PHILIPPIANS 1:9 - 11

And this is my prayer: that you may abound more and more in knowledge and depth of insight, so that you may be able to discern what is best and may be pure and blameless until the day of Christ, filled with the fruit of righteousness that comes through Jesus Christ.

COLOSSIANS 1:9 - 12

For this reason, since the day we heard about you, we have not stopped praying for you and asking God to fill you with the knowledge of his will through all spiritual wisdom and understanding. And we pray this in order that you may live a life worthy of the Lord and may please him in every way: bearing fruit in every good work, growing in the knowledge of God, being strengthened with all power according to his glorious might so that you may have great endurance and patience, and joyfully giving thanks to the Father, who has qualified you to share in the inheritance of the saints in the kingdom of light.

COLOSSIANS 2:2 - 3

May [you] have the full riches of complete understanding, in order that you may know the riches of God, namely, Christ, in whom are hidden all the treasures of wisdom and knowledge.

1 THESSALONIANS 5:21
Test everything. Hold on to the good.

JAMES 1:5
If any of you lacks wisdom, he should ask God who gives generously to all without finding fault, and it will be given to him.

JAMES 3:13, 17
Who is wise and understanding among you? Let him show it by his good life, by deeds done in the humility that comes from wisdom.... The wisdom that comes from heaven is first of all pure; then peace-loving, considerate, submissive, full of mercy and good fruit, impartial and sincere.

2 PETER 1:2
Grace and peace be yours in abundance through the knowledge of God and of Jesus our Lord.

2 PETER 3:18
Grow in the grace and knowledge of our Lord and Savior Jesus Christ. To him be the glory both now and forever. Amen.

"O Divine Master, grant that I may not so much seek
to be consoled as to console,
to be understood as to understand,
to be loved, as to love."

Saint Francis, died 1226
From the "The Peace Prayer of Saint Francis"

"The end of learning is to know God, and out of that knowledge to love Him, to imitate Him, to be like Him."

John Milton, 1608 – 1674
Tractate on Education (1644)

"Love follows knowledge. To love God is something greater than to know him."

St Thomas Aquinas, 1225 – 1274
Summa Theologica (1486)

"Therefore, do not seek to understand in order to believe, but believe that you may understand."

Saint Augustine, 354 – 430
"Tractates on the Gospel of John" (408 – 420)

"A humble knowledge of thyself is a surer way to God than a deep search after learning."

Thomas à Kempis, 1380 – 1471
The Imitation of Christ (circa 1418 – 1427)

"Wisdom is a right understanding, a faculty of discerning good from evil, what is to be chosen and what rejected; a judgment grounded upon the true value of things, and not the common opinion of them."

Wellins Calcott, 1726 – 1779
Thoughts Moral and Divine (1758)

"As a single footstep will not make a path on the earth, so a single thought will not make a pathway in the mind. To make a deep physical path, we walk again and again. To make a deep

mental path, we must think over and over the kind of thoughts we wish to dominate our lives."

Wilferd Arlan Peterson, 1900 – 1995
The Art of Living Day by Day (1972)
(Misattributed to Thoreau)

"What we need is a cup of understanding, a barrel of love, and an ocean of patience."

Saint Francis de Sales, 1567 – 1622

"I have been driven many times upon my knees by the overwhelming conviction that I had nowhere else to go. My own wisdom and that of all about me seemed insufficient for that day."

Abraham Lincoln, 1809 – 1865
Noah Brooks, "Harper's Weekly," (July 1865)

"Nothing in life is to be feared, it is only to be understood. Now is the time to understand more, so that we may fear less."

Marie Curie, 1867 – 1934
Attributed
Melvin A. Bernard, *Our Precarious Habitat* (1970)

"Mystery creates wonder and wonder is the basis of man's desire to understand."

Neil Armstrong, 1930 – 2012
James R. Hansen, *First Man* (2005)

"Any fool can know. The point is to understand."

Albert Einstein, 1879 – 1955
Attributed

"God has not been trying an experiment on my faith or love in order to find out their quality. He knew it already. It was I who didn't."

C. S. Lewis, 1898 – 1963
A Grief Observed (1961)

"Knowledge comes, but wisdom lingers."

Alfred, Lord Tennyson 1809 – 1892
Poem, "Locksley Hall" (1842)
Written 1835

"That is just the way with some people. They get down on a thing when they don't know nothing about it."

Mark Twain, 1835 – 1910
The Adventures of Huckleberry Finn (1885)

"This is the greatest wisdom: to seek the kingdom of heaven through contempt of the world."

Thomas à Kempis, 1380 – 1471
The Imitation of Christ (1418 – 1427)

"God assumed from the beginning that the wise of the world would view Christians as fools, and he has not been disappointed. If I have brought any message today, it is this: Have the courage to have your wisdom regarded as stupidity. Be fools for Christ. And have the courage to suffer the contempt of the sophisticated world."

Antonin Scalia, 1936 – 2016
Speech at the "Living the Catholic Faith Conference,"
Denver, Colorado, March 3, 2012

"God walks with the humble; he reveals himself to the lowly; he gives understanding to the little ones; he discloses his meaning to pure minds, but hides his grace from the curious and the proud."

Thomas à Kempis, 1380 – 1471
The Imitation of Christ (c. 1418 – 1427)

"Life: You live it forward but understand it backward."

Abraham Verghese
Cutting for Stone (2009)

"There is a wisdom of the head, and there is a wisdom of the heart."

Charles Dickens, 1812 – 1870
Hard Times (1854)

"*Wisdom is knowing what to do next. Skill is knowing how to do it. Virtue is doing it.*"

Thomas Jefferson, 1743 – 1826
Attributed

"Wisdom is to see the miraculous in the common."

Ralph Waldo Emerson, 1803 – 1882
Nature (1836)

"Tell me and I'll forget; show me and I may remember; involve me and I'll understand."

Chinese Proverb

"Wisdom is the daughter of experience."

Leonardo Da Vinci, 1452 – 1519
Thoughts on Art and Life (1906)

"It is the province of knowledge to speak and it is the privilege of wisdom to listen."

Oliver Wendell Holmes, Sr., 1809 – 1894
The Poet at the Breakfast Table (1872)

"Wise are they who have learned the truths:
Trouble is temporary.
Time is tonic.
Tribulation is a test tube."

William A. Ward, 1921 – 1994
Fountains of Faith (1970)

"Devout Christians are destined to be regarded as fools in modern society. We are fools for Christ's sake. We must pray for the courage to endure the scorn of the sophisticated world."

Antonin Scalia, 1936 – 2016
Speech, Mississippi College School of Law, Jackson, Mississippi, April 9, 1996

"If you desire to be wiser yet, think yourself not yet wise."

Wellins Calcott, 1726 – 1779
Thoughts Moral and Divine V (1758)

"How can we turn our knowledge about God into knowledge of God? The rule for doing this is simple but demanding. It is that we turn each Truth that we learn about God into matter for meditation before God, leading to prayer and praise to God."

J.I. Packer, 1926 – 2020
Knowing God (1973)

"Honesty is the first chapter in the book of Wisdom."

Thomas Jefferson, 1743 – 1826
Letter to Nathaniel Macon, January 12, 1819

"Like water in the desert is wisdom to the soul."

Edward Counsel, 1849 – 1939
Maxims Political, Philosophical, and Moral (1892)

"Love is the foolishness of men, and the wisdom of God."

Victor Hugo, 1802 – 1885
Les Misérables (1862)

"O come, thou Wisdom from on high,
And order all things far and nigh;
To us the path of knowledge show
And teach us in her ways to go."

From the Hymn, "O Come, O Come Emmanuel"
Latin, *Veni, veni Emmanuel,* 12th century
Translated, J. M. Neale (1851)

"Wisdom is the right use of knowledge. To know is not to be wise. Many men know a great deal, and are all the greater fools for it. There is no fool so great a fool as a knowing fool. But to know how to use knowledge is to have wisdom."

Charles Spurgeon, 1834 – 1892
Sermon No. 991, "The Fourfold Treasure," April 27, 1871

"Necessity teaches wisdom, while prosperity makes fools."

Wellins Calcott, 1726 – 1779
Thoughts Moral and Divine V (1758)

"One can be sophisticated and believe in God. Reason and intellect are not to be laid aside where matters of religion are concerned."

Antonin Scalia, 1936 – 2016
Speech, Mississippi College School of Law, April 9, 1996

"God never gives us discernment so that we may criticize, but that we may intercede."

Oswald Chambers, 1874 – 1917
My Utmost for His Highest (1924)

"It is the duty of human understanding to understand that there are things which it cannot understand."

Søren Kierkegaard, 1813 – 1855
Journals (1847)

"Grant me, O Lord, a mind to know you, a heart to seek you, wisdom to find you, conduct pleasing to you, faithful perseverance in waiting for you, and a hope of finally embracing you."

Saint Thomas Aquinas, 1225 – 1274

"Mere silence is not wisdom, for wisdom consists of knowing when and how to speak, and when and where to keep silent."

St. Francis De Sales, 1567 – 1622
Introduction to the Devout Life (1609)

Spirit of God, Descend Upon My Heart

Spirit of God, descend upon my heart;
Wean it from earth; through all its pulses move.
Stoop to my weakness, mighty as Thou art,
And make me love Thee as I ought to love.

Hast Thou not bid me love Thee, God and King?
All, all Thine own, soul, heart and strength and mind.
I see Thy cross; there teach my heart to cling:
Oh, let me seek Thee, and, oh, let me find!

Teach me to feel that Thou art always nigh;
Teach me the struggles of the soul to bear,
To check the rising doubt, the rebel sigh;
Teach me the patience of unanswered prayer.

Teach me to love Thee as Thine angels love,
One holy passion filling all my frame;
The kindling of the heav'n-descended Dove,
My heart an altar, and Thy love the flame.

George Croly, 1780 – 1860
Hymn (1854)

As you hear me when I pray, Lord, allow me to hear your voice, even in the midst of the whirlwind.

The Lord said, "Go out and stand on the mountain in the presence of the Lord, for the Lord is about to pass by." Then a great and powerful wind tore the mountains apart and shattered the rocks before the Lord, but the Lord was not in the wind. After the wind there was an earthquake, but the Lord was not in the earthquake. And after the earthquake a fire; but the Lord was not in the fire. And after the fire a still small voice. When Elijah heard it, he pulled his cloak over his face and went out and stood at the mouth of the cave.

1 Kings 19:11 – 13

DEUTERONOMY 4:7
The Lord our God is near us when we pray to him.

DEUTERONOMY 30:19 - 20
I have set before you life and death, blessings and curses. Now choose life, so that you and your children may live and that you may love the Lord your God, listen to his voice, and hold fast to him. For the Lord is your life.

1 SAMUEL 15:22
Does the Lord delight in burnt offerings and sacrifices as much as in obeying the voice of the Lord? To obey is better than sacrifice, and to heed is better than the fat of rams.

PSALM 5:1 – 3
Give ear to my words, O Lord, consider my sighing. Listen to my cry for help, my King and my God, for to you I pray. In the morning, O Lord, you hear my voice; in the morning I lay my requests before you and wait in expectation.

PSALM 19:1 – 4
The heavens declare the glory of God; the skies proclaim the work of his hands. Day after day they pour forth speech; night after night they display knowledge. There is no speech or language where their voice is not heard. Their voice goes out into all the earth, their words to the end of the world.

PSALM 29:4
The voice of the Lord is powerful; the voice of the Lord is majestic.

PSALM 66:19 – 20
But God has surely listened and heard my voice in prayer. Praise be to God who has not rejected my prayer or withheld his love from me.

PSALM 130:1 – 2
Out of the depths I cry to you, O Lord; O Lord, hear my voice. Let your ear be attentive to my cry for mercy.

ISAIAH 6:8
Then I heard the voice of the Lord saying, “Whom shall I send? And who shall go for us?” And I said, “Here I am. Send me!”

ISAIAH 30:21
Whether you turn to the right or left, your ears will hear a voice behind you, saying, "This is the way; walk in it."

ISAIAH 55:3
Incline your ear and come to me; hear that your soul may live.

ISAIAH 58:6 - 9
Is not this the fast that I choose: to loose the bonds of wickedness, to undo the straps of the yoke, to let the oppressed go free, and to break every yoke? Is it not to share your bread with the hungry and bring the homeless poor into your house; when you see the naked, to cover him, and not to hide yourself from your own flesh? Then shall your light break forth like the dawn, and your healing shall spring up speedily; your righteousness shall go before you; the glory of the Lord shall be your rear guard. Then you shall call, and the Lord will answer; you shall cry, and he will say, "Here I am."

MARK 9:7
Then a cloud appeared and enveloped them, and a voice came from the cloud: "This is my Son, whom I love. Listen to him!"

JOHN 5:24
Jesus said, "Truly I say to you, he who hears my voice and believes in him who has sent me has everlasting life, and shall not come to judgment, but has passed from death into life."

JOHN 5:25
Jesus said, "I tell you the truth, a time is coming and has now come when the dead will hear the voice of the Son of God and those who hear will live."

JOHN 10:27 - 29
Jesus said to them, "My sheep listen to my voice; I know them and they follow me. I give them eternal life and they shall never perish; no one can snatch them out of my hand."

HEBREWS 3:8
As the Holy Spirit says, "Today, if you hear his voice, do not harden your hearts."

REVELATION 3:20
The risen Christ, the Living One spoke to his servant John, "Here I am! I stand at the door and knock. If anyone hears my voice and opens the door, I will open the door and come in and eat with him, and he with me."

"Listen in silence because if your heart is full of other things you cannot hear the voice of God. But when you have listened to the voice of God in the stillness of your heart, then your heart is filled with God."

Mother Teresa, 1910 – 1997
In the Heart of the World (1995)

"Whenever there is stillness there is the still small voice, God's speaking from the whirlwind, nature's old song and dance...."

Annie Dillard, b. 1945
Teaching a Stone to Talk: Expeditions and Encounters (1982)

"There is hardly ever a complete silence in our soul. God is whispering to us well-nigh incessantly. Whenever the sounds of the world die out of the soul, or sink low, then we hear these whisperings of God. He is always whispering to us, only we do not always hear, because of the noise, hurry, and distraction which life causes as it rushes on."

Frederick William Faber, 1814 – 1863
Ed., Martin H. Manser; *The Westminster Collection of Christian Quotations* (2001)

"What is essential is not what we say but what God tells us and what He tells others through us. In silence He listens to us; in silence He speaks to our souls. In silence we are granted the privilege of listening to His voice."

Mother Teresa, 1910 – 1997
In the Heart of the World (1995)

"Prayer is not monologue, but dialogue; God's voice is its most essential part. Listening to God's voice is the secret of the assurance that He will listen to mine."

Andrew Murray, 1828 – 1917
Lesson 22, *With Christ in the School of Prayer* (1885)

"Among all nations there should be vast temples raised where people might worship in silence and listen to it, for it is the voice of God."

Jerome K. Jerome, 1859 – 1927
Diary of a Pilgrimage (1892)

The true guide of our conduct is no outward authority, but the voice of God, who comes down to dwell in our souls, who knows all our thoughts, to whom are owing all the truth we know, and all the good we do; for vice is voluntary, and virtue comes from the grace of the heavenly spirit within."

Lord Acton, 1834 – 1902
John E. E. Dalberg-Acton, *The History of Freedom* (1907)

"Whenever conscience speaks with a divided, uncertain, and disputed voice, it is not the voice of God. Descend still deeper into yourself, until you hear nothing but a clear, undivided voice, a voice which does away with doubt and brings with it persuasion, light, and serenity."

Henri Frederic Amiel, 1821 – 1881
Journal entry, April 6 1851
Amiel's Journal: The Journal Intime of Henri-Frédéric Amiel (1882)

"Prayer is not asking. Prayer is putting oneself in the hands of God, at His disposition, and listening to His voice in the depth of our hearts."

Mother Teresa, 1910 – 1997
In My Own Words (1996)

"Never trample on any soul though it may be lying in the veriest mire; for that last spark of self-respect is its only hope, its only chance; the last seed of a new and better life: the voice of God that whispers to it: 'You are not what you ought to be, and you are not what you can be. You are still God's child, still an immortal soul. You may rise yet and fight a good fight yet, and be a man once more, after the likeness of God who made you, and Christ who died for you!'"

Charles Kingsley, 1819 – 1875
Sermon XXXIII, *The Good News of God* (1880)

"God is not silent. It is the nature of God to speak. The second person of the Holy Trinity is called 'The Word.'"

A.W. Tozer, 1897 – 1963
The Pursuit of God (1948)

"Go forth, under the open sky, and list
To Nature's teachings, while from all around
Earth and her waters, and the depths of air—
Comes a still voice—"

William Cullen Bryant, 1794 – 1878
Poem, "Thanatopsis" (1817)

"God whispers to us in our pleasures, speaks in our conscience, but shouts in our pains: it is His megaphone to rouse a deaf world."

C. S. Lewis, 1898 – 1963
The Problem of Pain (1940)

"First of all, every time you begin a good work, you must pray to God most earnestly to bring it to perfection...Let us open our eyes to the light that comes from God and our ears to the voice from heaven that every day calls out this charge: 'If you hear his voice today, do not harden your hearts.' And again, 'He who has ears to hear, let him hear what the Spirit says to the churches.' And what does He say? 'Come, My children, listen to Me; I will teach you the fear of the Lord. Run while you have the light of life, lest the darkness of death overtake you.'"

Saint Benedict, 480 – 550
Rule of Benedict (516)

"Drop thy still dews of quietness,
till all our strivings cease;
take from our souls the strain and stress,
and let our ordered lives confess
the beauty of thy peace.

Breathe through the heats of our desire
thy coolness and thy balm;
let sense be dumb, let flesh retire;
speak through the earthquake, wind, and fire,
O still, small voice of calm!"

John Greenleaf Whittier, 1807 1892
From the Hymn, "Dear Lord and Father of Mankind" (1872)

"Conscience is the voice of the soul; passions are the voice of the body."

Jean-Jacques Rousseau, 1712 – 1778
Emile (1762)

"I found I had less and less to say, until finally, I became silent, and began to listen. I discovered in the silence, the voice of God."

Søren Kierkegaard, 1813 – 1855
Eds., *The Essential Kierkegaard* (1996) OMIT Source?

"Every happening, great and small, is a parable whereby God speaks to us, and the art of life is to get the message.

Malcolm Muggeridge, 1903 – 1990
Attributed

"Converse with men makes sharp the glittering wit,
But God to man doth speak in solitude."

John Stuart Blackie, 1809 – 1895
Comps., Hunt and Lee; *Highland Solitude, The Book of the Sonnets* (1867)

"There is not in the world a kind of life more sweet and delightful than that of a continual conversation with God; those only can comprehend it who practiced and experience it."

Brother Lawrence, 1614 – 1691
The Practice of the Presence of God (1692)

"Of all human activities, man's listening to God is the supreme art of his reasoning and will."

Pope Paul VI, 1897 – 1978
Attributed

"The silence of prayer is the silence of listening."

Elizabeth O'Connor, b. 1928
Eighth Day of Creation: Discovering Your Gifts and Using Them (1971)

"Open my ears that I may hear
Voices of truth Thou sendest clear;
And while the wave notes fall on my ear,
Everything false will disappear."

Clara Scott, 1841 – 1897
From the Hymn, "Open My Eyes, That I May See" (1895)

"God speaks in the silence of the heart. Listening is the beginning of prayer."

Mother Teresa, 1910 – 1997
In the Heart of the World (1997)

"Conscience is the authentic voice of God to you."

Rutherford B. Hayes, 1822 – 1893
Letter to his son, Scott R. Hayes, March 8, 1892

"Public opinion is held in reverence. It settles everything. Some think it is the voice of God."

Mark Twain, 1835 – 1910
Attributed

"The remarkable thing about the way in which people talk about God, or about their relation to God, is that it seems to escape them completely that God hears what they are saying."

Søren Kierkegaard, 1813 – 1855
Ed., Alexander Dru; *The Journals of Kierkegaard* (1938)

"It is in Silence that we hear the voice of Truth."

Jerome K. Jerome, 1859 – 1927
Diary of a Pilgrimage (1891)

"Listen carefully to the master's instructions, and attend to them with the ear of your heart."

Saint Benedict, 480 – 550
Rule of Benedict (516)

"The trouble with nearly everyone who prays is that he says 'Amen' and runs away before God has a chance to reply. Listening to God is far more important than giving Him our ideas... Prayer at its highest is a two-way conversation...."

Frank Laubach, 1884 – 1970
The Game with Minutes (1953)

"Lord, teach me to listen. The times are noisy and my ears are weary with the thousand raucous sounds which continuously assault them. Give me the spirit of the boy Samuel when he said to Thee, 'Speak, for thy servant heareth.' Let me hear Thee speaking in my heart. Let me get used to the sound of Thy Voice, that its tones may be familiar when the sounds of earth die away and the only sound will be the music of Thy speaking Voice. Amen."

A.W. Tozer, 1897 – 1963
The Pursuit of God (1948)

"In the Book of Nature, the Divine Teacher speaks."

Wellins Calcott, 1726 – 1779
Thoughts Moral and Divine IV (1758)

"Never had he thought, never once, that such a woman existed, one who stood so close to God that God's own voice poured from her. How far she must have gone inside herself to call up that voice. It was as if the voice came from the center part of the earth and by the sheer effort and diligence of her will she had pulled it up through the dirt and rock and through the floorboards of the house, up into her feet, where it pulled through her, reaching, lifting, warmed by her, and then out of the white lily of her throat and straight to God in heaven. It was a miracle and he wept for the gift of bearing witness."

Ann Patchett, b.1963
Bel Canto (2001)

"If this inner and critical voice has kept you safe for many years as your inner voice of authority, you may end up not being able to hear the real voice of God."

Richard Rohr, b. 1943
Falling Upward: A Spirituality for the Two Halves of Life (2011)

"To call out to God also means being ready to listen and to receive whatever he gives."

Augustine, 356 – 430
Confessions (397 – 400)

"However softly we speak, God is so close to us that he can hear us; nor do we need wings to go in search of him, but merely to seek solitude and contemplate him within ourselves, without being surprised to find such a good Guest there."

John of the Cross, 1542 – 1591
Living Flame of Love (1618)

"Humble yourself before God and your neighbors, for God speaks to ears that are bowed down."

St. Francis de Sales, 1567 – 1622
Introduction to the Devout Life (1609)

All thy ways are loving and good. Thy will, O Lord, is perfect.

As for God, his way is perfect and his word is flawless.
He is a shield to all who trust in him.

Psalm 18:30

This is the Lord's doing; it is marvelous in our eyes.

Psalm 118:23

The Lord is righteous in all his ways and loving toward all he has made.

Psalm 145:17

"For my thoughts are not your thoughts, nor are your ways my ways," declares the Lord. "For as the heavens are higher than the earth, so are my ways higher than your ways and My thoughts than your thoughts."

Isaiah 55:8 – 9

EXODUS 33:13
If you are pleased with me, teach me your ways so I may know you and continue to find favor with you.

DEUTERONOMY 8:2 - 3, 5 - 6
And you shall remember the whole way that the LORD your God has led you these forty years in the wilderness, that he might humble you, testing you to know what was in your heart, whether you would keep his commandments or not. And he humbled you and let you hunger and fed you with manna, which you did not know, nor did your fathers know, that he might make you know that man does not live by bread alone, but man lives by every word that comes from the mouth of the LORD. Know then in your heart that, as a man disciplines his son, the LORD your God disciplines you. So you shall keep the commandments of the LORD your God by walking in his ways and by fearing him.

DEUTERONOMY 30:16
For I command you today to love the Lord your God, to walk in his ways, and to keep his commands his decrees and his laws

DEUTERONOMY 32:4
Our God is the Rock, his works are perfect and all his ways are just. A faithful God who does no wrong, upright and just is he.

2 SAMUEL 22:31
As for God, his way is perfect; the word of the Lord is flawless. He is a shield for all who take refuge in him.

JOB 36:5
God is mighty, but does not despise men; he is mighty and firm in his purpose.

PSALM 19:7 – 9
The law of the Lord is perfect, restoring the soul; the testimony of the Lord is sure, making wise the simple. The precepts of the Lord are right, rejoicing the heart; the commandment of the Lord is pure, enlightening the eyes. The fear of the Lord is clean, enduring forever; the judgments of the Lord are true; they are righteous altogether.

PSALM 25:4 – 5
Show me your ways, O Lord, teach me your paths; guide me in your truth and teach me, for you are my God my Savior, and my hope is in you all day long.

PSALM 25:8 – 9
Good and upright is the Lord; therefore, he instructs sinners in his ways. He guides the humble in what is right and teaches them his way.

PSALM 25:10
All the ways of the Lord are loving and faithful for those who keep the demands of his covenant.

PSALM 40:8
I delight to do your will, O my God; your law is within my heart.

PSALM 86:11
Teach me your way, O Lord, and I will walk in your truth; give me an undivided heart, that I may fear your name.

PSALM 100:4 – 5
Be thankful unto him; bless his name. For the Lord is good; his mercy is everlasting and his truth endures for all generations.

PSALM 128:1 – 2
Blessed is everyone who fears the Lord, who walks in his ways. You shall eat the fruit of the labor of your hands; you shall be happy and it shall go well with you.
– ("Fear of the Lord" is often referred to as reverential awe.) –

PSALM 139:23 – 24
Search me, O God, and know my heart; test me and know my anxious thoughts, see if there is any offensive way in me and lead me in the way everlasting.

PROVERBS 19:21
Many are the plans in the mind of a man, but it is the purpose of the Lord that will stand.

PROVERBS 21:2
All a man's ways seem right to him, but the Lord weighs the heart.

ISAIAH 30:21
Whether you turn to the right or left, you will hear a voice behind you, saying, "This is the way; walk in it."

JEREMIAH 6:16
This is what the Lord says: "Stand at the crossroads and look; ask for the ancient paths, ask where the good way is and walk in it, and you will find rest for your souls."

DANIEL 4:37
Now I, Nebuchadnezzar, praise and exalt and glorify the King of heaven, because everything he does is right and all his ways are just.

HABAKKUK 3:6
His ways are eternal.

HABAKKUK 3:17 - 18
Though the fig tree does not bud and there are no grapes on the vines, though the olive crop fails and the fields produce no food, though there are no sheep in the pen and no cattle in the stalls, yet I will rejoice in the Lord, I will be joyful in God my Savior.

MATT 5:48
Jesus said, “Be perfect, therefore, as your heavenly Father is perfect.”

LUKE 18:19
And Jesus said to him, “Why do you call me good? No one is good except God alone.”

JOHN 14:6
Jesus answered, “I am the way and the truth and the life. No one comes to the Father except through me.”

ROMANS 8:27 - 28
And he who searches our hearts knows the mind of the Spirit, because the Spirit intercedes for God’s people in accordance with the will of God. And we know that in all things God works for the good of those who love him, who have been called according to his purpose.

ROMANS 12:2
And do not be conformed to this world, but be transformed by the renewing of your mind, so that you may prove what the will of God is, that which is good and acceptable and perfect.

REVELATION 15:3 - 4
Great and marvelous are your deeds, Lord God Almighty. Just and true are your ways, King of the ages. Who will not fear

you, O Lord, and bring glory to your name? For you alone are holy.

"Great God of wonders! All Your ways
Are matchless, Godlike, and divine."

Charles Spurgeon, 1834 – 1892
Sermon, December 27, 1877, *Sermons of the Rev. C.H. Spurgeon Vol. 23* (1878)

"We are not necessarily doubting that God will do the best for us; we are wondering how painful the best will turn out to be."

C. S. Lewis, 1898 – 1963
God in the Dock (1970)

"God never withholds from His child that which His love and wisdom call good. God's refusals are always merciful— 'severe mercies' at times but mercies all the same. God never denies us our hearts desire except to give us something better."

Elisabeth Elliot, 1926 – 2015
Loneliness (1988)

"Be ye perfect as your heavenly Father is perfect. Holy Scripture never orders and never counsels us to do the impossible. By these words, then, the Lord Jesus does not command us to accomplish the very works and ways of God, which no one can attain in perfection. But He invites us to model ourselves on them, as much as is possible, by applying ourselves to imitate them. We can do this with the help of grace and we should do so. And as the Bishop John said, 'nothing is more suitable to man than to imitate his Creator, and to carry out, to the degree that he is able, the will of God.'"

Thomas Aquinas, 1225 – 1274
The Ways of God (1793)

"Of one thing I am perfectly sure: God's story never ends with ashes."

Elisabeth Elliot, 1926 – 2015
These Strange Ashes (1975)

"Let us a thousand times a day turn our eyes upon the loving will of God, and make ours melt into it."

Saint Francis de Sales, 1567 – 1622
Treatise on the Love of God (1616)

"To understand the workings of God's will, you have to submit yourself to it unreservedly. Then you come to know that everything happens by his will, and for good."

Swami "Papa" Ramdas, 1884 – 1963
The Sayings of Ramdas (1936)

"In all His acts God orders all things, whether good or evil, for the good of those who know Him and seek Him and who strive to bring their own freedom under obedience to His divine purpose. All that is done by the will of God in secret is done for His glory and for the good of those whom He has chosen to share in His glory."

Thomas Merton, 1915 – 1968
No Man is an Island (1955)

"Blessed are you who lose your grip on the way things are—
For God shall lead you in the way things shall be."

Barbara Brown Taylor, born1951
Home By Another Way (1997)

"God knows better than we do what we need."

Victor Hugo, 1802 – 1885
Les Misérables (1862)

"Good morning, God.
This is your day.
I am your child.
Show me the way."

Unknown

"I am like a pencil in God's hand. That is all. He does the writing. The pencil has nothing to do with it. The pencil has only to be allowed to be used.

Mother Teresa, 1910 – 1997
The Joy in Loving: A Guide to Daily Living (1996)

"True worship of God consists quite simply in doing God's will, but this sort of worship has never been to man's taste."

Søren Kierkegaard, 1813 – 1855
Attack Upon "Christendom" (1854 – 1855)

"God is our owner. We are his property; his providence works for our good."

Immanuel Kant, 1724 – 1804

"There is no duty in religion more generally agreed on, nor more justly required by God almighty, than a perfect submission to his will in all things: Nor is there any disposition of mind that can either please him more or become us better, than that of being satisfied with all he gives, and contented with all he takes away."

Wellins Calcott, 1726 – 1799
Thoughts Moral and Divine (1756)

"He is truly very learned who does the will of God, and forsakes his own will. "Desire and pray always that God's will be perfectly fulfilled in you."

Thomas à Kempis, 1380 – 1471
The Imitation of Christ (1418 – 1427)

"You choose yourself to be a receiver of spiritual truth when you surrender your will to God's will. We all have the same potential. God is revealed to all who seek—God speaks to all who will listen. When you surrender your will to God's will you enter a very busy life—and a very beautiful one."

Peace Pilgrim, 1908 – 1981
Peace Pilgrim: Her Life and Work in Her Own Words (1991)

"Whatever Heaven ordains is best."

Confucius, 551 – 479 BC

"God does not will that we abound in knowledge, but that we lovingly and humbly submit ourselves in all things to His will."

Henry Suso, 1295 – 1366
Andy Zubko, *Treasury of Spiritual Wisdom* (1996)

"In His will is our peace."

Dante Alighieri, died 1321
"Paradiso," Part III, *The Divine Comedy* (circa early 3rd Century)

"Do God's will as if it were your will, and God will accomplish your will as if it were His own."

Rabbi Gamaliel, died 52 AD

"If we inquire the will of God, free from all doubt and all mistrust, we shall discover it."

Dietrich Bonhoeffer, 1906 – 1945
Sunday Morning Service, October 18, 1942
Quoted by Eric Metaxas, *Bonhoeffer: Pastor, Martyr, Prophet, Spy* (2011)

"We must neither ask anything nor refuse anything, but leave ourselves in the arms of divine Providence, without busying ourselves with any desires, except to will what God wills of us."

Saint Francis de Sales, 1567 – 1622
Conferences 21, "On Asking for Nothing," *Spiritual Conferences* (1869)

"Perfect conformity to the will of God is the sole sovereign and complete liberty."

Jean H. D'Aubigne, 1794 – 1872
History of the Reformation of the Sixteenth Century (1800)

"Restrain every wish that is not referred to God's will; banish all eager desires and anxiety; desire only the will of God; and seek Him alone and supremely, and you will find peace."

François Fénelon, 1651 – 1715
"On the Peace of the Soul," *Selections from Fenelon* (1892)

"Obeying God is listening to God, having an open heart to follow the path that God points out to us."

Pope Francis, born 1936
Morning Meditation, "The Obedience That Sets Us Free,"
Thursday, April 11, 2013

"All things that God would have us do are hard for us to do—remember that—and hence, he oftener commands us than endeavors to persuade."

Herman Melville, 1819 – 1891
Moby Dick (1851)

"The will of God must first live in us if it is to be done by us."

Andrew Murray, 1828 – 1917
Holy in Christ (1887)

"There are two kinds of people: those who say to God, 'Thy will be done,' and those to whom God says, 'All right, then, have it your way.'"

C. S. Lewis, 1898 – 1963
The Great Divorce (1945)

"The history of all the great characters of the Bible is summed up in this one sentence: they acquainted themselves with God, and acquiesced in His will in all things."

Richard Cecil, 1748 – 1810
J. H. Gilbert; *Dictionary of Burning Words of Brilliant Writers* (1895)

It will be very interesting one day to follow the pattern of our life as it is spread out like a beautiful tapestry. As long as we live here we see only the reverse side of the weaving, and very often the pattern, with its threads running wildly, doesn't seem to make sense. Someday, however, we shall understand. In looking back over the years, we can discover how a red thread goes through the pattern of our life: the Will of God."

Maria Augusta von Trapp, 1905 – 1987
The Story of The Von Trapp Family Singers (1949)

"There is one safe and happy place, and that is in the will of God."

David Livingstone, 1813 – 1873

"Fate! There is no fate. Between the thought and the success God is the only agent. Fate is not the ruler, but the agent of Providence."

Edward Bulwer-Lytton, 1803 – 1873
Andy Zubko, *Treasury of Spiritual Wisdom* (1996)

"Nothing comes by chance, for in all the world there is no such thing as chance."

Ralph W. Trine, 1866 – 1958
What All the World's A-Seeking: The Vital Law of True Life, True Greatness (1899)

"The doctrine of chance is the bible of the fool."

William G. Simms, 1806 – 1870
The Sword and the Distaff: A Story of the South at the Close of the Revolution (1852)
– (Written in response to Harriet Beecher Stowe's book, *Uncle Tom's Cabin*) –

"Perfection is founded entirely on the love of God: 'Charity is the bond of perfection;' and perfect love of God means the complete union of our will with God's."

St. Alphonsus Maria de Ligouri, 1696 – 1787
Conformity to the Will of God (1758)

"We must never pray to God that he may grant us what we desire, but that his will may be accomplished in us."

Saint Nilus of Sinai, died 430

"The will of God is never exactly what you expect it to be. It may seem to be much worse, but in the end it's going to be a lot better and a lot bigger."

Elisabeth Elliot, 1926 – 2015
Attributed

"We must follow, not force, Providence."

William Shakespeare, 1564 – 1616
Andy Zubko, *Treasury of Spiritual Wisdom* (1996)

"God Himself—His thoughts, His will, His love, His judgments are men's home. To think His thoughts, to choose His will, to judge His judgments, and thus to know that He is in us, with us, is to be at home."

George MacDonald , 1824 – 1905
J. H. Gilbert; *Dictionary of Burning Words of Brilliant Writers* (1895)

"There is always time to do the will of God. If we are too busy to do that, we are too busy."

Elisabeth Elliot, 1926 – 2015
Secure in the Everlasting Arms (2002)

"Only in peace with God, with others, and with ourselves will we hear and do God's will. In this we may have great confidence and need not become impatient or act rashly."

Dietrich Bonhoeffer, 1906 – 1945
Letter to Maria von Wedemeyer, November 19, 1942
Eric Metaxas, *Bonhoeffer: Pastor, Martyr, Prophet, Spy* (2011)

"Life teaches much, but to all thinking persons it brings ever closer the will of God—not because their faculties decline, but on the contrary, because they increase."

Madame de Stael, 1766 – 1817
J. Christopher Herold, *Mistress to an Age: The Life of Madame de Stael* (1958)

"Let us labor for an inward stillness—
An inward stillness and an inward healing.
That perfect silence where the lips and heart
Are still, and we no longer entertain
Our own imperfect thoughts and vain opinions,

But God alone speaks to us and we wait
In singleness of heart that we may know
His will, and in the silence of our spirits,
That we may do His will and do that only"

Henry Wadsworth Longfellow, 1807 – 1882
Christus: A Mystery (1872)

"I asked You, God, for strength that I might achieve,
I was made weak that I might obey;
I asked for health that I might do great things,
I was given infirmity that I might do better things;
I asked for riches that I might be happy,
I was given poverty that I might be wise;
I asked for power that I might have the praise of men,
I was given weakness that I might feel the need of God;
I got nothing that I asked for,
But everything I hoped for;
I am among all men most richly blessed."

Recovered from the body of a
Confederate soldier killed at Gettysburg

To the Supreme Being

"The prayers I make will then be sweet indeed,
If Thou the spirit give by which I pray:
My unassisted heart is barren clay,
Which of its native self can nothing feed:
Of good and pious works Thou art the seed,
Which quickens only where Thou say'st it may;
Unless Thou show to us Thine own true way,
No man can find it: Father! Thou must lead.
Do Thou, then, breathe those thoughts into my mind
By which such virtue may in me be bred
That in Thy holy footsteps I may tread;

The fetters of my tongue do Thou unbind,
That I may have the power to sing of Thee,
And sound Thy praises everlastingly."

Michelangelo Buonarroti (1475 – 1564)
Translated (circa 1805) into English by William Wordsworth (1770 – 1850)

X

Exalted art thou over all the earth! Rejoice and give thanks! From the rising of the sun to the place where it sets, may thy name, O Lord, be praised.

Be exalted, O God, above the heavens; let your glory be over all the earth.

Psalm 57:11

From the rising of the sun to the place where it sets, the name of the Lord is to be praised. The Lord is exalted over all the nations, his glory above the heavens. Who is like the Lord our God, the one who sits enthroned on high, who stoops down to look on the heavens and the earth?

Psalm 113:3-6

Rejoice in the Lord always. I will say it again: Rejoice!

Philippians 4:4

EXODUS 15:2
The Lord is my strength and my song, and he has become my salvation; this is my God, and I will praise him, my father's God, and I will exalt him.

2 SAMUEL 22:50
I will give thanks to You, O Lord, among the nations, and I will sing praises to your name.

1 CHRONICLES 16:8 – 11
Give praise to the Lord, proclaim His name; make known among the nations what He has done. Sing to Him, sing praise to Him; tell of all His wonderful acts. Glory in His holy name; let the hearts of those who seek the Lord rejoice. Look to the Lord and His strength; seek His face always.

NEHEMIAH 8:10
Do not be grieved, for the joy of the Lord is your strength.

PSALM 5:11
Let all who take refuge in you rejoice; let them ever shout for joy. May you shelter them that those who love your name may shout for joy.

PSALM 8:10
O Lord, our Lord, how excellent is your name in all the earth! You have set your glory above the heavens.

PSALM 9:1 – 2
I will give thanks to the Lord with all my heart; I will tell of all your wonders. I will be glad and exult in you; I will sing praise to your name, O Most High.

PSALM 18:46
The Lord lives! Praise be to my Rock! Exalted be God my Savior.

PSALM 34:1, 3
I will bless the Lord at all times; his praise shall continually be in my mouth... Oh, magnify the Lord with me, and let us exalt his name together.

PSALM 46:10
Be still, and know that I am God; I will be exalted among the nations, I will be exalted in the earth.

PSALM 66:1
Shout joyfully to God, all the earth.

PSALM 68:19
Praise be to the Lord, to God our Savior, who daily bears our burdens.

PSALM 95:6
Come, let us worship and bow down, let us kneel before the Lord our Maker.

PSALM 99:5
Exalt the Lord our God and worship at his footstool; holy is he.

PSALM 100:1 – 2, 4 – 5
Make a joyful noise unto the Lord all you lands. Serve the Lord with gladness: come before his presence with singing.... Be thankful unto him, and bless his name. For the Lord is good; his mercy is everlasting; and his truth endureth to all generations.

PSALM 103:1
Praise the Lord, O my soul: all that is within me, praise his holy name.

PSALM 104:1, 33 - 35
Let all that I am praise the Lord. O Lord my God, how great you are! You are clothed with splendor and majesty.... I will sing to the Lord as long as I live. I will praise my God to my last breath! May all my thoughts be pleasing to him, for I rejoice in the Lord. Let all that I am praise the Lord. Praise the Lord!

PSALM 117:1 - 2
Praise the Lord, all nations! Extol him, all peoples! For great is his steadfast love toward us, and the faithfulness of the Lord endures forever. Praise the Lord!

PSALM 145:1
I will exalt you, my God the King; I will praise your name forever and ever.

PSALM 148:13
Praise the name of the Lord, for his name alone is exalted; his splendor is above the earth and the heavens.

ISAIAH 25:1
O Lord, you are my God; I will exalt you, I will give thanks to your name; for you have worked wonders, plans formed long ago, with perfect faithfulness

ISAIAH 42:10
Sing to the Lord a new song, and his praise from the end of the earth.

ISAIAH 57:15
For this is what the high and exalted One says – he who lives forever, whose name is holy: "I live in a high and holy place, but also with those who are contrite and lowly in spirit, to revive the spirit of the lowly and to revive the heart of the contrite."

HABAKKUK 3:17 - 18
Though the fig tree does not bud and there are no grapes on the vines, though the olive crop fails and the fields produce no food, though there are no sheep in the pen and no cattle in the stalls, yet I will rejoice in the lord, I will be joyful in God my Savior.

LUKE 1:46 - 47
And Mary said: "My soul exalts the Lord and my spirit rejoices in God my Savior."

ROMANS 12:12
Be joyful in hope, patient in affliction, faithful in prayer.

EPHESIANS 1:3
Praise be to the God and Father of our Lord Jesus Christ, who has blessed us in the heavenly realms with every spiritual blessing in Christ.

PHILIPPIANS 2:6 - 11
Your attitude should be the same as that of Christ Jesus: Who being in very nature God, did not consider equality with God to be something to be grasped, but made himself nothing, taking the very nature of a servant, being made in human likeness. And being found in appearance as a man, he humbled himself and became obedient to death—even death on a cross. Therefore, God exalted him to the highest place and gave him

the name that is above every name, that at the name of Jesus, every knee should bow, in heaven and on earth and under the earth, and every tongue confess that Jesus Christ is Lord, to the glory of God the Father.

1 THESSALONIANS 5:16 – 18
Be joyful always; pray continually; give thanks in all circumstances, for this is God's will for you in Christ Jesus.

JAMES 4:10
Humble yourselves before the Lord, and he will exalt you.

1 PETER 2:9
Declare the praises, proclaim the excellencies of him who called you out of darkness into his marvelous light.

REVELATION 5:13
And I heard every creature in heaven, and on earth, and under the earth, and in the sea, and all that is in them, saying: "To Him who sits on the throne, and to the Lamb, be praise and honor and glory and power forever and ever."

"Praise God from whom all blessings flow;
praise him, all creatures here below;
praise him above, ye heavenly host:
Praise Father, Son, and Holy Ghost."

Thomas Ken, 1637 – 1711
Doxology (1674)

"From the fears that long have bound us,
Free our hearts to faith and praise."

Harry Emerson Fosdick, 1878 – 1969
From the Hymn, "God of Grace and God of Glory" (1930)

"Let all things their Creator bless,
and worship Him in humbleness,
O praise Him! Alleluia!
Praise, praise the Father, praise the Son
And praise the Spirit, Three in One,
O praise Him, O praise Him
Alleluia, Alleluia."

Francis of Assisi, died 1226
From the Hymn "All Creatures of Our God and King," circa 1225
Paraphrased by William H. Draper, 1855 – 1933

"Praise and bless my Lord, and give him thanks and serve him with great humility."

Francis of Assisi, died 1226
"Canticle of Brother Sun and Sister Moon," circa 1224

"We must praise Your goodness that You have left nothing undone to draw us to Yourself. But one thing we ask of You, our God, not to cease to work in our improvement. Let us tend towards You, no matter by what means, and be fruitful in good works, for the sake of Jesus Christ our Lord."

Ludwig von Beethoven, 1770 – 1827
Attributed

"Joy is the serious business of heaven."

C. S. Lewis, 1898 – 1963
Letters to Malcolm (1964)

"What I am anxious to see in Christian believers is a beautiful paradox. I want to see in them the joy of finding God while at the

same time they are blessedly pursuing Him. I want to see in them the great joy of having God yet always wanting Him."

A.W. Tozer, 1897 – 1963
Article, "*Men Who Met God,*" "Christianity Today", January 1987

Almighty God, unto whom all hearts be open, all desires known, and from whom no secrets are hid: cleanse the thoughts of our hearts by the inspiration of thy holy spirit, that we may perfectly love thee, and worthily magnify thy holy name: through Christ our Lord. Amen.

Thomas Cramer, 1489 – 1556
"Collect for Purity," *English Prayer Book* (1549)
Cranmer's translation from an 11th century Latin prayer

"Oh, for a thousand tongues to sing
My great Redeemer's praise,
The glories of my God and king,
The triumphs of His grace!"

Charles Wesley, 1707 – 1788
From the Hymn, "Oh, for a Thousand Tongues to Sing," (1739)

"What is the chief end of man? To glorify God, and to enjoy him forever."

The Westminster Shorter Catechism (1646)
First Question and Answer

Praise to the Lord, the Almighty

Praise to the Lord, the Almighty, the King of creation!
O my soul, praise him, for he is your health and salvation!
Come, all who hear; now to his temple draw near,
join me in glad adoration.

Praise to the Lord, above all things so wondrously reigning;
sheltering you under his wings, and so gently sustaining!
Have you not seen all that is needful has been
sent by his gracious ordaining?

Praise to the Lord, who will prosper your work and defend you;
surely his goodness and mercy shall daily attend you.
Ponder anew what the Almighty can do,
if with his love he befriends you.

Praise to the Lord! O let all that is in me adore him!
All that has life and breath, come now with praises before him.
Let the Amen sound from his people again;
gladly forever adore him. –

Joachim Neander, 1650 – 1680
Hymn (1680)

Praise My Soul, the King of Heaven

Praise, my soul, the King of Heaven;
To His feet thy tribute bring.
Ransomed, healed, restored, forgiven,
Who like thee His praise should sing
Praise Him ! Praise Him!
Praise the everlasting King.

Praise Him for His grace and favour
To our fathers in distress.
Praise Him still the same for ever,
Slow to chide, and swift to bless
Praise Him ! Praise Him!
Glorious in His faithfulness.

Father-like He tends and spares us;
Well our feeble frame He knows.
In His hands He gently bears us,
Rescues us from all our foes.
Praise Him ! Praise Him !
Widely as His mercy flows

Angels, in the height to adore Him
Ye behold Him face to face;
Sun and moon, bow down before Him,
Dwellers all in time and space
Praise Him ! Praise Him !
Praise with us the God of grace.

Tenderly He shields and spares us;
Well our feeble frame He knows;
In His hands He gently bears us,
Rescues us from all our foes
Praise Him, praise Him, alleluia,
Widely as His mercy flows.

Henry Francis Lyte, 1793 – 1847
Hymn (1834)

Y

God of the ages, you are the same yesterday, today and forever. A thousand years in thy sight, Lord, are but as yesterday when it is past; our times are in your hands.

But in you, I trust, O Lord; I say, "You are my God."
My times are in your hands.

Psalm 31:14 – 15

For a thousand years in thy sight are but as yesterday when it is past, and as a watch in the night.

Psalm 90:4

"I, the Lord, do not change."

Malachi 3:6

NUMBERS 23:19
God is not a man, that he should lie, nor a son of man, that he should change his mind. Does he speak and then not act? Does he promise and not fulfill?

2 SAMUEL 22:32
For who is God besides the Lord? And who is the Rock except our God?

JOB 37:23
The Almighty is beyond our reach and exalted in power, the number of his years is unsearchable.

PSALM 33:11
The counsel of the Lord stands forever, the purposes of his heart through all generations.

PSALM 39:4
Lord, remind me of how brief my time on earth will be. Remind me that my days are numbered—how fleeting my life is.

PSALM 89:34
"I will not violate my covenant or alter what my lips have uttered."

PSALM 102:12, 24 - 27
But you, Lord, sit enthroned forever; your renown endures through all generations.... Your years go on through all generations. In the beginning you laid the foundations of the earth, and the heavens are the work of your hands. They will perish, but you remain; they will all wear out like a garment. Like clothing you will change them and they will be discarded. But you remain the same, and your years will never end.

PSALM 118:24
This is the day the Lord has made; we will rejoice and be glad in it.

PSALM 119:89
Forever, O Lord, thy word is settled in heaven.

PSALM 139:16
All the days ordained for me were written in your book before one came to be.

ECCLESIASTES 3:1 - 4, 7 - 8, 15
For everything there is a season, and a time for every matter under heaven:
a time to be born and a time to die, a time to plant and a time to pluck up what is planted, a time to kill and a time to heal, a time to break down and a time to build up, a time to weep and a time to laugh… a time to keep silence and a time to speak, a time to love and a time to hate, a time for war and a time for peace…. That which is, already has been; that which is to be, already is; and God seeks out what has gone by.

ISAIAH 26:4
Trust in the Lord forever, for the Lord is the Rock eternal.

ISAIAH 46:3 - 4
"Listen to me… you whom I have upheld since your birth, and have carried since you were born. Even to your old age and gray hairs, I am he, I am he who will sustain you. I have made you and I will carry you; I will sustain you and I will rescue you."

ISAIAH 46:9 - 11
"Remember the former things, those of long ago; I am God, and there is no other. I am God, and there is none like me. I make known the end from the beginning from ancient times, what is still to come. I say, 'My purpose will stand, and I will do all that I please.' What I have said, that I will bring about; what I have planned, that I will do."

EZEKIEL 24:14
"I am the Lord. I have spoken; it shall come to pass; I will do it."

MATTHEW 24:35
"Heaven and earth will pass away, but my words will never pass away," said Jesus.

TITUS 1:2
[Ours is] a faith and knowledge resting on the hope of eternal life which God, who does not lie, promised before the beginning of time.

HEBREWS 1:10 - 12
"In the beginning, O Lord, you laid the foundations of the earth, and the heavens are the work of your hands. They will perish, but you remain; they will all wear out like a garment. You will roll them up like a robe; like a garment they will be changed. But you remain the same, and your years will never end."

HEBREWS 13:8
Jesus Christ the same yesterday, today and forever.

JAMES 1:17
Every good and every perfect gift is from above and cometh down from the Father of lights, with whom there is no variableness, neither shadow of turning.

2 PETER 3:8 - 9
But do not overlook this one fact, beloved, that with the Lord one day is as a thousand years, and a thousand years as one day. The Lord is not slow to fulfill his promise as some count slowness, but is patient toward you, not wishing that any should perish, but that all should reach repentance.

REVELATION 1:8
"I am the Alpha and the Omega," says the Lord God, "who is and who was and who is to come."

REVELATION 21:6
Then He said to me, "It is done. I am the Alpha and the Omega, the beginning and the end. I will give to the one who thirsts from the spring of the water of life without cost."

REVELATION 22:13
"I am the Alpha and the Omega, the first and the last, the beginning and the end."

"Jesus is Lord of the ages and is always with his own, even when things are difficult, and will abide with us; that is our comfort. If tribulation and anxiety come upon us, Jesus is with us and leads us over into God's eternal kingdom."

Dietrich Bonhoeffer, 1906 – 1945
The Collected Sermons of Dietrich Bonhoeffer Vol. II (2017)
Sermon, Barcelona Spain, April 15, 1928

"You, my God, are supreme, utmost in goodness, mightiest and all powerful, most merciful and most just. You are unchangeable and yet you change all things. You are never new, never old, and yet all things have new life from you."

Augustine, 354 – 430
Confessions (397 – 400)

"Time, as it grows old, teaches all things."

Aeschylus, circa 523 – 456
Prometheus Bound (c. 430)

"Time is too slow for those who wait, too swift for those who fear, too long for those who grieve, too short for those who rejoice; but for those who love, time is eternity."

Henry Van Dyke, 1852 – 1933
Music and Other Poems (1905)

"Now, five years is nothing in a man's life except when he is very young and very old..."

Pearl S. Buck, 1892 – 1973
The Good Earth (1931)

"Faith is to rest, not in the best of God's servants, but in His unchanging Word."

H. A. Ironside, 1876 – 1951
Full Assurance (1937)

"A thousand ages in Thy sight
Are like an evening gone;
Short as the watch that ends the night
Before the rising sun."

Isaac Watt, 1674 – 1748
From the Hymn, "O God, Our Help in Ages Past" (1719)

"Consider what you owe to His immutability. Though you have changed a thousand times, He has not changed once."

Charles H. Spurgeon, 1834 – 1892
Morning Devotion, February 3, *Morning and Evening* (1865)

"Grow old along with me!
The best is yet to be,
The last of life, for which the first was made:

Our times are in His hand
Who saith "A whole I planned,
Youth shows but half; trust God: see all, nor be afraid!'"

Robert Browning, 1812 – 1899
Poem, "Rabbi ben Ezra" in *Dramatis Personae* (1864)

"I will thank God for the day and moment I have."

Jim Valvano, 1946 – 1993
From his Arthur Ashe Courage Award acceptance address;
March 3, 1993

"Faith in God includes Faith in God's timing."

Neal A. Maxwell, 1926 – 2004
LDS Church Apostle, Speech, April 1991

"For the Present is the point at which time touches eternity."

C. S. Lewis, 1898 – 1963
The Screwtape Letters (1942)

"But there is something about Time. The sun rises and sets. The stars swing slowly across the sky and fade. Clouds fill with rain and snow, empty themselves, and fill again. The moon is born, and dies, and is reborn. Around millions of clocks swing hour hands, and minute hands, and second hands. Around goes the continual circle of the notes of the scale. Around goes the circle of night and day, the circle of weeks forever revolving, and of months, and of years."

Madeleine L'Engle, 1918 – 2007
The Small Rain: A Novel (1945)

"There is nothing of which we are apt to be so lavish as of Time, and about which we ought to be more solicitous; since without it we can

do nothing in this World. Time is what we want most, but what, alas, we use worst, and for which God will certainly most reckon with us when Time shall be no more."

William Penn, 1644 – 1718
Fruits of Solitude (1682)

"It is not in time that you precede all times, O Lord. You precede all past times in the sublimity of an ever-present reality. You have made all times and are before all times."

Augustine, 354 – 430
Confessions (397 – 400)

"Yesterday is gone.
Tomorrow has not yet come.
We have only today.
Let us begin."

Mother Theresa, 1910 – 1997
In the Heart of the World (1995)

"How did it get so late so soon?
It's night before it's afternoon.
December is here before it's June.
My goodness how the time has flown.
How did it get so late so soon?"

Theodor Seuss Geisel, (Dr. Seuss) 1904 – 1991
Poem, "How Did It Get So Late So Soon?" (1990)

"I wish it need not have happened in my time," said Frodo. "So do I," said Gandalf, "and so do all who live to see such times. But that is not for them to decide. All we have to decide is what to do with the time that is given us."

J.R.R. Tolkien, 1892 – 1973
The Fellowship of the Ring (1954)

"It is the time you have wasted for your rose that makes your rose so important."

Antoine de Saint-Exupery, 1900 – 1944
The Little Prince (1943)

"Don't spend time beating on a wall, hoping to transform it into a door."

Coco Chanel, 1883 – 1971
Robert Rohm, *You've Got Style: Your Personal Guide for Relating to Others* (2000)

"Time is a created thing. To say 'I don't have time,' is like saying, 'I don't want to.'"

Lao Tzu, born 601BC
Tao Te Ching, 4th Century BC
Published in English (1868)

"They say I'm old-fashioned, and live in the past, but sometimes I think progress progresses too fast!"

Dr Seuss, 1904 – 1991
The Lorax (1971)

"A man who dares to waste one hour of time has not discovered the value of life."

Charles Darwin, 1809 – 1882
The Life & Letters of Charles Darwin (1887)

"Remember always your end, and that time lost does not return."

Thomas à Kempis, 1380 – 1471
The Imitation of Christ (1418 – 1427)

"Those who make the worst use of their time are the first to complain of its brevity."

Jean de La Bruyère, 1645 – 1696
Les Caractères (1887)

"The strongest of all warriors are these two—Time and Patience."

Leo Tolstoy, 1828 – 1910
War and Peace (1869)

"The Moving Finger wites; and, having writ,
Moves on: nor all thy Piety nor Wit
Shall lure it back to cancel half a Line,
Nor all thy Tears wash out a Word of it."

Omar Khayyám, 1048 – 1131
Poem, "The Rubáiyát of Omar Khayyám," written circa 1120
Translator, Edward Fitzgerald; published (1859)
– (Khayyám dubbed "the Astronomer-Poet of Persia") –

"The great rule of moral conduct is, next to God, respect time."

John K. Lavater, 1741 – 1801
Andy Zubko, *Treasury of Spiritual Wisdom* (2003)

"A changeable God would be a terror to the righteous, they would have no sure anchorage, and amid a changing world they would be driven to and fro in perpetual fear of shipwreck… Our heart leaps for joy as we bow before One who has never broken His word or changed His purpose."

Charles Spurgeon, 1834 – 1892
Exposition, Psalm 100, The Treasury of David (1869)

"What is Time? The shadow on the dial,—the striking of the clock,—the running of the sand,—day and night,—summer and winter,—months, years, centuries,— these are but outward signs,— the measure of Time, not Time itself. Time is the life of the Soul."

Henry Wadsworth Longfellow, 1807 – 1882
Hyperion (1839)

"God gave you a gift of 86,400 seconds today. Have you used one to say, 'thank you?'"

William Arthur Ward, 1921 – 1994
Fountains of Faith (1970)

"Time is precious, but truth is more precious than time."

Benjamin Disraeli, 1804 – 1881
Speech, Aylesbury, Royal & Central Bucks Agricultural Assoc., September 21, 1865

Delays are not refusals; many a prayer is registered, and underneath it the words: "My time is not yet come." God has a set time as well as a set purpose, and He who orders the bounds of our habitation orders also the time of our deliverance.

Lettie Cowman, 1870 – 1960
Devotion, January 24, *Streams in the Desert* (1925)

"We tend to use prayer as a last resort, but God wants it to be our first line of defense. We pray when there's nothing else we can do, but God wants us to pray before we do anything at all. Most of us would prefer, however, to spend our time doing something that will get immediate results. We don't want to wait for God to resolve matters in His good time because His idea of 'good time' is seldom in sync with ours."

Oswald Chambers, 1874 – 1917
My Utmost for His Highest (1927)

"To all life Thou givest, to both great and small;
In all life Thou livest, the true life of all;
We blossom and flourish as leaves on the tree,
And wither and perish, but nought changeth Thee."

Walter C. Smith, 1824 – 1908
From the Hymn, "Immortal, Invisible, God Only Wise" (1867)

"Today is mine. Tomorrow is none of my business. If I peer anxiously into the fog of the future, I will strain my spiritual eyes so that I will not see clearly what is required of me now."

Elisabeth Elliot, 1926 – 2015
Keep a Quiet Heart (1995)

Whatever the attributes of God were before the universe was called into existence, they are precisely the same now, and will remain so for ever. Necessarily so; for they are the very perfections, the essential qualities of His being. Semper idem (always the same) is written across every one of them. His power is unabated, His wisdom undiminished, His holiness unsullied. The attributes of God can no more change than Deity can cease to be. His veracity is immutable, for His Word is "forever settled in heaven" (Psalm 119:89). His love is eternal: "I have loved thee with an everlasting love" (Jeremiah 31:3) and "Having loved His own which were in the world, He loved them unto the end" (John 13:1). His mercy ceases not, for it is "everlasting" (Psalm 100:5).

A.W. Pink, 1886 – 1952
His Immutability, *The Attributes of God* (1988)

"It fortifies my soul to know
That, though I perish, Truth is so:
That, howsoe'er I stray and range,
Whate'er I do, Thou dost not change.

I steadier step when I recall
That, if I slip, Thou dost not fall."

Arthur Hugh Clough, 1819 – 1861
Poem, "With Whom Is No Variableness, Neither Shadow of Turning," (1850)

"Frail as summer's flower we flourish,
Blows the wind and it is gone;
But while mortals rise and perish
God endures unchanging one,
Praise Him, praise Him,
Praise Him, praise Him,
Praise the High Eternal One!

Henry Francis Lyte, 1793 – 1847
From the Hymn, "Praise My Soul the King of Heaven" (1834)

Z

Give me zeal, O Lord, only for those things which you have prepared for me to do.

Whatever you do, work at it with all your heart, as working for the Lord, not for men, since you know that you will receive an inheritance from the Lord as a reward. It is the Lord you are serving.

Colossians 3:23 – 24

Never be lacking in zeal but keep your spiritual fervor, serving the Lord. Be joyful in hope, patient in affliction, faithful in prayer. Share with God's people who are in need. Practice hospitality. Bless those who persecute you; bless and do not curse. Rejoice with those who rejoice; mourn with those who mourn. Live in harmony with one another.

Do not be proud, but be willing to associate with people of low position. Do not be conceited. Do not repay anyone evil for evil. Be careful to do what is right in the eyes of everybody. If it is possible, as far as it depends on you, live at peace with everyone. Do not take revenge, my friends, but leave room for God's wrath, for it is written,

"It is mine to avenge; I will repay," says the Lord.
On the contrary: If your enemy is hungry, feed him;
if he is thirsty, give him something to drink.
In doing this you will heap burning coals on his head.
Do not be overcome by evil, but overcome evil with good.

Romans 12:11 – 21

DEUTERONOMY 6:5
Love the Lord your God with all your heart and with all your soul and with all your strength.

DEUTERONOMY 13:4
You shall follow the Lord your God and fear Him; and you shall keep His commandments, listen to His voice, serve Him, and cling to Him.

DEUTERONOMY 31:6, 8
Be strong and courageous. Do not be afraid or terrified, for the Lord your God goes with you; he will never leave or forsake you.... The Lord himself goes before you and will be with you; do not be discouraged.

JOSHUA 1:9
Have I not commanded you? Be strong and courageous. Do not be terrified; do not be discouraged, for the Lord your God will be with you wherever you go.

JOSHUA 24:14 - 15
Now fear the Lord and serve him with all faithfulness. Throw away the gods your ancestors worshiped beyond the Euphrates River and in Egypt, and serve the Lord. But if serving the Lord seems undesirable to you, then choose for yourselves this day whom you will serve, whether the gods your

ancestors served beyond the Euphrates, or the gods of the Amorites, in whose land you are living. But as for me and my household, we will serve the Lord.

1 SAMUEL 12:24
But be sure to fear the Lord and serve him faithfully with all your heart; consider what great things he has done for you.

1 CHRONICLES 16:10 – 11
Glory in his holy name; let the hearts of those who seek the Lord rejoice! Seek the Lord and his strength; seek his presence continually!

1 CHRONICLES 28:20
David also said to Solomon his son, "Be strong and courageous, and do the work. Do not be afraid or discouraged, for the Lord God, my God, is with you. He will not fail you or forsake you until all the work for the service of the temple of the Lord is finished."

PROVERBS 19:2
It is not good to have zeal without knowledge, nor to be hasty and miss the way.

PROVERBS 22:29
Do you see a man skillful in his work? He will stand before kings.

ECCLESIASTES 9:10
Whatever your hand finds to do, do it with all your might.

JEREMIAH 29:11 – 13
"I know the plans I have for you," declares the Lord, "plans to prosper you and not to harm you, plans to give you hope and

a future. Then you will call upon me and come and pray to me, and I will listen to you. You will seek me and find me when you seek me with all your heart."

JOEL 2:12 – 13
"Even now," declares the Lord, "Return to me with all your heart.... Rend your heart and not your garments."

MATTHEW 3:8
Bear fruit in keeping with repentance.

MATTHEW 6:20 – 21, 24
Jesus said, "Do not store up for yourselves treasures on earth, where moths and vermin destroy, and where thieves break in and steal. But store up for yourselves treasures in heaven, where moths and vermin do not destroy, and where thieves do not break in and steal. For where your treasure is, there your heart will be also.... No one can serve two masters. Either you will hate the one and love the other, or you will be devoted to the one and despise the other. You cannot serve both God and money."

MATTHEW 22:36 – 40
Jesus was asked, "Teacher, which is the greatest commandment in the law?" He replied, "'Love the Lord your God with all your heart and with all your soul and with all your mind.' This is the first and greatest commandment. And the second is like it: 'Love your neighbor as yourself.' All the Law and the Prophets hang on these two commandments."

MATTHEW 23:11
Jesus said, "The greatest among you will be your servant."

MATTHEW 25:21
"His master replied, 'Well done, good and faithful servant! You have been faithful with a few things; I will put you in charge of many things. Come and share your master's happiness!'"

MATTHEW 25:40
Jesus said to them, "The King will reply, 'Truly I tell you, whatever you did for one of the least of these brothers and sisters of mine, you did for me.'"

LUKE 6:38
Jesus said, "Give, and it will be given to you. A good measure, pressed down, shaken together and running over, will be poured into your lap. For with the measure you use, it will be measured to you."

JOHN 2:14 - 17
In the temple courts Jesus found people selling cattle, sheep and doves, and others sitting at tables exchanging money. So he made a whip out of cords, and drove all from the temple courts, both sheep and cattle; he scattered the coins of the moneychangers and overturned their tables. To those who sold doves he said, "Get these out of here! Stop turning my Father's house into a market!" His disciples remembered that it is written: "Zeal for your house will consume me."

JOHN 4:34
"My food," Jesus said, "is to do the will of him who sent me and to finish his work."

JOHN 9:4
Jesus said, "As long as it is day, we must do the work of him who sent me."

ROMANS 8:28
And we know that in all things God works for the good of those who love him, who have been called according to his purpose.

ROMANS 12:2
Do not conform any longer to the pattern of this world, but be transformed by the renewing of your mind. Then you will be able to test and approve what God's will is—his good, pleasing and perfect will.

ROMANS 12:11
Never be lacking in zeal, but keep your spiritual fervor, serving the Lord.

1 CORINTHIANS 10:31
So... whatever you do, do it for the glory of God.

1 CORINTHIANS 12:31
But earnestly desire the higher gifts. And I will show you a still more excellent way.

1 CORINTHIANS 15:58
Therefore, my dear brothers and sisters, stand firm. Let nothing move you. Always give yourselves fully to the work of the Lord, because you know that your labor in the Lord is not in vain.

1 CORINTHIANS 16:13 – 14
Be on your guard; stand firm in your faith; be courageous; be strong. Do everything in love.

2 CORINTHIANS 4:1
Therefore... by the mercy of God we do not lose heart.

2 CORINTHIANS 9: 6 - 8
Remember this: Whoever sows sparingly will also reap sparingly, and whoever sows generously will also reap generously. Each man should give what he has decided in his heart to give, not reluctantly or under compulsion, for God loves a cheerful giver. And God is able to make all grace abound to you, so that in all things at all times, having all that you need, you will abound in good work.

GALATIANS 6:9 - 10
Let us not grow weary in doing good, for at the proper time we will reap a harvest if we do not give up. Therefore, as we have opportunity, let us do good to all people

EPHESIANS 2:8 - 10
For it is by grace that you have been saved, through faith—and this is not of yourselves, it is the gift of God—not by works so that no one can boast. For we are God's workmanship, created in Christ Jesus to do good works which God prepared in advance for us to do.

EPHESIANS 5:15 - 16
Be very careful then how you live—not as unwise but as wise, making the most of every opportunity.

EPHESIANS 6:7 - 8
Serve wholeheartedly, as if you were serving the Lord, not men, knowing that whatever good anyone does, this he will receive back from the Lord, whether he is a slave or free.

PHILIPPIANS 1:9 - 10
And it is my prayer that your love may abound more and more, with knowledge and all discernment, so that you may approve what is excellent, and so be pure and blameless for the day of Christ.

PHILIPPIANS 3:13 – 14
Forgetting what is behind and straining toward what is ahead, I press on toward the goal to win the prize for which God has called me heavenward in Christ Jesus.

PHILIPPIANS 4:8
Finally, brothers, whatever is true, whatever is honorable, whatever is just, whatever is pure, whatever is lovely, whatever is commendable, if there is any excellence, if there is anything worthy of praise, think about these things.

COLOSSIANS 1:9 – 12
We have not stopped praying for you, asking God to fill you with the knowledge of his will through all spiritual wisdom and understanding. And we pray this in order that you may live a life worthy of the Lord and may please him in every way: bearing fruit in every good work, growing in the knowledge of God, being strengthened with all power according to his glorious might so that you might have great endurance and patience, joyfully giving thanks to the Father.

COLOSSIANS 3:17
And whatever you do, whether in word or deed, do it all in the name of the Lord Jesus, giving thanks to God the Father through him.

COLOSSIANS 3:23 – 24
Whatever you do, work at it with all your heart, as working for the Lord, not for human masters, since you know that you will receive an inheritance from the Lord as a reward. It is the Lord Christ you are serving.

2 TIMOTHY 2:15
Do your best to present yourself to God as one approved, a

workman who does not need to be ashamed and who correctly handles the word of truth.

TITUS 2:7 - 8
Show yourself in all respects to be a model of good works, and in your teaching show integrity, dignity, and sound speech that cannot be condemned.

HEBREWS 12:12
Strengthen your feeble arms and weak knees.

HEBREWS 13:16
And do not forget to do good and to share with others, for with such sacrifices God is pleased.

JAMES 1:12
Blessed is the one who perseveres under trial, because when he has stood the test, he will receive the crown of life that God has promised to those who love him.

JAMES 2:14 - 17
What does it profit, my brethren, if someone says he has faith but does not have works? Can faith save him? If a brother or sister is naked and destitute of daily food, and one of you says to them, "Depart in peace, be warmed and filled," but you do not give them the things which are needed for the body, what does it profit? Thus, also faith by itself, if it does not have works, is dead.

1 PETER 4:10
As each has received a gift, use it to serve one another, as good stewards of God's varied grace.

2 PETER 1:5 – 8
For this reason make every effort to add to your faith goodness, and to goodness, knowledge, and to knowledge, self-control, and to self-control, perseverance, and to perseverance, godliness and to godliness brotherly kindness, and to brotherly kindness, love.

2 PETER 1:10
Therefore, brothers, be all the more diligent to confirm your calling and election, for if you practice these qualities you will never fall.

"My candle burns at both ends;
It will not last the night;
But ah, my foes, and oh, my friends—
It gives a lovely light."

Edna St. Vincent Millay, 1892 – 1950
A Few Figs from Thistles (1920)

"True zeal is a soft and gentle flame that will not scorch anyone's hands."

Ralph Cudworth, 1617 – 1688
Article, "On Truth and Love," (1678)

"We ought not to be weary of doing little things for the love of God, who regards not the greatness of the work, but the love with which it is performed."

Brother Lawrence, 1614 – 1691
The Practice of the Presence of God (1692)

"Zeal is that pure and heavenly flame,
The fire of love supplies;
While that which often bears the name,
Is self in a disguise.

True zeal is merciful and mild,
Can pity and forbear;
The false is headstrong, fierce and wild,
And breathes revenge and war."

John Newton, 1725 – 1807
Olney Hymns (1779)

"Zeal is an ardent and vehement love, it requires guidance; otherwise, it can become excessive."

Saint Francis de Sales, 1567 – 1622
Treatise on the Love of God (1616)

"Overzealousness is the mother of all imperfections."

Saint Francis de Sales, 1567 – 1622
Introduction to the Devout Life (1609)

"Zeal without knowledge is like expedition to a man in the dark."

John Newton, 1725 – 1807
Ed., Harold J. Chadwick; *The Amazing Works of John Newton* (2009)

"Just as there is a wicked zeal of bitterness which separates from God, so there is a good zeal which separates from evil and leads to God. This, then, is the good kind of zeal which monks must foster with fervent love."

Saint Benedict, died 547
Rule of Benedict (516)

"None are so old as those who have outlived enthusiasm."

Henry David Thoreau, 1817 – 1862

"Do little things as if they were great, because of the majesty of the Lord Jesus Christ who dwells in thee."

Blaise Pascal, 1623 – 1662
Pensées (1669)

"May we not say, that true zeal is not mostly charitable, but wholly so? That is, if we take charity in St. Paul's sense, for love: the love of God and neighbor. For it is a certain truth (although little understood in the world), that Christian zeal is all love. It is nothing else."

John Wesley, 1703 – 1791
Sermons on Several Occasions (1746)

"Zeal should not outrun discretion."

Aesop, 621 – 565BC
Moral of "The Thirsty Pigeon"

"Zeal must be yoked with humility."

William Cave, 1637 – 1713
Comp., Edward Parsons Day; *Day's Collacon* (1884)

"Zeal without judgment is like gunpowder in the hands of a child."

Eliza Cook, 1818 – 1889
Diamond Dust (1865)

"Zeal is only fit for wise men, but it is chiefly in fashion among fools."

John Tillotson, 1630 – 1694
Works (1820)

"Do not then spend the strength of your zeal for your religion in censuring others. The man that is most busy in censuring others is always least employed in examining himself."

Thomas Lye, 1621 – 1684
Sermon preached August 17, 1662
Farewell Sermons of Some of the Most Eminent of the Nonconformist Ministers (1816)

"Rebellion against your handicaps gets you nowhere. Self-pity gets you nowhere. One must have the adventurous daring to accept oneself as a bundle of possibilities and undertake the most interesting game in the world—making the most of one's best."

Harry Emerson Fosdick, 1878 – 1969
Ed., H. V. Prochnaw; *The New Speaker's Treasury of Wit and Wisdom* (1958)

"All work is empty save when there is love. And when you work with love you bind yourself to yourself, and to one another, and to God."

Kahlil Gibran, 1883 – 1931
Poem, "On Work," *The Prophet* (1923)

"We can be truly successful only in the work to which we have been called. The work is not ours, it's God's, and we are privileged to be worked through by God. How foolish, then, for anyone to think and proclaim that he has a certain work to do for God. God may have a certain work to do through him, that is if he is sufficiently humble, but that is quite a different thing."

Henry T Hamblin, 1873 – 1958
Andy Zubko, *Treasury of Spiritual Wisdom* (2003)

"Men seldom die of hard work; activity is God's medicine."

Robert S. McArthur, 1841 – 1923
Andy Zubko, *Treasury of Spiritual Wisdom* (2003)

"Have thy tools ready; God will find thee work."

Charles Kingsley, 1819 – 1875
The Works of Charles Kingsley (1820)

"It is a happy moment when our desire crosses with the will of Heavenly Father."

C. S. Lewis, 1898 – 1963
Sermon, "The Weight of Glory," June 8, 1941
University Church of St Mary the Virgin, Oxford

"Everyone has been made for some particular work, and the desire for that work has been put in his heart."

Rumi, 1207 – 1273

"Every calling is great when greatly pursued."

Oliver W. Holmes, Jr., 1841 – 1935
Speech, "The Law," Suffolk Bar Association, February 5, 1885,
Speeches (1891)

"And when you discover what you will be in your life, set out to do it as if God Almighty called you at this particular moment in history to do it. Don't just set out to do a good job. Set out to do such a good job that the living, the dead or the unborn couldn't do it any better."

Martin Luther King, 1929 – 1968
Speech to Barratt Junior High School in Philadelphia,
October 26, 1967

"It is not your business to succeed, but to do right. When you have done so the rest lies with God."

C. S. Lewis, 1898 – 1963
Yours, Jack: Spiritual Direction from C. S. Lewis (2008)

"No man is born into the world whose work
Is not born with him. There is always work,
And tools to work withal, for those who will;
And blessed are the horny hands of toil."

James Russell Lowell, 1819 – 1891
A Glance Behind the Curtain (1843)

"We must run and do now what will profit us forever."

Saint Benedict, died 547
Rule of Benedict (516)

"Do all the good you can, in all the ways you can, to all the souls you can, in every place you can, at all the times you can, with all the zeal you can, as long as ever you can."

John Wesley, 1703 – 1791
Paraphrase from Sermon, "On the Use of Money,"
Sermons on Several Occasion (1799)

"Pursue some path, however narrow and crooked, In which you can walk with love and reverence."

Henry David Thoreau, 1817 – 1862
Journal (1855)

"And even should you lose your zeal, never forget that the Lord has not lost His."

Msgr. Charles Pope, born 1961
Sermon, "Never Give Up: St Augustine's stirring Call to Pastors", October 2, 2016
Community in Mission – the Archdiocese of Washington DC

"May you live every day of your life."

Jonathan Swift, 1667 – 1745
A Complete Collection of Genteel and Ingenious Conversation (1738)

"Zeal is like fire; in the chimney it is one of the best servants; but out of the chimney it is one of the worst masters."

Thomas Benton Brooks, 1608 – 1680
Ed., The Rev. C. Bradley, *The Select Works of the Reverend Thomas Brookes Volume* I (1824)

"Every day you make progress. Every step may be fruitful. Yet there will stretch out before you an ever-lengthening, ever-ascending, ever-improving path. You know you will never get to the end of the journey. But this, so far from discouraging, only adds to the joy and glory of the climb."

Winston Churchill, 1874 – 1965
"Painting as a Pastime," The Strand Magazine
(December 1921/January 1922)

"Diligence is the mother of good luck."

Benjamin Franklin, 1706 – 1790
"The Way to Wealth," *Poor Richard's Almanac* (1758)

"Do everything calmly and peacefully. Do as much as you can as well as you can. Strive to see God in all things without exception, and consent to His will joyously. Do everything for God, uniting yourself to Him in word and deed. Walk very simply with the Cross of the Lord and be at peace with yourself."

Saint Francis de Sales, 1567 – 1622

"Never let your zeal outrun your charity.
The former is but human, the latter is divine."

Hosea Ballou, 1781 – 1852
Comp., C.N. Douglas; *Forty Thousand Quotations: Prose and Poetical* (1917)

"Give me the Love that leads the way
The Faith that nothing can dismay
The Hope no disappointments tire
The Passion that'll burn like fire
Let me not sink to be a clod
Make me Thy fuel, Flame of God"

Amy Carmichael, 1867 – 1951
From the Poem, "Make Me Thy Fuel"
Mountain Breezes: The Collected Poems of Amy Carmichael (1999)

"Kindness has converted more sinners than zeal, eloquence, or learning."

Frederick W. Faber, 1814 – 1863
J. H. Gilbert, *Dictionary of Burning Words of Brilliant Writers* (1895)

"The key to winning is choosing to do God's will,
and loving others with all you got."

Lou Holtz, born 1937
The Fighting Spirit: A Championship Season at Notre Dame (1990)

"Be interesting, be enthusiastic... and don't talk too much."

Norman Vincent Peale, 1898 – 1963

"Refuse to be average. Let your heart soar as high as it will."

A.W. Tozer, 1887 – 1963
The Pursuit of God (1948)

"The terrible thing, the almost impossible thing, is to hand over your whole self—all your wishes and precautions—to Christ."

C. S. Lewis, 1898 – 1963
Mere Christianity (1952)

"Doing little things with a strong desire to please God makes them really great."

Saint Francis de Sales, 1567 – 1622

"It matters little how one begins, provided that he be resolved to go on well and to end well."

Saint Francis de Sales 1567 – 1622

"Be who you are and do that well."

Saint Francis de Sales, 1567 – 1622
Introduction to a Devout Life (1609)

"Blind zeal is soon put to a shameful retreat, while holy resolution, built on fast principles, lifts up its head like a rock in the midst of the waves."

William Gurnall, 1617 – 1679
The Christian in Complete Armour (1865)

"The place God calls you to is the place where your deep gladness and world's deep hunger meet."

Frederick Buechner, born 1926
Wishful Thinking (1973)

"Excellence is an art won by training and habituation. We do not act rightly because we have virtue or excellence,

*but we rather have those because we have acted rightly.
We are what we repeatedly do. Excellence, then, is not an act
but a habit."*

Aristotle, 384 – 322 B.C.

"Burning the candle at both ends for God's sake may be foolishness to the world, but it is a profitable Christian exercise — for so much better the light. Only one thing in life matter: being found worthy of the Light of the World in the hour of His visitation. We need have no undue fear for our health if we work hard for the kingdom of God; God will take care of our health if we take care of His cause. In any case it is better to burn out than to rust out."

Fulton J. Sheen, 1895 – 1979
Venerable Fulton J. Sheen Collection [3 Books] (2016)

"Every vocation becomes more agreeable when united with devotion."

Saint Francis de Sales, 1567 – 1622

"Work first, then rest."

John Ruskin, 1819 – 1900
Essay, "The Seven Lamps of Architecture" (1849)

"Believe with all of your heart that you will do what you were made to do."

Orison Swett Marden, 1848 – 1924
The Miracle of Right Thought (1910)

"Work as though you would live forever, and live as though you would die today. Go another mile!"

Augustine A. (Og) Mandino, 1923 – 1996
A Better Way to Live: Og Mandino's Own Personal Story of Success (1990)

"To do anything truly worth doing, I must not stand back shivering and thinking of the cold and danger, but jump in with gusto and scramble through as well as I can."

Augustine A. (Og) Mandino, 1923 – 1996
Quoted by Louis Montgomery, Jr., *A Year's Worth of Inspiration* (2011)

"Take care of your health that it may serve you to serve God."

Saint Francis de Sales, 1567 – 1622

"The person who knows one thing and does it better than anyone else, even if it only be the art of raising lentils, receives the crown he merits. If he raises all his energy to that end, he is a benefactor of mankind and is rewarded as such."

Augustine A. (Og) Mandino, 1923 – 1996
The Greatest Salesman in the World (1968)

"Every memorable act in the history of the world is a triumph of enthusiasm. Nothing great was ever achieved without it because it gives any challenge, no matter how frightening or difficult, a new meaning. Without enthusiasm you are doomed to a life of mediocrity but with it you can accomplish miracles"

Augustine A. (Og) Mandino, 1923 – 1996

"We must believe that we are gifted for something, and that this thing, at whatever cost, must be attained."

Marie Curie, 1867 – 1934
Eve Curie Labouisse, *Madame Curie: A Biography Part 2* (1937)

"What is nobler than a man wresting and wringing his bread from the stubborn soil by the sweat of his brow and the break of his back for his wife and children!"

William Morris Hunt, 1824 – 1879
Julia D. Addison, *The Boston Museum of Fine Art* (1910)

"It's faith in something and enthusiasm for something that makes life worth living."

Oliver Wendell Holmes, Jr., 1841 – 1935

"With all humility, I think, 'Whatsoever thy hand findeth to do, do it with thy might.' Infinitely more important than the vain attempt to love one's neighbor as one's self."

Oliver Wendell Holmes, Jr., 1841 – 1935
"Speech to the Bar Association of Boston," *Speeches* (1913)

"Teach me to love thee as thine angels love,
one holy passion filling all my frame;
the kindling of the heaven-descended Dove,
my heart an altar, and thy love the flame."

George Croly, 1880 – 1860
From the Hymn, "Spirit of God, Descend Upon My Heart" (1854)

"Lord, grant that I may always desire more than I can accomplish."

Michelangelo, 1475 – 1564

"Is your place a small place? Tend to it with care; He set you there. Is your place a larger place? Guard it with care; he set you there. Whate'er your place, it is not yours alone, But His Who set you there."

John Oxenham, 1852 – 1941
Bees in Amber: A Little Book of Thoughtful Verse (1913)

"The sense of this word among the Greeks affords the noblest definition of it: Enthusiasm signifies 'God in us.'"

Madame de Stael, 1766 – 1817
Germany (1813)

"Of all human sentiments, enthusiasm creates the most happiness; it is the only sentiment that gives real happiness, the only sentiment that can help us bear our human destiny in any situation in which we may find ourselves."

Madame de Stael, 1766 – 1817
M. L. Goldsmith; *Madame de Stael: Portrait of a Liberal in the Revolutionary Age* (1938)

"I had determined never to stop until I had come to the end and achieved my purpose...Nothing earthly will make me give up my work in despair. I encourage myself in the Lord my God, and go forward."

David Livingstone, 1813 – 1873
Entry, March 25, 1873, *The Last Journals of David Livingstone in Central Africa* (1874)

"Live joyously among your occupations."

Saint Francis de Sales, 1567 – 1622
Introduction to the Devout Life (1609)

"God is a kind Father. He sets us all in the place where he wishes us to be employed, and that employment is truly "our Father's business." He chooses work for every creature which will be delightful to them, if they do it simply and humbly. He gives us always strength enough, and sense enough, for what he wants us to do. And we may always be sure, whatever we are doing, that we cannot be pleasing Him if we are not happy ourselves.".

John Ruskin, 1819 – 1900
Ed., J.H. Gilbert; *Dictionary of Burning Words and Brilliant Writers* (1895)

"All find what they truly seek."

C. S. Lewis, 1898 – 1963
The Last Battle 1956

"You shall love the Lord your God with all your heart and with all your soul and with all your might. And these words that I command you today shall be on your heart. You shall teach them diligently to your children, and shall talk of them when you sit in your house, and when you walk by the way, and when you lie down, and when you rise."

Moses

"Seek first the kingdom of God and his righteousness and all these things will be added to you."

Jesus, The Christ

POSTSCRIPT

And I said to the man who stood at the gate of the year:

"Give me a light that I may tread safely into the unknown."

And he replied:

"Go out into the darkness and put your hand into the Hand of God. That shall be to you better than light and safer than a known way."

So I went forth, and finding the Hand of God, trod gladly into the night and He led me towards the hills and the breaking of day in the lone East."

Minnie Louise Haskins (1875 – 1957)
Preamble to the poem, "God Knows," *The Desert* (1908)

– Spoken by George VI in his Christmas 1939 broadcast to the Empire, these words struck a chord with a country facing the uncertainty of war. Haskins' words live on inscribed at the entrance to the George VI memorial chapel in St George's Chapel, Windsor, and in a window at the Queen's Chapel of the Savoy. The poem was read at the funeral of Elizabeth, the Queen Mother, in 2002. –

ACKNOWLEDGEMENTS

I have said in jest, but actually seriously, that many who knew me in my college days and as a young adult would find it hard to believe that a favorite pastime for me would become browsing in Christian bookstores or pouring over commentaries. That's probably not the girl they may remember on Thursday nights at Clarence's on Franklin Street in Chapel Hill.

How did I get here? All the way from then to now and there to here, God allowed me a very long leash, and though I wandered far and wide, He never lost sight of me. It is very humbling to realize His constant love, presence, and provision. He never left me alone.

I see the faces of so many who pointed me toward "home," helped keep me on the path, and even walked with me along the way—some all my life and others just for part of the journey.

From the very beginning, on Sundays my parents faithfully took us to our tiny church, where the congregation was composed mostly of members of my father's family and close neighbors. I realize now how good it is for children to observe the Sabbath firsthand, to sit in the pew, be (mostly) quiet, and experience worship with others as part of the rhythm of life.

I think of my aunts and uncles, always there, dressed for church in coat and tie, hats and heels, even white gloves. One particularly vivid memory is of a great aunt who often wore one of those mink things wrapped around her shoulders with the jaws of one mink locked on the tail of another. (The weirdness of that still fascinates me.)

Miss Audrey and Miss Ophelia, our Sunday School teachers, set such an example of commitment to their calling, being there with lessons planned for us, Sunday by Sunday, without fail.

I think of the genuine affection I felt from my Grandmother Scott who helped me memorize scripture when I was a very little girl. Those verses are still with me, permanently etched into my mind, as is the ditty from one of the books she seemed to always be reading:

I had a little party this afternoon at three,
'twas very small, three guests in all,
just I, myself, and me.
I ate the sandwiches, while myself drank the tea.
And it was I that ate the pie and passed the cake to me.

Today I have no idea the context of that little rhyme, but obviously it caught my attention in a powerful way, never to be forgotten.

There are so many others whose faith increased my faith and continues even to this day to do so.

As iron sharpens iron, so one person sharpens another.

Proverbs 27:17

I will always remember the Buettners who, in the tragedy of the death of their young daughter Lisa, demonstrated in an unforgettable way the "peace that passes understanding." Their faith which enabled them to comfort others in the midst of their own suffering inspired me. I longed for what they had, realizing that it was absent in my life.

So many of my friends and mentors in faith I met through my years at Bible Study Fellowship. My first teacher there,

Patty Crossley, whose intellect, love for, and grasp of Scripture assured me I was on the right track and inspired me to diligently study the Bible.

There are so many angels in my life whom I first met at BSF: Muffin Grant, my dear friend and Class Leader, who asked me to do the things for which I felt no natural inclination: be organized, follow rules, and see to it that several hundred other women do the same. Apparently, she saw something in me that was invisible to everyone else... especially me!

Terry Brantley, my first Bible Study friend, sat with me at Patty's feet as we soaked in every word she taught us, marveling at her knowledge of Scripture and her deep spiritual wisdom. Though Terry's life was not long in years, she left a great legacy of faith. She once told me of her amazement at God's faithfulness to her throughout her illness, of her overwhelming sense of His constant and palpable presence with her, and the peace she felt. Her words have never left me and they assure me that His grace is indeed sufficient, even in the suffering that leads to death.

Evelyn Cheek, is truly my sister in Christ. She teaches me what it means to love God with all your heart, and mind, and strength, while serenely trusting Him in all things, moment by moment. She is one who prays without ceasing. How many times I have fled to her in my most difficult times asking her to pray for and with me, and how many times she has opened her heart to me in love, genuine concern, and fervent prayer. In Evelyn, the light of the Holy Spirit is ever visible.

Martha Gray Edwards, who literally walked with me daily for years sharing untold hours of conversation on all topics from the ridiculous to the sublime. Her love and prayers for my son keep her close to my heart.

Pam Williams and Martha Bridge have revealed the courage that comes by undaunted faith.

These women are not only models of faithfulness—but my heroes.

For affording me the greatest honor and the joy of a lifetime, I will never be able to adequately express my thanks to the women of the Tuesday Morning Bible Study at First Presbyterian Church in Charlotte who allowed me to lead our group for the better part of a decade. I still see their faces before me and I realize that their affection, encouragement, affirmation, and expressions of gratitude made it the most fulfilling and, I believe, most meaningful work I have ever done.

There are hundreds more who have touched my life in ways for which I am profoundly grateful. For all these friends, named and unnamed, I say with eternal gratitude and confidence in Christ and his promises that the words of Saint Francis De Sales are true:

"Friendships begun in this world will be taken up again, never to be broken off."

It is impossible to think of my life's blessings without thinking first of my family. My mother and father, Jean and John Scott, gave me roots on the farm that connect me to so many others who have meant so much to me, but none more than my brothers, Martin and Brad, and my sister and best friend, Emily. How grateful I am for our shared memories—all of them—and for every day of our lives together. My brothers and sister have given me a new generation to love, my nieces and nephews, Mary Wilson, Tommy, Catherine, Louisa, Caroline, Missy, Lauren and Thomas. And, a next generation: Reese, Jack, Tuck and Charley!

Desmond Tutu wrote,

"You don't choose your family. They are God's gift to you, as you are to them."

Yes, they truly are.

Finally, I think of my Johns, my husband and my son, peas in a pod. They are God's greatest earthly gifts to me. My great disturbers, my great encouragers, they have led me (sometimes dragged me... thank goodness!) to places and experiences I would certainly have missed if not for their enthusiasm to go, see, and do. My life with them has been a great adventure, and they make every day richer and more interesting than I would ever have dreamed. I cannot imagine me without them.

And now our trio has become a quintet! In 2017 our daughter-in-law, Duncan, joined us on the journey. Moving nearly 5000 miles from the familiar comforts of the East Coast, family, home, friends, and career, she took on the role of "Navy wife" with energy, an adventurous spirit, and enthusiasm that is contagious. Our "Ginger Uprooted" has done an amazing job of putting down new roots, building an interesting and vibrant new life in the Pacific and beyond. There's more: our precious grandson, the newest John Keener, came into this world in the early evening of a bright blue Pacific day!

"To have a happy family is to enjoy an earlier heaven."

Og Mandino

All these dear souls, as well as innumerable others with whom I have shared the path are gifts from the One who is the source of "every good and perfect gift," the One who has blessed me "exceedingly abundantly beyond all that I can think or imagine," the One who has led me to Himself, the One who has shown me mercy every day of my life, and proven over and over that His love is truly the "love that will not let me go."

Now unto him that is able to do exceedingly abundantly above all that we ask or think, according to the power that worketh in us,

Unto him be glory in the church by Christ Jesus throughout all ages, world without end. Amen.

Ephesians 3:20 – 21

To Him, I owe everything. – **CSK**

INDEX

ABOUT ATMOSPHERE PRESS

Atmosphere Press is an independent, full-service publisher for excellent books in all genres and for all audiences. Learn more about what we do at atmospherepress.com.

We encourage you to check out some of Atmosphere's latest releases, which are available at Amazon.com and via order from your local bookstore:

The Great Unfixables, by Neil Taylor

Soused at the Manor House, by Brian Crawford

Portal or Hole: Meditations on Art, Religion, Race And The Pandemic, by Pamela M. Connell

A Walk Through the Wilderness, by Dan Conger

The House at 104: Memoir of a Childhood, by Anne Hegnauer

A Short History of Newton Hall, Chester, by Chris Fozzard

Serial Love: When Happily Ever After... Isn't, by Kathy Kay

Sit-Ins, Drive-Ins and Uncle Sam, by Bill Slawter

Black Water and Tulips, by Sara Mansfield Taber

Ghosted: Dating & Other Paramoural Experiences, by Jana Eisenstein

Walking with Fay: My Mother's Uncharted Path into Dementia, by Carolyn Testa

FLAWED HOUSES of FOUR SEASONS, by James Morris

Word for New Weddings, by David Glusker and Thom Blackstone

It's Really All about Collaboration and Creativity! A Textbook and Self-Study Guide for the Instrumental Music Ensemble Conductor, by John F. Colson

A Life of Obstructions, by Rob Penfield

Troubled Skies Over Quaker Hill: A Search for the Truth, by Lessie Auletti

ABOUT THE AUTHOR

Carolee Keener is a wife, mother, and shamelessly-doting grandmother. With her husband, John, she divides her time between their mountain home in Linville, NC and the family farm on the North Carolina/Virginia border where she grew up. She is once again appreciating life on the farm with its vistas of lush green pastures, woodlands, Carolina blue skies, and unobstructed sunrises and sunsets.